BOSNIA: A CULTURAL HISTORY

Ivan Lovrenović

BOSNIA:
A CULTURAL HISTORY

Foreword by
Ammiel Alcalay

NEW YORK UNIVERSITY PRESS
Washington Square, New York

First published in the U.S.A. in 2001 by
NEW YORK UNIVERSITY PRESS
Washington Square
New York, NY 10003

© 2001 by Saqi Books Publishers, London
Translation © 2001 The Bosnian Institute (London), based on a version by
Sonja Wild Bičanić
Maps prepared for this edition by Ivo Žanić and Krešo Turčinović

Originally published as *Unutarnja Zemlja: kratki pregled kulturne povijesti
Bosne i Hercegovine* [Inner Land: A Short Survey of the Cultural History of
Bosnia-Herzegovina] by Durieux, Zagreb
copyright © 1998 Durieux, Zagreb

Manufactured in the United Kingdom

Library of Congress Cataloging-in-Publication Data
Lovrenovic, Ivan.
Bosnia : a cultural history / Ivan Lovrenovic.
p. cm.
Includes bibliographical references and index.
ISBN 0-8147-5179-2 (cloth : alk. paper)
1. Bosnia and Hercegovina--Civilization. I. Title
DR1672 .L668 2001
949.742--dc21   2001037020

Contents

Illustrations

Colour Plates (between pages 128 and 129)

Maps

Foreword

by
Ammiel Alcalay

One of the more ironic and unfortunate by-products of war in the age of mass media is that it too often tends to be the only conduit through which we can grasp some sense of seemingly distant or hitherto unknown cultures. While the war against Bosnia was initially fought by the media machine directed from Belgrade, all the might and technology of the Western world's journalistic resources were soon concentrated on a part of the world that few had any real conception or knowledge of. In many ways, particularly in the American context (though somewhat less so in Europe), the extent, depth and quality of the coverage on Bosnia was quite surprising, despite numerous lingering misconceptions. At the same time, while it was exceedingly difficult if not impossible to translate works from Bosnia before the war, a critical mass of translated texts has since found its way into English. This, too, is somewhat surprising. After all, if one considers some of the major post-World-War-II conflicts – Vietnam, the Gulf War or Algeria (both presently and in its struggle against colonialism) – one can see just how little Vietnamese, Iraqi or Algerian culture has penetrated the anglophone world.

In this sense, we know more about Bosnia now than many other places we should have at least some knowledge of. Yet, when one encounters the work of Ivan Lovrenović, we are immediately confronted with a profundity of knowledge and an integrity of approach that makes us realize how little we actually do know about Bosnia's multiple and palimpsestial history. Poet, novelist, essayist and journalist, Lovrenović's uncompromising work seems almost antithetical to what generally passes for 'informed' intellectual discourse. Fiercely local, his erudition goes to the deepest roots of language's connection to place, while conveying the sense that no human culture can ever really be 'foreign' to other humans.

Yet, Lovrenović's sense of humanity is never nostalgic or reductive as he remains constantly and acutely aware of the barbarism that only humans are capable of perpetrating. In another book representing a very different tone, *Ex tenebris: Sarajevo Diary* [1994], Lovrenović writes:

Moral accommodation – this is the mark of modern Europe and the world, perhaps the highest achievement (why not even the goal?) of technologically conceived Western consumer civilization at the end of the 20th century, going into the 21st. When you think, even in a quick panoramic scan, of what Europe has gone through in only the last two thousand years, or even the last two hundred years – from the guillotines of Paris, the French-Austrian-German-Russian-Turkish slaughter, bloody revolutions, world wars, Hitlerism and Stalinism, Auschwitz and the Gulag – then you see that it's only now, in the last couple of years, that she has had a historical second to doze off a bit, to take a breather from these awful goings-on and the even more awful need to be morally awake. What a terrible strain – to remain morally alert, to always have your uneasy conscience plugged in! So just as Europe finally succumbed to sweet indulgence, to the idyll of prosperity and affluence, the fairy-tale of democracy–boom: the Balkan slaughterhouse! You can just imagine how much they hate us in European parliaments – each and every one of them, and all of them together (no kidding). Irretrievably, mercilessly, with wanton irresponsibility, their whole dream has been ruined . . . Isn't there perhaps in this hatred just a nuance more rage vented on the victims than on the murderers (even without taking into account the fact that everyone knows precisely who is who)? I mean, what the hell did you have to get us into all this for anyway? And once you started, why weren't your reflexes on the alert, the reflexes of potential victims, instead of naively and sheepishly peeking your half-wailing, half-accusing gaze over here at us, at a world that has gotten out of the throat-cutting business . . . And besides, what the hell do we need this whole bloody, morbid circus for anyway? War criminals, victims, mass graves, camps, hunger, sickness, rivers of people carrying things, hysterical children . . . What's in it for us if we identify with the victims and try the murderers?

With the world seemingly connected by the feel-good imagery of global capitalism in which everyone is equally different but the same, Lovrenović defines a new humanism that never descends into the bathetic platitudes of a selective liberalism in which politics become a fashion statement.

The importance of this, following Europe's acquiescence in allowing the destruction of Bosnia to take place, cannot be over emphasized. Moreover, the increased homogeneity of intellectual discourse through academic migration between Europe and America, and the almost total victory of theory without active politics, makes Lovrenović's work ever more urgent and relevant. Like so many intellectuals outside the pale of academic moulds and models, Lovrenović's career has encompassed many facets of productive cultural and public life. Author of more than ten books, Lovrenović also worked as the editor in chief of *Svjetlost*, one of Europe's best publishing houses before the war. He has worked and continues to work as a journalist, while remaining active in both establishing and promoting a diverse range of cultural and political projects. Given the post-war measures of political and intellectual conformity, as well as the death and migration of so many important Bosnian intellectuals, his presence and example in Sarajevo cannot be underestimated.

Needless to say, any translation of Lovrenović's work is long overdue. Despite many good books on Bosnia, there is still nothing comparable to *Inner Land* [the present work's original title]. While it may at times remind us of Claudio Magris or Amin Maalouf, Lovrenović's style represents a unique and incredibly condensed mix of geography, politics, history, culture and poetics. The staying power of this mix derives from his profound sense that the accumulated experience of a place can be possessed by a people and contained in its buildings, books, music, and language, and that this complex amalgam must be conveyed in all its richness.

The great Guyanese novelist Wilson Harris has spoken of 'inequalities, harboured by one-sided traditions' that become stamped into narratives as 'injustices'. Speaking of Dante, Harris writes:

> You may recall how Virgil – who had laboured for Dante in guiding him through the Inferno and the Purgatorio – was unjustly excluded from the Paradiso. He was deemed a pagan because his address lay in

a pre-Christian age. How one-sided is such a Paradiso? Does it not need a profound, re-visionary momentum of the frame of language in which it was cast? Once such deep-seated inequalities remain within traditions, the Soul of tradition itself is orphaned. It suffers cosmic abandonment in that it appears to *nurture absolutes which polarize* humanity irreconcilably. Unless such absolutes can *yield their particularities within* plural masks that question themselves, the Soul is cut adrift and may lose its potency to arbitrate, with profoundest creativity, between divisions in humanity.

In the labyrinth of inherited assumptions, willful manipulations and grotesque mythologies that Bosnia has come to represent, we have never been in greater need of a guide to arbitrate between these wounding and wounded divisions. Yet, despite the obliteration of so much, Bosnia still represents a place and a people that embodies human, geographic, historical and cultural plurality in ways other peoples and places are only beginning to fathom. In acting as our guide, Ivan Lovrenović never lets go, holding our hand throughout the journey as we meander through pagan sites, synagogues, churches, mosques and flaming libraries, places that – no matter how beautiful or horrid – are never unfamiliar.

Ammiel Alcalay, poet, translator, critic and scholar, has written on a wide range of subjects from diaspora, memory and modernism to sacred texts. His books include After Jews and Arabs; Remaking Levantine Culture *[1993],* The Cairo Notebooks *[1993] and* Keys to the Garden: New Israeli Writing *[1996]. His selected essays have been published as* Memories of our Future *[City Lights Books, San Francisco, 1999].*

ONE

From Palaeolithic Times to Illyrian Tribal Leagues

People have lived in what is today Bosnia-Herzegovina from far back in prehistory. In the long period stretching from the Palaeolithic right down to the emergence of Illyrian tribal leagues, all the stages on the ladder of European cultural development can be traced here, sometimes enriched with local variants of considerable refinement.

Research into the early Stone Age shows that the northern parts of Bosnia, the area between the Bosna, Ukrina and Usora rivers, were most developed at that time. But there have also been important Palaeolithic finds in Herzegovina, at Crvena Stijena near Trebišnjica and Varvra near Prozor.

At some point during this prehistoric past the important leap forward took place when Neanderthal man of the Middle Palaeolithic was supplanted by *Homo sapiens* of the Late Palaeolithic, which lasted until about 10,000 BC. The first cave drawing from that period in Bosnia-Herzegovina, a rare example of its kind, was found in the Badanj cave near Stolac.

The end of the Palaeolithic Age was marked by great climatic changes. The temperature rose, the ice sheets melted, the glaciers withdrew to the north and huge swamps and forests emerged into a climate so humid as to be fatal for all forms of Palaeolithic life. This improvement in the climate so humid had catastrophic consequences for Palaeolithic man; from the Middle Stone Age until about 4,000

PALAEOLITHIC, MESOLITHIC AND NEOLITHIC SITES IN PRESENT-DAY BOSNIA-HERZEGOVINA

○ Prehistoric sites

⌒ Prehistoric cave drawings

—·—·—·— Present-day borders of Bosnia-Herzegovina

1. Palaeolithic rock engraving from Badanj near Stolac, 12,000 BC.

BC Bosnia-Herzegovina was largely uninhabited except for the Mediterranean coast, as may be seen from finds of the period in Crvena Stijena, a locality of great interest, its cultural levels stretching right back to pre-Neanderthal times.

After this long, dark Mesolithic pause, in the third millennium BC a rich Neolithic culture developed in present-day Bosnia-Herzegovina, testified to by many finds with a rich variety of objects and forms. Conditions were now favourable for the formation of settlements, for the skilled production of stone tools and weapons, and for the development of agriculture and stockbreeding. With the formation of settlements came the development of a new kind of social organization. Above all it was a period for the production of pottery. Moreover until the second millennium it was peaceful and did not suffer from any great invasions or drastic breaks in continuity.

Neolithic culture developed in Bosnia-Herzegovina in the overlap of two great cultural regions: the Mediterranean, with its characteristic impressed pottery, and central Europe where banded

2. Neolithic terracotta sculpture from Butmir near Sarajevo, 3,000 BC.

3. Neolithic pottery from Butmir near Sarajevo, 3,000 BC.

pottery was made; but many common elements suggest a single Neolithic culture with a large number of local variants. The oldest finds came from the Gornja Tuzla and Zelena Pećina caves above the Buna near Mostar, while the most prominent cultural groups were those of Kakanj (with sites in Kakanj and Arnautovići), Vinča (embracing north-eastern Bosnia), Butmir (at Butmir, Kraljevine near Novi Šeher, Obre near Kakanj, Nebo near Travnik, Crkvina near Turbe, and Kiseljak), Lisičići (near Konjic), and Posavina (Donji Klakar near Bosanski Brod, Donja Mahala near Orašje).

The beauty of the pottery produced at Butmir is enough to show the rich variety of forms and high degree of skill reached in these regions by Neolithic man. An abundance of pottery with a dark lustre and wealth of decorative fantasy; countless dishes, vases, burial urns; an unerring sculptural sense that reached its peak in the modelling of heads, with a creative use of material ranging from rigid stylization to precise realism. All this indicates a long-gone 'golden age', a developed spiritual life matched by creative talent, enjoyed by these now-vanished prehistoric peoples who, after a splendid epoch, disappeared without trace, as did all the Neolithic culture of Bosnia-Herzegovina, lost in the dark chaos of Europe in the transition between the third and second millennia.

The great process of shift and change that swept over the Balkans began in a movement among the nomads of the Black Sea steppes. They brought the use of copper to the Balkans, opening the door to a new Copper Age. In this transitional Aeneolithic period the use of stone and metal developed in parallel, and pottery continued to flourish, marked with important cultural characteristics. This period lasted to about 1800 BC. The use of metal in Bosnia came mainly across the Sava from the north, as may be seen from the considerable number of finds in the north of the country along the Bosna: Dobrinja, Vranovići, Džakule, Tešanj, Bosanski Svilaj, and Vrbas, Bočac, Griča, Laktaši. Elements of Neolithic culture were completely obliterated with the arrival and settlement of new groups of people, among whom the most important were the Vučedol, Lasinja, Kostolac, and Baden groups. This period, along with the subsequent Bronze Age covering the rest of the second millennium, saw great changes in production and social organization. Towards the end of the millennium, well-armed and aggressive tribes from the west Pannonian area began a powerful movement of expansion to the south and south-east. In those uncertain times metal began to be increasingly prized, especially for weapons, for wars were frequent. This placed Bosnia in a very favourable position, because of its rich mines and because of the safety offered by its mountains and forests, deep valleys and rugged peaks.

TWO

The Illyrian World

From early forms of political organization to the Baton Rising

In the early centuries of the first millennium BC, in Bosnia-Herzegovina as throughout the western Balkans, the permanent settlement of a variety of ethnic and cultural groups began. New forms of social organization started to evolve, tending more and more towards the formation of sizeable territorial communities. The ethnic group associated with the Iron Age culture in these regions is known under the collective name of Illyrian. The Illyrians began to develop the widespread political and cultural synthesis which has come to bear their name. Recent research has brought into serious question the degree of ethnic unity of all the nations and tribes involved; but we shall continue to use the word Illyrian here, since it is impossible to avoid using such an established term and its derivatives.

The Illyrian tribes settled the western Balkans from the Adriatic Sea to the Morava, and from Albania to Istria. During the first millennium BC, and especially during its latter half, this extensive area became increasingly important; it was the scene of frequent armed incursions and of trading, cultural and political penetration. For two centuries the Illyrians put up resistance to Roman expansionism, but finally at the beginning of the new era they became part of the Roman Empire.

By about the middle of the first millennium BC the process of

ILLYRIAN TRIBES AND HELLENISTIC CULTURE

Colapiani
Siscia
Sava
PANNONIA
Iapodes
Una
Donja Dolina
Oseriates
Sava
Breuci
Sava
Una
Jezerine
Ribići
Ripač
Sana
Sanski Most
Vrbas
Vis
Iapodes
Maezaei
Bosna
Drina
Ditiones
DALMATIA
Deuri
Pod
Daesitiates
Dindari
Scardona
Delmatae
Debelo Brdo
Drina
Tragurium
Salona
Delminium
Neretva
Mahrevići
Strpci
Ardiaei
Gorica
Narensii
Daorsi
Siculotae
Autariates
Pharia
Issa
Narona
Daorson (Ošanići)
Kačanj
Meleumani
Adriatic Sea
Rhizon

● Major urban centres in Antiquity

□ Illyrian sites

▬ ▬ ▬ Roman provincial border

—·—·—·— Present-day borders of Bosnia-Herzegovina

forming larger territorial and economic tribal leagues was well advanced among the Illyrians, as was the process of developing beyond the clan system. This seems to have been particularly true in the south, but it could be observed throughout the territory, and included the tribes which partially or wholly, continuously or sporadically, settled in what is today Bosnia-Herzegovina. Best known among these tribes were the Daesitiates, Maezaei, Daorsi, Delmatae, Japodes, Ardiaei, Autariatae, Deuri and Deretini.

In the fourth century BC two events occurred which vitally affected the future of the Illyrians: the great Celtic migration, and the foundation of the first Greek colonies on the Adriatic coast.

Warlike, well-armed Celtic horsemen swept over these wide lands towards Greece, which was their ultimate goal. In the first surge forwards the Illyrians fell an easy prey to the long swords of the Celts, who then paused for a time, resolving to attack Greece only once Alexander the Great was dead. But they were beaten in battle and repulsed, and in the first half of the third century withdrew to the Danubian plains. Although the Celts may not have had any deep effect on Illyrian culture (as was once supposed), in global terms their descent affected the fate of the Illyrians by isolating the territory they inhabited from the Alpine regions and Italy to the north and north-west.

The establishment of Greek colonies in the Adriatic, on Vis, Hvar and Korčula, in the early fourth century marked the beginning of a new epoch in Illyrian history. It opened the way to powerful cultural and economic influences which soon began to affect the spiritual and material culture of the Illyrians. At the same time there were important changes in the political situation, which initiated and speeded up Roman conquest and expansion in all these areas. This development, which became ever more inclusive and ambitious, began when the process of inter-tribal political cohesion was well advanced, and with it more extensive state organization. The Romans made a series of attacks on the Illyrians. Starting in 229 with the capture of the islands, which broke the power of the Illyrian navy, in 168 they defeated the famous Illyrian king Gentius. They

4. Japod horsemen on a stone tablet from Založja near Bihać,
circa 2nd–1st centuries BC.

now stood firmly on Illyrian soil, but another century and a half of
bloody fighting followed, during which the tribes from inland Illyria
put up tenacious opposition, sometimes pitted against the entire military might of Rome and its best commanders.

The territory of the Delmatae was the first to be attacked. In 156
after a two-stage siege their capital Delminium fell, but despite this
the Delmatae long remained unconquered. After them the Ardiaei,
skilful and daring pirates who had settled the right bank of the
Neretva, were crushed in a fierce attack in 135. The Romans, following the age-old method of conquerers, moved the conquered peoples
inland where, forced to lead a settled agricultural life, they soon died
out. From 129–119 the Romans next fought an indecisive and for

them exhausting war against the powerful Japodes, conducted in several stages but ending in conquest and a further strengthening of Roman power over the Illyrians, a power now also recognized by many other tribes. The Delmatae continued to conduct risings with varied success, several times even managing to conquer Salona. Finally, from 35 to 33 BC, the Emperor Octavian personally led the army in a massive attack. Once again the Delmatae were in the forefront of the opposition, led by their skilful commanders Verzo and Testimus, who used guerrilla tactics with great success. Octavian was wounded in battle and went back to Rome, only to return in 33. Decimated and famished, the Delmatae were forced to surrender and Octavian finally occupied Illyria. (In the fashion of the time and with a conqueror's irony he founded the great Octavian Library with the plunder of these wars, just as from earlier plunder the poet-general Asinius Pollio had founded the first public library in Rome.) In 12 BC the Dalmatae once again staged a rising and conquered Salona, but this rising was quickly crushed.

The last scene in this centuries-long Illyrian drama, grand in concept but inescapably tragic, was played out in a last fatal finale between 6 and 9 AD in the very heart of what today is Bosnia. It is known as the *Bellum Batonianum,* the Batonian Rising, called after the two namesakes Bato leader of the Daesitiates and Bato leader of the Breuci. In this rising, at the moment of their final defeat, the Illyrian tribes presented a united front for the first time. The seriousness of the rising can be gauged by the panic tales that spread through Rome of 800,000 insurgents, including 200,000 elite warriors and 9,000 horsemen! Also by the fact that the Emperor Augustus sent two of his most experienced military leaders, Tiberius and Germanicus, to crush it. In face of this strong offensive the Breuci front broke in a great battle on the river Bathinus (the Bosna?), and Bato of the Breuci surrendered. Bato of the Daesitiates, who at the time was operating somewhere in the lands of the Delmatae, escaped to Pannonia, captured the Breuci leader and executed him by order of the tribal court.

In this continuous fighting, in which conquest and defeat alternated, the Illyrian tribes had some important victories, for example at the battle of Raetinum (Golubić near Bihać?), but their resistance was confined to an ever narrower area. The last citadel to fall was Arduba (Vranduk). It was a terrible battle in which, according to Roman historians, the Illyrian women with their children in their arms threw themselves into the fire when Bato surrendered, rather than be enslaved by the Romans. In this battle the Batonian Rising was finally crushed, and with it Illyrian history may be said to have ended; for Illyria was now divided into the provinces of Pannonia and Dalmatia, which the Romans began administratively, politically and culturally to incorporate into their Empire. All that was Illyrian was progressively diminished by overall Romanization, surviving only as some kind of amalgam or in relics which sometimes remain even today. Probably some isolated villages or groups were never completely Romanized, and their culture most likely melded with that of the Slavs when the latter settled the land.

Since the Illyrians never developed a literature, our only written sources concerning their life, language, social organization, culture, wars and customs come from other hands. Our only direct witnesses are the large number of archaeological sites, mainly settlements such as hill-forts and pile-dwellings – and graves. The most usual kinds of settlement were well fortified and built on some small hill or mountain slope. They range from quite small ones, probably little more than refuges, to large and monumental ones fortified with what are known as Cyclopean walls (from the gigantic stones used in their construction), like those of the citadel in Ošanići near Stolac. Pile-dwellings have been found in only two places: Ripač near Bihać and Donja Dolina near Bosanska Gradiška. The intricacy of their construction and the large number of finds providing information about the culture of their inhabitants make them of first-class importance.

The Illyrian custom was to bury their dead in barrows or under grave mounds of stones. A large number of barrows have been excavated, especially significant being those in the immediate vicinity of Glasinac Polje, one of the most important archaeological sites of the Bronze and Iron Ages. Glasinac was obviously the site of a dense concentration of some Illyrian tribe over a long period. It has yielded a large number of finds, one of special note dating from the fourth or fifth century BC in the Pod district near Bugojno. It has Umbrian-Etruscan writing on an earthenware pot, the oldest writing from this region. There are also Japod funeral urns of great aesthetic value with various motifs executed in shallow relief. About the character and structure of the Illyrian language little is known. The scant traces that have come down in funeral inscriptions, in a few geographical names, or in the roots of some words, are far too meagre to allow any reconstruction.

The defeat of the Batonian Rising and the incorporation of Illyria into the Roman empire meant that any continuous development of an Illyrian ethos was broken, so that its life began to conform to the forms and models of classical antiquity. Sometimes it did very obviously fill these with its own Illyrian content, but it could not hope to withstand the might of a far more developed civilization.

Illyrian Hellenism

In the historical periodization of the peoples of southern Europe, the prehistoric period is taken to have ended with the coming of Greek and Roman civilization. For the region of what is today Bosnia-Herzegovina and its original Illyrian inhabitants, the threshold was traditionally located in the first century BC. More precisely, it was considered that the Roman variant of classical civilization came to the Illyrians of Bosnia-Herzegovina with the Roman conquerors. Recent archaeological research has challenged this view, however, indicating that the culture of antiquity came much earlier and in its Hellenistic form.

This important historical correction was the result of research at the hill-fort in the village of Ošanići near Stolac in Herzegovina. This was the site of Daors, capital of the Daorsi from the fifth to the middle of the first century BC. Finds here and in other Daorsi settlements in Herzegovina have yielded a rich and splendid archaeological harvest, which shows to what extent the tribal lands of the Daorsi were from some point in the third century BC the most northerly branch of the great Hellenistic tree.

It seems that the inhabitants of this region had contact very early on with the Greek world. This can be seen in certain similarities between Illyrian and Greek mythology, according to which the Daorsi tribe came from mother Daortha, daughter of Illyrios, whose parents were the Cyclops Polyphemus and the nymph Galatea. From later antiquity there are written records relating to the Daorsi and some other tribes in Hecataeus of Miletus, about 500 BC.

All such contacts may well have been made originally through maritime connections. This is suggested by some finds from Daors, such as fragments of proto-Corinthian and ancient pottery from the second half of the eighth century BC, and Greek amphorae of slightly later date. The fourth century BC is crucial for tracing links between Greece and the Daorsi. By that date there were already Greek colonies in southern Italy and Albania, while on the eastern Adriatic coast Greek culture had already made an impact inland. It was in this period that the Daorsi experienced cultural and economic development. Firm maritime links were established with Issa, Pharos, Corcyra and other Greek colonies on the islands of the eastern Adriatic, as also with southern Italy and more distant parts of the Hellenic world. Of this there is ample archaeological evidence in Ošanići. The importance of seafaring for the Daorsi is vividly illustrated by the ships portrayed on all their coins. Even the later Roman wars did not affect this Hellenistic connection, since even after the fall of the Illyrian state in 168 BC the Daorsi, by supporting the Romans, managed very cleverly to retain a considerable degree of autonomy until the end of the first century BC, when with the fall of the Roman Republic and the creation of the Empire they lost their independence. Thus, however important an influence Rome was in the life of the Daorsi, their culture was formed by Hellenism, while retaining important elements of their own Illyrian tradition. It is particularly interesting to see how Daorsi craftsmen mastered Hellenistic techniques but used them for forms of their own, unknown in other parts of the Hellenistic world.

The hill-fort of Ošanići was constructed on an exceptionally favourable plateau above the Radimlje stream and could be approached only from one side. It was continuously inhabited from the fifth century BC and developed into the true cultural and administrative centre of the Daorsi.

To the west, on the Neretva, Daorsi territory bordered on that of the more numerous and militant Delmatae who had so long defied the power of Rome.

Thanks to the natural boundary of the Neretva and the Roman protectorate, the Daorsi were long able to repulse the attacks of the Dalmatae. As part of their unrelenting opposition to Rome, in the middle of the first century BC the Delmatae brought together a great force and managed to push the Roman legions back. They then overran the Daorsi, which was the beginning of the end of Daorsian autonomy and cultural development. Their capital city was overrun and burned and was never restored nor even to any great extent inhabited.

Archaeologists have not yet fully researched Ošanići. But what they already know is enough to show a town with many typically Hellenistic features. Defensive structures and dwellings, pottery, writing, money, craftsmen, and in particular small scale ceramics all show Ošanići to be among the most important cultural sites of its time in this part of the Balkans.

Its very layout shows strong Greek influence: a settlement with a fortress above it, all protected by powerful Cyclopean walls. The traces of houses cannot be clearly seen but archaeological investigation has uncovered their character. They are built of stone with well-planned interiors, using plaster and tiled roofs, and there is a well-developed urban infrastructure including a horizontal street plan and vertical steps. The most impressive feature is without doubt the massive Cyclopean walls which protected the hill-fortress on its only accessible side. They are constructed of finely dressed stone without bonding, just like those that appeared in Greece in the fourth and third centuries BC. Their defensive power is reinforced by a zig-zag wall that would have been an obstacle to any enemy attack.

5. Cyclopean walls at Ošanići near Stolac, Hellenistic period, 4ᵗʰ–3ʳᵈ centuries BC.

The most important item found in the town was pottery, which is not only vital for dating purposes but also first-class cultural material. Of special importance are the remains of 'Gnathian ware'. The vessels found in Ošanići have many elements exactly corresponding to the Hellenistic ceramics of southern Italy in the fourth and third centuries BC. But here, with altered shapes and ornamentation, they continued to be used right down to the first century BC. It is characteristic that in Ošanići, parallel with these Hellenistic forms, remains of local pottery have also been found, handmade and very archaic in form and ornamentation. It dates from the last two centuries BC and is similar to far earlier Bronze and Iron Age discoveries made at Prozor and Livno. This shows the long and interesting retention of elements of autochthonous Illyrian culture even in territories which were largely Hellenized.

Helmets from the third and second centuries, belonging to the Illyrian cultural tradition, have also been found in the ruins of Daors. But these also show something else – the symbiosis of two cultures. A helmet of Illyrian shape bears the owner's name in Greek letters, a shortening of the typical Illyrian name *Pinnes*.

Even such scant information shows the Hellenization and level of civilization attained in Ošanići. Greek writing was long in use here, not only among the elite but in everyday life. This is shown not only by the inscription on the helmet, but even better by the considerable number of fragments of pottery of various kinds bearing Greek letters. The inscription DAORSON on coins believed to have been minted and in circulation in Ošanići in the second century BC uses the Greek alphabet and the Greek grammatical form. This is the basis for the presumed name of the settlement. Its similarity to the inscriptions on coins in many Greek towns allow us to presume that this use of the Greek genetive case refers to the inhabitants of the city, from which we can form the name of the city as Daors, and call the people the Daorsi, having no further basis for reconstructing the name. The form of the coins and the method of minting are also Greek, but they retain certain elements of a local tradition: the Illyrian ship and the cap on the ruler's head. These are analogous with other Illyrian coins from the reign of King Gentius.

All this sheds new light on the cultural history of these regions during the Hellenistic period. But it is all put in the shade by finds made in a storage place below the hill-fort containing several hundred articles of enormous cultural value. These include a large set of implements for the use of smiths and goldsmiths, together with a lot of original artifacts and a number of items from farther away. The store was cleverly hidden in a stone hole, dating from the second century BC, and until discovered by archaeologists it had obviously never been touched. Judging from the number and character of the items, they probably represent the contents of an excellent and well-developed workshop. Why the owners were forced to hide them we shall never know, but probably fighting or invasion forced them to flee and for some reason they were never able to return. So this exceptionally interesting hoard has come down to us untouched, just as it was when it was buried two thousand years ago.

Of the treasures found in the Ošanići deposit, we will here mention only some of the most important in artistic terms and for cultural history. When the deposit was opened, one small bronze casket of

6. Mould from a jeweller's workshop at Ošanići near Stolac, Classical Greek period, 5ᵗʰ–4ᵗʰ centuries BC.

masterly workmanship found inside could not be dated or culturally identified. But later, when the world was astounded by the treasure discovered in the grave of the Macedonian King Philip II in the village of Vergina near Thessalonica, it was found to contain two gold caskets that bore a startling likeness to the Ošanići casket. Thus the puzzle about date and cultural provenance was solved, and the two discoveries were placed in significant cultural and historical relationship.

Among the many finds, some of which have not yet been identified, were two apparently simple bronze squares. More careful examination showed that they were moulds for casting miniature metal figures and decorative elements. For some figures there were two symmetrical moulds, which would produce a three-dimensional figure, perhaps to serve for some religious purpose. The other moulds were halves, and no doubt used to produce decorative metalwork. The only logical conclusion is that the casting required the use of a flat piece of stone, probably marble. The technical and artistic perfection involved required a highly skilled artist, a sculptural miniaturist.

Miniatures were popular in the Hellenistic age, of course. But a large number of the moulds from Ošanići represent patterns not found elsewhere in the Hellenistic world: Pegasus, hippocamps, gryphons, eagles' wings, palmetta, stars from Olympus, muses, sphinxes, Aphrodite, Nike, goddesses of death, Helios, doves, snakes' heads, Medusa, spears, thunderbolts etc. Equally unknown elsewhere is the production and use of decorated belt discs. Again, Daors is unique in its evidence of continuous mass-production. These finds show the existence of a high level of craftsmanship among the Illyrians and have revealed some forms of Hellenistic miniature art as yet unknown. This leads us to the important conclusion that the Daorsi were not simply passive receivers of Greek culture, but were already involved in it in the fourth century BC and even in a position to enrich it.

ILLYRICUM, EARLY CHRISTIANITY
AND THE ADVENT OF THE SLAVS

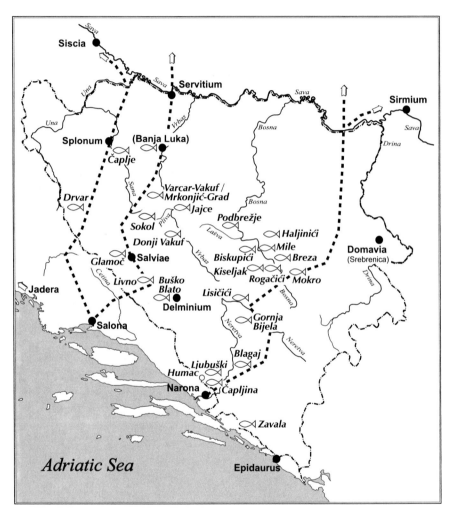

THREE

Ancient Illyricum

At the outset of our era the territory of what is today Bosnia-Herzegovina thus became part of the immense Roman Empire, at the height of its power and stretching into three continents. From now on the Illyrians would share the Empire's fate and the changes that overtook it – the early days of Roman expansion, the conversion to Christianity which ushered in the late classical period, the division of the empire into East and West, the whirlwind of the barbarian invasions, the fall of Rome – right up to the arrival and settlement of a wholly new, Slav, ethnic element at the beginning of the seventh century AD, when the South Slav history of this region began.

The early centuries under the Romans were for the Illyrians a time of peace and stability. Of course some Illyrian tribes and communities faced a long period of punishment for their intractability. The Daesitiates, for example, did not achieve equal rights of citizenship until the third century.

In establishing their rule the Romans, with their great energy and experience of such tasks, at once set about taming Illyricum and adapting it to their own needs. The forms of this undertaking quickly became evident, and later also highly developed: an administrative apparatus, a road network, mining and metallurgy centres. Iron, gold, silver, lead, rock salt, a labour force and military potential, and other 'gifts' of Illyricum were for long a mainstay of the Empire's might.

Luxuriously appointed bathing establishments at the numerous hot springs; well-run estates with richly appointed villas; a large number of settlements ranging from small places of refuge to strong military camps; stopping places for travellers and well-developed municipal centres, such as Domavia near Srebrenica in the Argentaria valley, Delminium on Duvansko Polje, Bistue Nova (Bugojno?, Zenica?), Bistue Vetus (Duvno?), Diluntum (Stolac?), Salviae on Glamočko Polje, Splonum near Stari Majdan, Stanecli in the Lašva valley, Baloie (Šipovo?), Castra (Banja Luka), and many more. Illyria also became an important source of manpower, ranging from workers for big public works and soldiers for the legions to those who ascended the imperial throne (Diocletian, for example) or even those who, like St Jerome, enriched the history of human thought and spiritual life.

One of the first tasks the Romans set themselves immediately after crushing the Batonian Rising was building a whole network of roads in all important directions. Throughout the entire period of Roman rule these solidly built and ingeniously constructed roads, sometimes passing through intractable country, were maintained and extended. Main thoroughfares were interlinked, large towns were connected to smaller ones by subsidiary roads. The Roman roads throughout all subsequent history were the foundation for later communications, sometimes even down to today. One of these that has never lost its importance is the ancient Roman artery '*a colonia Salonitana ad fines provinciae Illyrici*', leading from Salona to Bosanska Gradiška. Built in 17 AD it went through Sinj, Prolog, Livansko Polje (station at Pelva), Glamočko Polje, (Salviae, Hlapić), Mlinište, Pecka (Sarnade), with connections to Leusaba (Varcar Vakuf, today Mrkonjić-Grad) and Baloie (Šipovo?). It crossed the Vrbas at Krupa (Lamatis), continued to Banja Luka (Castra), Trn (Ad Ladios) and Laktaši (Ad Fines), and ended in Bosanska Gradiška (Servitium). A parallel road ran from Salona through Knin, Bosansko Grahovo, Drvar, Sanski Most, Prijedor and Bosanska Dubica. In the Neretva valley a main road was constructed from Narona via Čapljina, Nevesinjsko Polje, Boračko Jezero, Konjic, Sarajevsko Polje and Romanija to Drinjača and on towards the Sava.

The most populated areas, as in pre-Roman, Illyrian times, continued to be the region round Bihać, the mining areas in the Sana valley, the region round Srebrenica, Glamočko, Duvansko and Livansko Polje, the region round Gornji Vakuf, Bugojno and Donji Vakuf (Uskoplje), the Lašva valley, the region between Ljubuški and Posušje, the Neretva valley, Mostar and Konjić, Stolac and its surroundings, Sarajevsko Polje, and so on.

Subject to recurrent crises, and times of great difficulty, too large to administer, exposed to increasing attacks from Huns, Ostrogoths and Visigoths, in 395 the Roman Empire divided into the Eastern and Western Empires, of which the latter fell apart in 476. Archaeological research has brought to light in much detail the terrible devastation of the lands that are now our country.

By the third century Illyricum had developed from a colony into a flourishing Roman province, which played a considerable role in the political and economic life of the empire. Its people not only had equal citizenship but could even aspire to the supreme imperial power. Their cultural development had always included certain interesting autochthonous elements, whose creative contribution was now enhanced. Sculpture of all kinds clearly showed that the framework of Roman forms and style could be enriched by elements with a different artistic approach and treatment. In traditional art histories these are treated as a kind of rustic classicism, the product of barbaric inability to follow Roman models. But should we not rather marvel at the vitality of a cultural tradition which not even the centuries-long supremacy of a different culture was able to eradicate? It shows us that even in civilized centres Romanization need not be considered absolute.

Not long after the disintegration of the Western Empire, the Illyrian lands fell to the Ostrogoths, who integrated them into their state so that for several decades they enjoyed a period of peace and reconstruction. By about 535 the Eastern Empire had managed to get most of Illyria back, but not for long. The northern frontiers once again came under attack, this time from Avars and Slavs.

As the power of Rome waned, the spiritual void that it left be-

7. Relief of Sylvanus from Duvansko Polje, 1st century AD.

8. Relief of Mithras from Jajce, 4th–5th centuries AD.

hind was filled with a heterogeneous assortment of interpenetrating cults, mythologies and beliefs. These provided a rich mix, not all of which was obliterated when, in 391, the Edict of Theodosius made Christianity the official religion. Many of the pagan elements of the indigenous population and those brought with them by the incoming barbarians had already become established on the frontiers of the Empire. Syncretism, Mithraism, neo-Platonism, in complex interaction with the world of the Roman gods and against the background of the general systemic breakup, formed unexpected and unpredictable combinations, even spilling over into Christianity, in which they sometimes gained acceptance and can be found embedded even today.

This *mixtum compositum* of varied cults embracing the Roman pantheon and Christianity, together with the important episode of the Arian heresy brought by the Ostrogoths, left abundant traces observable in finds in various parts of Bosnia-Herzegovina. They may be seen in Mithraic reliefs (Jajce, Konjic) and in carvings with different cultural messages which often retain, as part of the Roman canon, traces of the Illyrian rustic spirit already referred to.

The few decades of relative peace and attempts at reconstruction within the Ostrogothic state were no more than a breathing space in a chaotic historical period of barbarian inroads and fighting during the migration of nations which began in the fourth century and lasted several hundred years, and from which a spiritually and socially changed Europe emerged.

From that uncertain period date some buildings worthy of note in both historical and cultural terms. These include the remains of early Christian church architecture and religious or memorial carving. It is striking that local people still call the places where the remains of these late Roman basilicas are to be found *crkvine*, a Slav word [*crkva* = church] testifying to their long use. Although in general terms late classical architecture in Bosnia-Herzegovina followed the model of the Roman basilica, many elements of the *crkvine* show them to represent a separate form of church building in the Europe of their time. Leaving aside specificities of building technique, it is necessary only to contemplate the special world revealed in stone carvings and the details of churches and gravestones. Carving and symbolism follow the lines and associations of classical art – as well, of course, as the universal symbols of early Christianity. But the style and motifs of the carvings hark back, in their dominant tone, to an autochthonous culture and artistic tradition.

Remains of early Christian basilicas have been found in Nerezi (Čapljina), Mokro, Klobuk near Ljubuški, Dabravina near Breza, in Breza, Zenica, Majdan (near Mrkonjić-grad), Oborci near Donji Vakuf, Blagaj (on the Japra) and Mošunj near Travnik, while new finds have been made in Buško Blato, Kiseljak, Banja Luka . . .

FOUR

The Early Slav Centuries

The Illyricum that emerged from the chaos of the great movements marking the fall of the Western Empire and the dawn of a new epoch was largely populated by Slavs. Moving easily and fast along the roads the Romans had built for movement in the opposite direction, unstoppable waves of Slavs flooded in from the east, from the sixth century onwards, moving in tandem with the warlike Avars. This was the final blow delivered against a weakened Roman world whose transformation had already begun.

In 614 the great Roman town of Salona (Solin) fell to the newcomers, and in 626 they besieged Constantinople itself. After their defeat before the capital of the Byzantine Empire, the military power of the Avars began to wane and they gradually withdrew to their state in Pannonia. But the Slav tribes, with their different agricultural and stock-breeding background, remained in the new homeland; it is now that the Slav history of these lands begins.

Details of the first century of Slav settlement are scant and for Bosnia-Herzegovina almost non-existent. States were formed in neighbouring Croatia, Duklja and Raška, but the process went more slowly in Bosnia. Its first mention in a known historical source dates from the tenth century, in Constantine Porphyrogenitus' *De Administrando Imperio*. Two centuries later, in the middle of the twelfth century during the rule of the Bosnian ban Borić, another Byzantine writer Ivan Kinamos records: 'Bosnia is not a vassal state . . .

but is independent; the people lead their own life and rule themselves.'

The overriding characteristic of mediaeval Bosnia, as we shall see, was stubbornly to preserve archaic forms of social life and nurture a specific cultural tradition. It is difficult to give a precise answer to the question why Bosnia, among all the Slav states of the Middle Ages, retained and developed its own special forms. Certainly one reason was its inland situation, which in many ways cut it off from both east and west.

In the dark and little known centuries this location, preceding as it did the political formation of Bosnia in the twelfth century, was probably responsible for two interlinked processes that formed the basis of a specific way of life. The first favoured the prolongation of certain Slav forms of social life and culture, while the second fostered cultural interaction between indigenous inhabitants and newcomers. The indigenous Illyrians were themselves an ethnically complex mix: there was a Romanized component inherited from the centuries of classical antiquity, and a non-Romanized or semi-Romanized population nourished by the springs of prehistoric Illyrian tradition. These regions differed from the Adriatic coastal towns and islands, which were long able to fend off Slav influence from behind the walls of fortified towns. In Bosnia assimilation may have been quicker, which strengthened the Slav component; but the new amalgam carried within itself much more of the indigenous tradition. Some of these so-called ancient Balkan elements can still be discerned today. Ethnographers have not yet found a completely satisfying explanation for them, but have indicated certain aspects that are not common to the Slav folk background. These are the puzzling vestiges still found today in toponyms, mountain yelling, dance rhythms, tattooing, certain details of rural architecture and costume, and certain traces of pagan beliefs.

With the arrival of the Slavs in the Balkans, this large region between two centres of Christianity – the Roman and later Frankish to the west and the Byzantine to the east – was once more de-Christianized. So one of the first great undertakings of these centres was its reconversion. In the parts nearer the centres of power and in the more accessible places this happened fairly quickly, and its early traces can be seen in the architecture and carving of early Croatian churches in Dalmatia, built in the ninth and tenth centuries. But we can only surmise the progress of conversion in Bosnia in the early days of Slav settlement; not until the end of the tenth century is there any direct evidence, and that comes from the western regions in natural contact with Dalmatia. Bosnia was probably open to powerful conversion moves from the ninth century onwards, as a result of the important work of the Slav missionaries Cyril and Methodius and their successors. This can be seen from the early and long-lasting establishment of literacy in Bosnia, using both the Glagolitic and Cyrillic alphabets.

No architecture, sculpture or dressed stonework has been found from the early Slav period in Bosnia. A number of archaeological finds show that for a long time the prehistoric hill-fort settlements which the Slavs found when they arrived continued to be used. These ancient sites have come down to us under the general Slav name *gradina* [*grad* = town]. In smaller numbers in lowland areas there are traces of traditional circular Slav settlements known as *gradišta*, and constructed from earth and wood.

Graveyards are the most important source for study of the culture of that time, especially because of considerable finds of locally-made metal ornaments, jewellery and weapons. These graveyards are found near still earlier necropolises or places with religious significance, and thus show cultural continuity, in spite of all wars and perturbations, from prehistory through classical times down to early Slav days and on into the Middle Ages. These early Slav burial places confirm belief in the cultural and ethnic intermeshing of the original inhabitants of the region and the Slavs during the early period of their settlement. This is confirmed by many items of Slav personal adornment, the fashioning of which incorporates motifs and forms that have been traditional here since classical and even pre-classical times.

An important innovation was the development of skill in working with stone, something that in later centuries was to surface in the amazing art of the stećci.* The earliest finds were fragments of church architecture and carving in a transitional style between pre-Romanesque and Romanesque. These date from the eleventh, twelfth and thirteenth centuries and are products of the same carving and building skills that were responsible for early Croatian architecture and carving. Examples include fragments of interlacing work found near Glamoč and Livno, similar motifs in the church of St Peter in Zavala,

9. The Humac Tablet, from Humac near Ljubuški, 10th–11th centuries.

---

* The mediaeval gravestones found in many parts of Bosnia-Hercegovina and a small number of other places are known as *stećci* (plural of *stećak*). The folk name for them is *mramorovi*, but except where essential we have used the more common name of stećci.

and the fragment of a ciborium from a church in Rogačici near Sarajevo.

Writing, another important aspect of the Bosnian and Herzegovinian cultural heritage, has also been preserved in stone – though not very much of it. The oldest such memorial is the Humac Tablet from Humac near Ljubuški. It bears the dedicatory inscription *A se crki Arhanpela Mihaila . . . a zida ju Krsmir . . . i žena Jega Pavica* ['This is the church of the Archangel Michael . . . and was built by Krsmir . . . and his wife Pavica']. It has been dated to the tenth or early eleventh century and is important evidence for archaeologists, historians and linguists. It is also of considerable palaeographic interest. In front of this ancient inscription, we feel that we are standing before the very source of what in Bosnia-Herzegovina was to become a special variant of the written language. Basically the text is Cyrillic, but Glagolitic elements can be clearly seen. It is obviously the beginning of the transformation of one graphic system into another: Bosnian Cyrillic or *Bosančica*, which in the following centuries was to become the dominant and generally accepted form of writing in Bosnia, also used in Dubrovnik and other Dalmatian towns.

MEDIAEVAL BOSNIA

CROATIA

Una

Sava

Đakovo

Sava

Otoka
Krupa
Bihać
Kamengrad

Sana

Zvečaj

Vrbas

Lijevče

St. Helyae Dobor

USORA

Skakava
Srebrenik

Bijeljina

SOLI

Drina

Ključ Greben/Krupa

Bosna

Teočak

DONJI KRAJI

BOSNA

Tuzla

Jezero

Vranduk

Zvornik

SERBIA

Sokol Jajce

Zgošća

Bobovac

Lab

ZAVRŠJE

Travnik
Lašva

Vrbas

Olovo

Glamoč

Mile
Fojnica

Curia Bani

Srebrenica

Moštre Vrhbosna

Zadar

Cetina

Kupres

Bjelosavljevići

Bistrica

Dreževice

Podvisoki

Borač

Duvno

Kreševo Hodidjed

Drina

Split

Blidinje

Konjic

Pavlovac

Prača

Samobor

Neretva

Gvozno

Foča

Mileševo

Blagaj

Podborač

Sokol

Drijeva
(port)

Krekovi

HUM

Ključ

Radimlja
& Boljuni

Adriatic Sea

Dubrovnik

Kotor

O Mining and metal-working centres	⋯⋯⋯⋯ Bosnia under ban Kulin
⚜ Roman Catholic (Franciscan) monastery	▬▬▬ Bosnia under king Tvrtko
◇ Major stećak necropolis	–·–·–·– Present-day border of Bosnia-Herzegovina
⚜ Royal palace	
⌂ Noble fortress	

FIVE

The Middle Ages

General overview

In the early Middle Ages the South Slavs found themselves between two great cultural entities – Byzantium and Rome, the Christianity of West and East. They underwent conversion to Christianity and in a very general sense became part of the social and spiritual world of mediaeval Europe. But after the eleventh century break between Byzantium and Rome, between Orthodox and Catholic Christianity, the two parts began to develop each in its own direction and their polarization has left an indelible mark on the cultural history of the South Slav lands, which because of their very position gravitated in both directions. One of the most important developments of the Middle Ages, moreover, was the successful attempt to evade religious assimilation, reflected in many branches of cultural and artistic life. Thanks to the epoch-making achievements of Cyril and Methodius in the ninth century, the South Slavs obtained their own script in the shape of the Glagolitic alphabet, and soon afterwards the Cyrillic, their own variant of the Greek alphabet. This made possible in succeeding centuries the rich development of literacy and literature in the vernacular language and script, thus placed on an equal footing with the 'holy' languages of Latin, Hebrew and Greek.

Situated in the very heart of these contending lands, inaccessible and impenetrable, Bosnia was last of the early feudal states to emerge and last to be registered in written history. But for the same reasons it survived longest politically and took on the most specific cultural and spiritual profile among the South Slav mediaeval lands. No other region was so completely overlapped by the two great contending civilizational blocs. It was inevitably affected by both and integrated by them into the Europe of the Middle Ages. But lying as it did on the periphery of each, neither had a sufficiently intense influence upon it to achieve its radical assimilation.

Thus the whole spiritual and material culture of mediaeval Bosnia had a bifocal development, open to impulses from abroad but able to refashion these in accordance with its own living South Slav traditions, grafted in turn onto prehistoric Illyrian roots. This produced a mediaeval culture with a high degree of creative self-reliance. It is also at the root of the multiform cultural parallelism that has characterized Bosnia-Herzegovina throughout history and down to the present day. In the Middle Ages the cultures of east and west coexisted here, enriched each other and were themselves enriched by the relics of autochthonous tradition. Side by side with the Catholic and Orthodox churches – the Bosnian Church. Side by side with the Cyrillic, Greek, Latin and Glagolitic scripts – *Bosančica*. Side by side with Byzantine and Serbian art, and west European Romanesque and Gothic transmitted through the Croatian coastal towns – a native tradition of stećci, manuscript illumination and fine craftsmanship. One atypical trait of mediaeval Bosnia that should be noted here is the degree of secularism that characterized all spheres of life, especially the spiritual and the creative. In this Bosnia differed from the rest of Europe, where the Middle Ages was a time of ecclesiastical domination, dogmatism and religious exclusiveness.

As we have said, the first mention of Bosnia is in Constantine Porphyrogenitus' *De administrando imperio* written in the tenth century. As the political territory of what is today Bosnia-Herzegovina he mentions Bosnia and the towns of Desnek (near Visoko), and Katero (Kotorac near Sarajevo), Hum, Trebinje, with Konavlje and part of the Neretva area. Thus when there was already a fairly advanced form of feudal development in other South Slav areas such as Croatia, Duklja, and Raška, Bosnia in the inaccessible interior was little known.

Thanks to its undefined level of political independence, Bosnia was successively claimed by various neighbours – Croatia, Duklja, Raška and sometimes, in a spirit of global domination, by the Byzantine Empire and even by Hungary. The oldest recorded Bosnian ruler was a Prince Stjepan, installed by Bodin King of Duklja in the ninth century. In the time of Ban Borić in the middle of the twelfth century, Hungarian interest in Bosnia became evident.

Political and territorial stabilization and expansion began in the reign of Ban Kulin (1180–1204), when trade links were opened especially to Dubrovnik. Dubrovnik had a key role in Bosnia's development throughout the Middle Ages and beyond into the period of Ottoman power. The city was also important for its impact on cultural life. It was at this time that the first Papal accusations of heresy began and the first threats of punitive expeditions and crusades.

The whole of the thirteenth century, under the bans Matej Ninoslav, Prijezda, and Stjepan Kotromanić, was marked by political disturbance and inter-dynastic rivalries almost entirely provoked by Hungary.

With Ban Stjepan Kotromanić II (1322–53) a more general state of well-being began which culminated in the reign of Tvrtko I Kotromanić (1353–77 as ban, 1377–91 as king). It was in this period that Bosnia attained its maximum size, stretching up the Adriatic coast from Kotor to Biograd na Moru, including the islands of Korčula, Brač and Hvar and extending east to the Sava and Drina.

An event now occurred which affected the fate of the whole of Bosnian religious life and cvilization in the Middle Ages, and the influence of which has persisted into the present day – the foundation of the Bosnian Franciscan Vicariate. Franciscan missionaries began to operate in Bosnia at the end of the thirteenth century, when the missionary work of the Dominicans collapsed (1240) and after the seat of the Bosnian bishopric had been transferred in 1251 to Đakovo in Slavonia (Croatia). From the beginning, one of the basic tenets of the Franciscans was to understand local conditions and traditions and to adapt to the social and cultural ambience. As soon as possible their mission was continued by people born in Bosnia, who were therefore bilingual. This allowed the Franciscans to obtain the confidence both of the people and of the rulers, who saw them as a support in their efforts to attain political emancipation both from unrelenting Hungarian pressure, and from the ambitions of the Catholic bishopric in Đakovo. By an agreement reached between Ban Stjepan Kotromanić II and Friar Peregrine of Saxony the work of the Franciscans in Bosnia was given a firm permanent organizational basis with the establishment in 1340 of the Bosnian Vicariate. Despite all the changes that have taken place in the Bosnian state and in Bosnian society, this has survived to the present day in the shape of the Province of Bosna Srebrena [Bosnia Argentina or 'Silver Bosnia'].

From this time onwards, Franciscan monasteries began to proliferate – Srebrenica, Mile near Visoko, Kraljeva Sutjeska, Tuzla, Gradovrh, Zvornik, Lašva, Olovo, Fojnica, Kreševo, Vranduk, Tešanj, Bihać, Otoka, Krupa on the Una, Zvečaj, Krupa on the Vrbas, Jajce, Jezero, Livno, Glamoč, Duvno, Konjic, Mostar, Ljubuški etc – and many Franciscan churches were built. The Franciscans worked mainly in the urban areas, which were developing at that time in the form of trading and mining centres. But they were also active in more remote places. They played a part in ruling circles as diplomats, advisers, intermediaries and spiritual advisers. Their influence went far beyond spiritual concerns, it was all encompassing, there was no aspect of mediaeval Bosnian life in which they were not involved, either directly or in an advisory capacity.

Fourteenth-century Bosnia was thus the scene of dynamic processes and important events, both productive and conflictual, typifying a time of fast and many-sided expansion. Fortified towns and residences for those in power were built; links with European courts were strengthened. There was intensive development of certain branches of economic life, especially mining, in order to expand which people were brought in from Saxony, and trade, for which the leading partner continued to be Dubrovnik. There was work for increasing numbers of craftsmen as urbanization and trade increased. The mediaeval market town of Drijevo in the lower Neretva valley was one of the most dynamic and open markets on the Mediterranean. Fojnica, Olovo, Podvisoki, Srebrenica, Foča, Prača, Podborač were all Dubrovnik colonies or open market towns. Increased connections with the outside world can be seen in the growing number of people who went abroad to study various crafts and trades in the more developed Croatian towns, such as Dubrovnik, Zadar and Split. Caravans of up to 300 horses were a common sight and required inns to accommodate them. Bosnian coins were minted, and records describe the jewellery, ornaments, clothes and other items for everyday use that could be seen in castles and town mansions, where standards of living and taste were in no way inferior to those prevailing in contemporary European castles. It is said that at the great tournament held at Buda in 1412, Dukes Hrvoje and Sandalj made a great impression on the feudal elite with their clothing, harness, weapons and bearing. A high artistic level had already been reached in the stećci and in the illumination and calligraphy of manuscripts.

In religious life, as we have seen, there was a duality between the Catholic Church, embodied in the Franciscan Order, and the Bosnian Church, which gradually over time also gained a place of authority in political life. From the beginning of the fifteenth century the Orthodox Church began to operate in Herzegovina, supported by Sandalj Hranić and later Duke [Herceg] Stjepan Kosača. When looking at religion in fifteenth-century Bosnia and Hum (today Herzegovina) we need to realize that beside these three components a fourth was already active. Several decades before the coming of the Ottoman Empire, Islam began to gain a foothold. In the first part of the century the Turks had already conquered some towns and areas in eastern Bosnia and formed administrative units there. The presence of Islam was not confined to the political and military level; along with the new religion a new civilization began to develop and new kinds of towns to be built.

At the end of the fourteenth century, following Tvrtko's death, the general level of prosperity began to favour the malign development of a powerful nobility with hereditary estates, typical of feudalism everywhere but reinforced in Bosnia by the tenacious remains of earlier tribal relations in the shape of the'noble hereditament': inalienability of landed property, whether inherited or acquired. This formed a basis for the creation of a powerful feudal class of territorial lords such as Hrvoje Vukčić Hrvatinić in Donji Kraji, Sandalj Hranić Kosača and later Stjepan Vukčić Kosača in Hum, Pavao Radinović (and later his son Radoslav Pavlović) in Podrinje, and the Zlatonosovićes, Dinjičićes, Kovačevićes, Radivojevićes . . .

From 1386 the first skirmishes with the Turks began in the Neretva valley. Before the great Battle of Kosovo the Turks once more attacked Bosnia and were defeated at Bileća in 1388. These first encounters marked the beginning of an endless series of wars against the Turks, lasting a full 140 years until the fall of Jajce in 1528.

In the early years of the fifteenth century, after Tvrtko's death, Bosnia was harassed by continuous Turkish raids and suffered from the anarchy of the territorial nobility, among whom there was continuous rivalry for the crown, clearly shown by the fact that in only thirty years, from 1391 to 1421, the throne was occupied by Stjepan Dabiša, Jelena, Stjepan Ostoja, Tvrtko II, Stjepan Ostoja once again and Stjepan Ostojić.

In Europe, fear of the advance of the Ottoman Empire was increasing. Rome strengthened Catholicism in Bosnia, promising in return organized defence against the Turkish advance. The territorial lords Hrvoje, Sandalj and Pavao Radinović were interested only in gaining power for themselves and making themselves independent of the crown. To achieve this they would go to any lengths, such as forming alliances with the Turks, who, knowing how to use their rivalry for their own ends, strengthened their position in the east of the country, even demanding tribute from the king.

In 1415 the Turks defeated the Hungarians in a great battle near Doboj and from then on their direct influence over political conditions in Bosnia became ever stronger.

In the second half of the century during the reigns of Stjepan Tomaš (1443–61) and Stjepan Tomašević (1461–3), when all the feudal lords with the exception of Stjepan Vukčić Kosača had either died or been killed as a result of revenge or intrigue, a process was taking place that was more and more clearly dividing the country in two. On the one hand were the parts under royal administration, with a considerable degree of centralization – the Bosna, Usora and Soli valleys, Podrinje, Donji Kraji etc – and on the other was Hum under Stjepan Vukčić Kosača, who in 1448 took the title of Herceg [duke], whence was derived the later name of Herzegovina.

The momentum achieved in the fourteenth century, thanks to the political, administrative and economic stability of Tvrtko's rule, made the fifteenth century the high point of culture in Bosnia and Hum. This was realized in many and diverse ways. The most beautiful illuminated manuscripts written in Bosnia date from these sixty years, the most imposing fortified towns, and above all the art of the stećci, which in this century reached its high point.

The Bosnian Church

In the whole history of mediaeval Bosnia there is nothing that has become so entangled in various theories, romantic ideas, controversy and mystification as the Bosnian Church and the supposed 'Bogomil' heresy of its adherents. Ever since the middle of the nineteenth century the Bosnian Church has been a constant preoccupation of scholars (both serious and less serious), politicians, writers and poets. Ideological motives have lain behind much of this interest, which has been used to support various current political and national ideas. This, of course, has complicated any critical approach to a complex and obscure subject.

The number of conflicting theories and suppositions may be reduced in substance to two. According to the older one the Bosnian Church was heretical and had similarities with the teaching and organization of the dualistic heresies that flooded into parts of Europe in the Middle Ages. The newer approach considers it a national church based on the traditions of Cyril and Methodius reflected in the Slav liturgy, which theologically and doctrinally is not in conflict with Christianity but represents an attempt to achieve jurisdictional independence from Rome.

The first of these theories started from the anathema against the Bosnian Church issued by the Roman curia and repeated mechanically and uncritically by later writers. According to this theory the Bosnian Church was a form of Bogomilism and preached a 'dualistic' theology in which the power of good and the power of evil were equal. It rejected the Christian sacraments and symbols, especially the Cross, and in a social and political sense was a more or less complete rejection of the system of its time. Those following this interpretation have a tendency to explain all cultural developments in mediaeval Bosnia in terms of a dualistic Church with esoteric gnostic teaching. It is interesting to observe how this interpretation, given a scholarly pedigree by the Zagreb priest and historian Franjo Rački in his *Bogomili i patareni* (Bogomils and Patarenes, 1870), has been used like others derived from it for all kinds of fancy theories. These range from political notions characterized by every kind of ideological invention (from an Austro-Hungarian academic 'Bosnianism', through later socialistic suggestions about – and sympathy for – Bosnia's supposed 'anti-clericalism' and 'social non-conformism', down to fairy-tales about a 'Bogomil nation' that went over en masse to Islam after the Turkish invasion) to poetical constructions in which the basic idea has been endowed with magical powers of suggestion, and in the greatest examples – above all, the essays of Miroslav Krleža (1893–1981) and the poetry of Mak Dizdar (1917–71) – summoned forth potent visions, with a new poetic and aesthetic reality developing quite independently of the original dubious premises or even quite false or imaginary 'facts'.

In the middle of the twentieth century a new interest arose in the culture of the Middle Ages, and complex inter-disciplinary research became the order of the day (stećci, manuscripts, towns, epigraphy, art). This made it clear that the spiritual profile of mediaeval Bosnia was very different from, and much more complex than, the black-and-white romanticized picture.

For any reliable study it was necessary to take into account the full context of Bosnian society and political and spiritual life. The basic elements of that context are: geographical location; the heritage of the liturgy of Cyril and Methodius; the crisis in, and loss of power by, the Byzantine Empire; the political pressure of Hungary; the political and ecclesiastical strengthening of Serbia, especially after its church became autocephalous in 1219; the ever present antagonism between the Hungarians and the Roman curia, and the claim of both to influence in Bosnia; the continuous efforts of Bosnian rulers to achieve as high a level as possible of legitimacy and independence, which in the Middle Ages inevitably involved the Church; and, finally, the continuous antagonism in Bosnia between King and nobles within which, in line with their interests, the former invoked the authority of Rome and the latter the long tradition of the Bosnian Church.

It became increasingly obvious that all the denunciations, threats and accusations against the Bosnian Church for heresy were always more political than religious in motivation, and always made use of standard incriminating formulae quite inapplicable to the real Bosnian context.

In all the cultural material of mediaeval Bosnia there are no Bogomil elements, nor those of any other heresy. The key texts – from the *Bilino Polje Abjuration* of 1203 down to the 1466 *Will of Gost Radin* – quite explicitly operate with orthodox Christian formulae and terminology.

Ban Kulin was accused by King Vukan of Duklja and Bishop Bernard of Split of having provided hospitality to heretics and himself been present at their teaching, and they denounced him to Pope Innocent III. Ban Kulin then proposed that the Pope should send representatives to ascertain the position in Bosnia, which was agreed. Ivan de Casamaris went to Bosnia as papal legate, and the result of his visit was made public at a meeting at Bilino Polje near Zenica on 8 April 1203. The meeting ended with a statement by representatives of the Bosnian Christians (later ratified in Buda before the King of Hungary) known as the *Bilino Polje Abjuration,* in which they undertook to abide by the general code of the Catholic Church. This clearly shows what they were like in organizational terms: a monastic community (perhaps with 'dual monasteries', for female and male

members) like many in Europe at the time, concerning whose discipline the reformed Catholic Church was greatly exerting itself.

Gost Radin Butković, a dignitary of the Bosnian Church, with 50
or 60 of his followers took refuge in Dubrovnik from the Turks, and
sought leave from the Venetians to go on into their dominions. His
request was granted, but he remained in Dubrovnik until his death
(and in 1455 was even given a fine house there). On 5 January 1466
Gost Radin drew up his will, in which the text and a whole host of
details and explicit expressions of faith put it beyond any doubt that
the signatory could not possibly have been part of any heretical sect
or organization.

Abusive names such as Patarenes, Cathars, Manichaeans, cursed
baboons and 'the Bosnian plague', applied to Bosnians and members
of the Bosnian Church, are found only in foreign sources. The accu-
sation of Bogomilism was a nineteenth-century academic invention.
The Bosnians always and exclusively referred to themselves as Christians.

It is, however, true that the Bosnian Church existed as a specific
form of religious organization, developed in Bosnia, and lasted as
long as the Bosnian state lasted. It had its own hierarchy with the
titles *dida* [*djed* = grandfather], *strojnik* [steward], *gost* [visitor] and
starac [elder], and some kind of monastic organization in *hiže* [homes],
as the Franciscan friars still call their monasteries. Respected and play-
ing an important role in the political life of the country, its dignitaries
were people of great social standing and secure status, quite different
from the fate of Europe's heretical sects and their followers, subjected to brutal repression.

Although this unresolved and enigmatic subject is likely to go on
intriguing the scholarly, the political and the artistic imagination,
recent critical research suggests the following conclusion. The church
in Bosnia was a continuation of, and substitute for, the Bosnian
bishopric in the period after the unsuccessful attempt to Latinize it
and its subsequent transfer to Đakovo in Croatia in the mid thirteenth century. In the tradition of Cyril and Methodius, use of the
national language and liturgy continued after the foundation of the

Bosnian Franciscan Vicariate (1340) and lived on in parallel with it, in a mixture of rivalry and coexistence, almost until the end of the Kingdom of Bosnia in 1463.

Building

The ruins of walled castles are the most evocative monuments of mediaeval Bosnia and an enduring part of the country's landscape. Experts know of about 200 of them all throughout Bosnia-Herzegovina, but it is estimated that during the Middle Ages there were some 350.

Intensive building began in the time of Stjepan Kotromanić II, in the first half of the fourteenth century (though some predate his reign). At that time Bosnia was a strong state stretching 'from the sea to the Sava, from the Cetina to the Drina', and it continued to expand during the reign of Tvrtko and into the fifteenth century. In style and building technique these fortified Bosnian castles were in step with the same kind of building in Europe, keeping abreast of improvements in both building methods and developments in the offensive power of weaponry. They also evolved certain stylistic elements unknown outside Bosnia; one was the strengthening of walls with horizontally placed tree trunks, a characteristic of all Bosnian walled castles.

The principal purpose of these buildings was defensive. This is particularly evident in some of the larger ones, such as the whole chain of castles and walled towns constructed along the Vrbas and Bosna rivers. In many cases suburbs grew up outside the walls, and some of these became centres of local life and the strongholds of regional nobles.

The oldest political centre of mediaeval Bosnia, as confirmed by many finds and records, was around Visoko in the gentle and more accessible open country on the banks of the Bosna. It was probably this area, and the surrounding country with its settlements of various sizes, which originally provided the name Bosnia, later extended to the rest of the country.

10. Mediaeval Stjepangrad, Ljubuški.

11. The castle at Vranduk on the River Bosna.

A large number of finds have been made in this small area. Kulin's church with its famous dedicatory stone inscriptions was in Biškupići (Muhašinovići). The Bosnian parliament sat at Mili (today Arnautovići), where Tvrtko the first Bosnian king was crowned. His tomb is there in St Nicholas' church and so too is the tomb of his great predecessor Ban Stjepan Kotromanić. There were royal places in Podvisoko and Moštre, and the walled city of Visoko, though destroyed during the Turkish occupation, was long remembered as one of the most important places in Bosnia.

The story of the discoveries made at Mili deserves a few more lines. In 1909 and 1910 the National Archaeological Museum in Sarajevo organized excavations in the expectation of discovering some Roman remains. What they did find was probably the most important discovery of mediaeval Bosnia – the remains of the Franciscan church of St Nicholas, sited on the ruins of two still older structures, a Romanesque chapel and a small Gothic chapel, within which was a large stećak *(sic)* and below it the crypt of the royal burial chamber, containing rich material: jewellery, brocade embroidered with the royal coat-of-arms in gold thread, etc. Instead of careful study, protection of the site and publication of the find, the discovery was followed by total silence. The stećak was broken up for stone to fill in the grave, the site and finds were never properly researched, the small objects (all of them? who can say?) were taken to the museum but never submitted to professional scrutiny, just carelessly thrown in, some not even labelled and classified. A narrow-gauge railway was later constructed through Mili, and after the Second World War a wide-gauge railway, with a road beside it. Very little would have been known about all this if certain of the museum's curators (Irma Čremošnik and Đuro Basler) had not, at first sporadically and later systematically, become interested in the puzzle of what these objects in the museum might be. Later (1967–77) Pavao Anđelić undertook a systematic study of the site and the museum material. On the basis of what was left of that important discovery, made only fifty years earlier, it was possible to ascertain the important facts we have related. The church was the very church of St Nicholas built by Ban

12. Coat of arms over the entrance to the king's court, Jajce, 15th century.

Stjepan Kotromanić, immediately after his agreement with Friar Peregrine of Saxony confirming the establishment of the Franciscan order in Bosnia, and had been the first centre of the Franciscan Vicariate.

It is difficult to explain the vandalism of 1910. Probably the nearest to the truth are authors like Marian Wenzel who think it was a consequence of Austro-Hungarian cultural policy in Bosnia. Its agents were perhaps over-committed to the theory of 'Bogomil Bosnia', believing that it could serve to neutralize the national movements of the time, which they perceived as a direct threat; the discovery that the two most famous rulers of Bosnia were buried in a Catholic church, one of them under a stećak, was seen as too destructive of their ideological constructions. Certainly there must have been a well-organized cover-up at a very high level for all traces of such an important find to have been lost.

Not far from this earliest centre of the Bosnian state, and naturally connected to it, are two towns of outstanding importance for Bosnian history – Sutjeska (Kraljeva, i.e. royal, Sutjeska) and Bobovac, both seats of Bosnian rulers. Another important centre was Jajce, city of the noble Hrvatinić family and at the end of Bosnia's independence a royal city and the place where the last king was killed.

A considerable number of other towns were built at this time by the big feudal families at places where some of them had castles: Borač, Ključ in Hum, Travnik, Pavlovac, Ključ on the Sana, Prozor, Sokol on the Pliva (more exactly, on the Pliva's tributary the Sokočnica), Blagaj, Samobor, Sokol on the Drina, Dobor.

The larger and more important towns formed nuclei around which political, commercial and cultural activities began to grow up. We may discern the development of three mediaeval cultural areas: Central Bosnia, with centres in Bobovac, Sutjeska and Visoko; Jajce, especially after it became a royal seat in the middle of the fifteenth century; and Hum, which in the decades immediately before the Turkish occupation was important for its connection with the Kosača family.

Not only in Bosnia itself but beyond its borders Bobovac was regarded as the capital, and its fate was somehow symbolic: at the very beginning of the Turkish occupation it was looted, torched and finally reduced to ruins, later to be adapted for the use of a small military garrison. It was first mentioned in 1350. In 1356 Tvrtko wrote in a letter of his castle as *curia nostra sub castro Bobovaz*. It was a typical mountain citadel, cut off from the world below by dizzy heights of more than 1000 metres, and had eleven towers.

13. Capital from the lower palace at Bobovac, 14th century.

14. Bronze basin in the Renaissance style excavated from Bobovac.

Within the walls was a well developed town dominated by two palaces, it had a granary, water cisterns, stables, a blacksmith's and other workshops, and was well supplied with defensive positions. At the end of the town was a small square in front of a church and mortuary chapel. Although it had originally been designed as a military base, it developed into a centre of commerce and crafts, and beyond the walls two suburbs of different sizes grew up. Contemporary records put the Bobovac suburbs on almost the same level as nearby Sutjeska, where there was a royal residence. Its amenities, architectural details and works of art made Bobovac an outstanding illustration of the European standards attained by the Bosnian feudal nobility. Glass and metal ware, ceramics and gilding, capitals, portals and Romanesque-Gothic distyles, carving and heraldry, the remains of wall paintings and details indicating the use of wall hangings, all demonstrate the living standards and taste of the upper class of mediaeval Bosnia. The sources from which all this came show that there was a brisk trade with European cultural centres, while the distinctive features of Bosnian architecture displayed in the fortifications and buildings at Bobovac show the important part played by highly skilled local craftsmen. The material remains and fragmentary records of life in these Bosnian castles show that, in kind if not in degree, they matched all the features and richness of life and culture of western European developed feudalism. This seems largely to have been true also of life in towns, castle outskirts, trading posts and mining settlements, which have only recently become the object of systematic scientific investigation.

Of churches, the most important buildings of the Middle Ages and most characteristic of the mediaeval spirit, there is little significant trace in Bosnia, although they were built throughout the Middle Ages and from the fourteenth century with the arrival of the Franciscans their number increased. This absence should not be interpreted as showing any lack of skills, especially since in the late fourteenth and the fifteenth century Bosnia was relatively wealthy and had many builders, stone masons and master craftsmen. It would also be wrong to interpret it as rejection by the Bosnian Church of imposing churches. The fact that there are almost no churches left is the result of destruction, and of a later history which was not conducive either to building new churches or to repairing old ones. The very small number that have come down to us today include the ruins of St Mary's chapel and St Luke's belfry in Jajce; ruins in Ošanići near Stolac, in Vareš, in Podmilačje near Jajce, in Sopotnica near Goražde, and in Dobrun near Višegrad; and churches in Srebrenica, Bihać and Jajce which were later turned into mosques. On the basis of what is left we can see the interaction of Romanesque and Gothic, the latter being dominant. St Luke's belfry is the only extant mediaeval tower in Bosnia and its construction is interesting. The bottom part has strong Romanesque elements, the second stage was built in the Gothic style, and then quite unexpectedly in the fifteenth century the bell-tower was provided with typically Romanesque distyles.

There is an interesting story associated with St Luke's tower and St Mary's church, a typical mediaeval story about bones. Today it seems amusing and slightly grotesque, but it exercised and disturbed mediaeval minds from Jajce to Dubrovnik, Buda and Venice, Padua and Rome. When in 1459 Stjepan Tomašević, heir to the Bosnian throne, married Jelena-Mara, daughter of the Despot of Serbia Lazar Branković, she brought with her from Smederovo, as the most valuable part of her dowry, relics of St Luke the evangelist. These were deposited in St Mary's church. The church never officially changed its name, but from that time on both clergy and people knew the tower as St Luke's tower.

But the journey of the relics did not end there. When the Turks conquered Bosnia in 1463 and for a short time took Jajce, Queen Mara came to recover her treasure and, of course, took the saint's bones away with her. She immediately put them up for sale, and for some time there was lively competition to possess them. King Matthias of Hungary offered her three castles, the Venetian Republic offered money. Although Queen Mara wrote in a letter that she considered the Venetian offer mean, she was finally forced to accept it. St Luke's bones were then ceremonially transported to Venice and given burial

15. Belfry of St Luke's Church, Jajce (1461–5).

in a luxurious coffin. The ceremony was organized by Doge Cristoforo Moro himself. But even this was not the end. The Benedictines of Padua now began a lawsuit questioning the authenticity of the Smederevo-Jajce relics. Until the matter should be settled the Venetians desposited the bones in an outlying church and placed the whole case before the Pope. But to this day the matter has never been settled, and what averred to be the bones of St Luke still lie, anonymous and forgotten, in the gloom of the church of San Giobbe on the outskirts of Venice.

Mortuary chapels are of especial interest in Bosnia. Besides that already mentioned in Bobovac there are others, the mausoleum of Batal Santić in Turbe near Travnik, and the chapel of Duke Vlado Bjelić in Vlahovići near Ljubinje.

In Jajce there is an underground chapel which is of especial interest. Lack of historical memory, characteristic of a country with a fate like Bosnia's, led to its being known as 'the catacombs', reminiscent of the underground sanctuaries and hidden places of worship used by the first Christians in Roman times. This one (according to

16. The Fojnica Bowl, hammered silver, from a Bosnian workshop, 15th century.

recent historical research) was probably associated with rites of initiation into knighthood inaugurated at the end of the fourteenth century by Hrvoje Vukčić. Hewn out of the living rock and constituting a coherent and quite highly developed architectural whole, it is in conception and execution alike a curiosity of its time.

The names of some Bosnian builders are recorded in stone inscriptions or historical sources. We know for example that Master Braja built the tomb of Župan Grd of Trebinje in the twelfth century, and that Draže Ohmučanin built the church and tomb of the great Judge Gradiša in Podbrežja near Zenica. We also know that many master-craftsmen came from the Croatian coastal towns of Dubrovnik, Split and Zadar, and that many Bosnians went to those places to learn from some of the best architects and sculptors of the time. Juraj Gradomilović, for example, from Vesela Straža (Bugojno) became pupil to Andrija Aleši and Mihovil Vučihnić in 1499; Antun Drastić from Livno in 1467 and Radovan Radoslavčić from Jajce in 1451 were pupils of the famous Juraj of Dalmatia.

Of smaller works of art such as reliefs and paintings, both prone to destruction, we know very little today. The only traces of their existence are fragments like those at Bobovac. We can talk with more certainty and on the basis of better evidence about a number of forms of fine craftsmanship in which a special Bosnian style developed, mentioned in many documents of the time especially from Dubrovnik and Italy. Bosnian metalwork especially gold, and costumes '*al modo de bossina*', were prized in many European courts, and a special place goes to the seals of the Bosnian nobility, which in beauty and workmanship are equal to the best European products.

Writing, books and miniatures

Writing and literacy perhaps provide the best gauge of the spiritual and cultural profile of mediaeval Bosnia, and of the catastrophic fate of that culture. Charters, documents, letters, canonical books, gospels, inscriptions in stone are witnesses both of the spirit of the time and of the cultural currents that splashed upon these lands, witnesses also of successful efforts to avoid blind mechanical copying of accepted models. They show a distinct striving for personal expression according to local standards and needs.

In mediaeval Bosnia and in Hum four different alphabets were in use, albeit not equally: Greek, Latin, Glagolitic and Cyrillic. Contrary to the generally held belief of a cultural vacuum in mediaeval Bosnia there was a high level of literacy as well as an interesting and unusual poly-alphabetism. Cyrillic was the local alphabet, but it developed marked characteristics of its own both in script and characters, to the extent that it came to be known as Bosnian Cyrillic or Bosančica. There are indications that a similar process had begun to take effect in Glagolitic.

17. Ban Kulin's charter to the people of Dubrovnik, 1189.

Another distinguishing mark of Bosnian literacy is that it was overwhelmingly secular, much more under the influence of the nobility and their administrators than of monks and monasteries. The famous Kulin Charter (*Kulinova povelja*) to the people of Dubrovnik, dated 1189, is an important document, the first official act written in the national language in the whole of the Slav south.

Radoje (in Kulin's court), Desoje (in Ninoslav's), Vladoje (in Tvrtko's), Tomaš Lužac (in Dabiša's), Stjepan Dobrinović and Hrvatin (in Ostoja's) are the names of only a few of the professional scribes (*dijak*), the work of whose hands testifies to the high level of their skill and learning. From their manuscripts lively and original flashes shine out, showing verbal creativity in what might otherwise have been routine copy-writing.

Numerous documents and records show that many nobles, merchants and craftsmen reached a relatively good standard of literacy.

Inscriptions hold a special place in mediaeval written records; they are found in churches, on stećci and on seals. The oldest known in Bosnia and Hum are the dedicatory epigrapha on the *Humac Tablet* (10 c), fragments from the church in Kijevci near Prijedor (11–12 c, Glagolitic), the Cyrillic writing in Biskupići church near Visoko and that in the church of Kulin's great judge Gradiša.

An eloquent proof of the considerable level of literacy and the need for it are two books commissioned by Duke Hrvoje: *Hrvoje's Missal*, and in Glagolitic, one in Cyrillic. It is logical to suppose that these were not the only ones written.

This brings us back to the subject of the Bosnian Church and the supposed heresy of its believers. These two manuscripts show Hrvoje as affirming the practice of the Bosnian Church, in the tradition of Cyril and Methodius, while the use of both alphabets – the older Glagolitic and the newer Cyrillic – demonstrated a good knowledge of both and held them both in equal respect. The language of these books is the liturgical form of the national language, showing Hrvoje to be a Christian and a declared follower of the Bosnian Church; in neither manuscript are there elements of divergence from the canonical Christian writings or suggestions of any heretical leanings.

That both alphabets were simultaneously used in Bosnia and that both were well known is shown by the fact that a number of texts written in Cyrillic were copied from Glagolitic and vice versa. Again, some Cyrillic manuscripts have marginal glosses in Glagolitic. Glosses, commentaries and extracts from the Apocrypha in old MSS are important for literary history as showing a step away from simple copying towards personal creativity.

The oldest Glagolitic manuscript believed to have been written in Bosnia in the tenth century, is the *Codex Marianus*. Other famous Bosnian texts are the twelfth century Glagolitic Gršković fragments, with Cyrillic notes added sometime in the fourteenth century, Mihanović's twelfth-century Cyrillic fragment, and the missal already mentioned written for Hrvoje Vukčić by the scribe Butko, which is one of the finest and best preserved and is today in Istanbul.

The Cyrillic *Miroslav Missal* (12 c) matches in fineness *Hrvoje's Missal*. It was produced in the time of Miroslav, Duke of Hum, brother

18. Initial from the Divoš Tihoradić Gospel, first half of the 14th century.

of Nemanja, and written and illuminated by Varsamelon and the scribe Gligorje.

The *Divoš Tihoradić Gospel* (14 c) is interesting for its non-canonical glosses and additions and for texts of an apocryphal character; the four folios of the *Balatal Gospel*, written in the fourteenth century for Batal, the great lord of Lašva, by the scribe Stanko Kromirjanin, and the *Srećkovićev Gospel* (14–15 c) are interesting for the questions and answers in their margins – a kind of folk encyclopedia of their time. The Venetian Codex, the *Čajniče Gospel* (14 c), is the only mediaeval codex still in Bosnia. The *Hval Codex* (14–15 c) and the *Radosava Codex* (15 c) are known together as the *Apocalypse of Bosnian Christians*.

Along with the stećci, the most important art of mediaeval Bosnia is found in the miniatures and illumination of the above manuscripts. In part they reflect various artistic traditions (Old Slav, Byzantine and even Coptic and Armenian) but more importantly they are part of western European Romanesque, as found in the *Miroslav Gospel*, and extending to mature Gothic in *Hrvoje's Missal*. Many original aspects can be seen in the miniatures, constituting a separate South Slav miniaturist style. It can be seen in choice of subject, in draftsmanship, in use of colour, ornament and composition. A wealth of subjects and artistic maturity can be seen especially in the miniatures of the *Miroslav Gospel*, with its wealth of animal and human figures, and in *Hrvoje's Missal* with its unusual calendar division and the portrait and coat-of-arms of Hrvoje; and also in the *Venetian Codex* and the *Divoš Tihoradić Gospel*.

Bosnian mramorovi *or stećci*

The mediaeval Bosnian and Hum gravestones known as stećci are unique in Europe and gave free rein to the national creative spirit. In the whole of mediaeval south Slav art there is almost nothing that is still so strangely moving even today, both for scholars and for artists. Historians, art historians, folklorists and specialists in many fields have studied the Bosnian stećci for 150 years. They are a permanent challenge to fresh interpretation. The creative suggestiveness of these strange burial monoliths is shown by the number of works they have inspired not only in art and sculpture but in poetry and music.

Little is known about them before the twelfth or thirteenth century, that is until the age of Kulin when they first appeared. Historiography is largely silent, a little more is known by archaeologists but we are still far from being able to reconstruct anything about the life and culture of the times out of which they emerged. How did the incoming Slavs and the Romanized Illyrians blend with each other? What forms emerged in the process of achieving a stabilized Illyro-Romanic-Slav amalgam? What is Illyrian-Romanic and what is Slav? And what is the place of Christianity in all this? To what extent do the stećci contain echoes of eastern culture and what role did western European culture play? We must not forget that we are here considering something that spanned almost half a millenium during which there are no reliable records until the time of Ban Kulin. Where did the stećci come from and why are they found only in Bosnia? The riddle of this unique ritual art will only be solved when we know more about the centuries before them, and about their genesis and lineage.

Bosnia-Herzegovina, with 60,000 mediaeval stećci, is a great gallery of fascinating and unmatched stone art. The secret of their origin, in spite of great interest and numerous publications, has not been solved, nor has their aesthetic impact been fully explained. But perhaps this is not important. What is important is that the contemporary spirit recognizes in these stećci an exciting artistic expression and cultural wealth that should asssure them a place as yet unrealized, in some imaginary world museum of the future.

Stećak art developed during the thirteenth, fourteenth, fifteenth and sixteenth centuries in an area that can be precisely mapped within the borders of the mediaeval Bosnian state at its most extensive. Thus besides those in Bosnia-Herzegovina, they can only be found in some parts of Dalmatia, a few in inland Croatia, and a few in Serbia and Montenegro. Chronologically this art coincided with the period of the Bosnian state, but it did not end with the Turkish occupation and continued down to the sixteenth century, undergoing an interesting transformation, including symbiosis with Islamic nuances.

Their original folk names are *mramor* [marble], *kami* [stone], *bilig* [mark], *kuća* [house], *zlamenije* and the graveyards were called *mramorje, grčko groblje* [Greek graveyard], *mašeti, divsko groblje* [giants' graveyard]

Stećci are basically huge stone monoliths, with or without a base. As time went on they developed new forms known as *ploča* [slab], *sanduk* [chest] and *sljemenjak* – a block with a pitched 'roof'. These are the basic forms but there are many transitional ones. The stones are also categorized according to the carvings on them: pure, anthropomorphic, crosses and gravestones.

19. The stećak necropolis at Radimlja near Stolac, 15ᵗʰ century.

How stylistically varied this form of art was and how much it was an expression of an autochthonous tradition can be seen from the fact that over the centuries, while the basic form was retained, a number of variants emerged in Bosnia and Hum each with its own distinguishing features and modifications. The two styles that have been most thoroughly studied to date are those of Herzegovina and east Bosnia. Detailed comparison and analysis shows certain characteristics common to central Bosnian stećci and those from west Herzegovina and the Duvno-Kupres region. The smallest number, and the least decorated, come from that part of Bosnia known in the Middle Ages as Donji Kraji, among which are a number with certain specific forms.

Artistic tension is achieved through the massive shape of the stećak itself and the reliefs and inscriptions carved on its sides. There are a smaller number of stećci with symbolic, ornamental or figural carving;

their subjects are varied, and they are composed with masterly skill and a feeling for the total effect which in the best examples reaches perfection.

The sun, crosses, crescent moon and stars, stylized lilies, rosettes, weapons, shields, arcading, twisted braiding, vines with trefoil leaves, grapes, spirals, processions of deer, scenes showing the *kolo* [round dance], hunting, tournaments, and figures with a puzzlingly uplifted right arm ending in a huge hand are some of the motifs which the master-craftsmen of long ago carved with great imagination on thousands of these stone blocks.

The inscriptions, which are an essential part of the structural patterning, show a fine sense of overall composition and integration. They are controlled both by the living forms of the national language and by the nature of the stone and the seriousness of their purpose. It was on the stećci that the mediaeval Bosnian Cyrillic script developed its most outstanding artistic and graphic characteristics. But the greatest importance and strength of these stones lies in their poetic and philosophical charge and character. They stand outside any conventional burial formulas. The sudden flame of some important insight often breaks through terse inscriptions, or exciting lyrical fragments hint at some unexpected drama.

Thanks to some of these inscriptions the names have come down to us of a few of the masons who cut and carved the stone of these huge shapes, weighing as much as thirty tons, and of the scribes who carried out the taxing literary and artistic discipline of chiselling in stone. Sometimes there were two people involved, sometimes scribe and mason were one and the same person. Names that have come down to us are Prodan and Miogost from central Bosnia, Ugarak from Vrhbosna, Veseoko Kukulamović and Vukašin from Jajce and Lašva, Bratjen from Travunija, Nikola Dragoljević and the scribe Dragoje from Podrinje, and Krilić and Miogost from near Stolac. Among all these engraver-sculptors the name that stands out is that of the mason Grubač, who lived in the second half of the fifteenth century in the Stolac area and whose easily distinguishable masterpieces are scattered throughout the graveyards of the region. His

20. End face of a stećak from Donja Zgošća near Kakanj, 14th–15th centuries.

contemporary and often co-signatory was the scribe Semorad, who composed many of the most quoted inscriptions.

There are a number of extensive graveyards in Bosnia-Herzegovina with stećci of varying shapes and varying beauty. By far the best known and most complete, though not the largest, is at Radimlja near Stolac. Almost all kinds of stećak can be found there and most of them are carved, ranging from the purely decorative to human portraits. Some of them bear inscriptions. Radimlja lies in a gentle valley on the road to Stolac, its stećci stir the imagination by the sheer effect of numbers: it is almost a town of stones. They form a spontaneous anthology of stećak art.

Other graveyards with these great stones are in Boljuni also near Stolac, on Krekovi near Nevesinje, on Lake Blidinje, in Bjelosavljevići near Sokolac, on Gvozan near Kalinovik, and on Ravanjska Vrata near Kupres.

It is difficult and unnecessary to single out individual masterpieces from so many, but in any account of them it is impossible not to mention the great stećak that once stood in Donja Zgošća near Kakanj and is now in the National Museum in Sarajevo. It seems to be a synthesis and sublimation of everything that is greatest in the stećak tradition. And, as if it were under the protection of some higher power, the only thing that over the centuries has been defaced as a result of destruction by the elements and by humans is the writing of the inscription that it once bore. Thus it stands before us today in stark beauty, untrammeled by any extraneous information.

The guarded hypotheses of archaeologists have sometimes surmised (Ćiro Truhelka) that this stećak, and the whole small graveyard from which it came, was that of the Bosnian kings; but recently and more convincingly it has been suggested by Marian Wenzel that it was the stećak of the Hrvatinić family.

The lay eye can discern little regularity in the placing of the stones. But something in their ambience suggests that these burial grounds were chosen with a feeling for surrounding nature. Like much ancient stone art they seem to come alive in the sunlight, to have been worked, carved and placed to make use of the full play of light at all seasons and at all times of the day. At one moment they are so lit that we suddenly stop amazed by their expressive power, at others we may pass them by almost unnoticed, seeing nothing on them but the lichens which merge them into the background. These aspects of the stećci are particularly noticeable in the photographs that were taken when they first became a focus of systematic study and aesthetic attention.

Of course, a little research shows that the stećak graveyards were almost always placed near contemporary settlements and highways. But many of these settlements disappeared long ago, and the highways ceased to be used so that some of the burial places can only be found today if we search for them with the help of a large-scale map. Although the golden age of the stećci was in the fifteenth century, up to the collapse of the mediaeval Bosnian state, they continued to be made even after the Turks had conquered Bosnia and Hum. They retained many of their original motifs and inscriptions, but they underwent an interesting evolution, taking on the taller and more slender form of an obelisk. From the seventeenth century these gravestones were differentiated according to religion – Muslim, Catholic, Orthodox, Jewish. New forms developed with specific Bosno-Herzegovinian characteristics, but their original monumentality and beauty had been lost.

The stećci are an unusual development in mediaeval European art, partly because of the strictly limited area in which they are found. The culture and art of the Middle Ages was always international with regional variations. In many aspects of life the Bosnian upper class was indisputably part of mediaeval Europe. Yet the art of the stećci is quite individual in style, unique even in the South Slav context. The sheer weight of the stone, the creative and technical difficulties of working it, the constant urge for monumentality, the simplicity of the basic form yet the wealth of representations, the development of regional 'schools', the long and continuous period of their production over more than three centuries all show the dimensions of an art that demands recognition as an independent stylistic formation, realized over a whole creative epoch.

It would not, however, be right to consider stećak art as something original in the absolute sense: indeed, this would be impossible. A large number of its elements and features belong to the wider spirit of European mediaeval art, indeed to its two dominant periods: Romanesque and Gothic. In the first place there is the use of symbolism as a means of presenting and understanding the essence of the world, and many of the same symbols and patterns are found, such as the cross, sun, crescent moon, lilies, rosettes, as in European art, Animals are frequently represented; sometimes the accent is on the fantastic as in Romanesque, or we find elegant, finely stylized figures and compositions more like those found in Gothic. Both of these faces of mediaeval art, and the techniques of the sculptors and architects who realized them, were easily accessible to the old Bosnian masters from their contacts with the coastal towns of Dalmatia.

There are many depictions on the stećci of what must have been bloody scenes, but these too were part of the mediaeval mentality: armed combat, hunting, fights between animals etc. Another mediaeval trait arises from the spirit of syncretism and aesthetic coexistence, which allowed the introduction on the faces of the stećci of elements, carvings and symbols from varied often far off spiritual and cultural systems.

The world of the *mramorovi* is thus, through a whole complexity of spiritual interconnections and presentations, an organic part of the world of mediaeval Europe, and it would require force to tear it artificially out of that world and explain it in isolation.

Even so their originality and variety in relationship to mediaeval art mean that in spite of obviously common elements, stećci cannot be wholly equated with that art nor explained by their relationship to it. The stećak sculptors did not only use common elements in unconventional ways, placing them in unknown symbolic and artistic relations: but they also had a considerable repertoire of symbols of their own, used only by them, and resistant to any comparative analysis.

Another aspect of stećak art is that they largely escape the usual sharp distinction between folk art and high culture. The distinction was present in Bosnian mediaeval society, but it is not found in the stećci. From the sociological point of view, the fact that stećci did not show any sharp hiearchical divisions has a meaning of its own. The most we can say is that the upper feudal class were 'enstoned' in richer and finer memorials, which is logical since they had more money. But a firm link with the broad folk base is suggested by many decorative details, which are identical with those found on textiles, in wood carving and tatooing and still present in the folk art of to-day.

This conjunction of rustic folklore and urban refinement, pagan and Christian, ironically grotesque and high art is unusual, and seldom found in the Middle Ages. The world which created the stećci obviously did not yet care about the strictly canonical artistic presentation of a central cult, the cult of death. So although they mark graves, these monuments portray more of life than they do of death. They do not embody any set of formalized norms or clichés. The decorated surfaces offer us a hospitable syncretism, an acceptance of elements from the most varied cultures and traditions, and of different artistic genres ranging from the purely ornamental to more realistic figurative motifs.

The whole conceptual world here fixed in marble was embodied in the highly charged meanings of the old term *bilig* [mark]. Associated with this, as a clearly defined symbol, is the idea of a house, named as such in inscriptions and portrayed on numerous stećci: the *sljemenjaci*. Bilig, pobiližiti [to record], vični dom [eternal home], vična kuća [eternal house] – to be recorded, never to be forgotten . . . never to be erased . . . never to die. The appeals recorded in Bosančica pray, bless, threaten, entreat, even today:

O God
I lay down a long time ago
And I will have to lie for a long time.

I made and built
This tomb in my lifetime
For my future life.

Be blessed he who passes by
And damned he who damages it.

I beg of you
do not touch it.

And who should destroy this record
May God destroy him.

This is the house
Of Milutin Marojević
And his wife Vladislava
And their children.

I set up this record of happiness
In my lifetime
While waiting for my death.

With the help of my kinsfolk
I built this honourable tomb
And I put this stone on my tomb
And I completed this eternal home
In my lifetime.

Brothers
Come and approach
My eternal home
But do not dig it over.

Man
Leave me in peace
That you be not damned. (*translated by Jasna Vince-Marinc*)

Today the stećci are only what they are – sculptures, bas reliefs and inscriptions of immediate beauty and suggestive power, a form of direct communication which, after four, five, six centuries still fulfill their basic function, to last through time, in their own land: creative signs testifying to death and life, yet delivered from life and death, showing themselves enduring.

The end of mediaeval culture

All that was left of mediaeval Bosnia after the turbulence of the Turkish invasion of 1463 were the old towns and castles and the stećci. Everything of cultural or material value either fell into decay or was looted or found its way, together with streams of refugees, to other European towns and countries, to become part of a desperate struggle for existence, or an object of intrigue, sale or contraband. Everything in the museums, archives, treasuries and collections of Europe which is identified as Bosnian, even if it could be brought together and systematized, could never really provide a complete picture of what had been. Of course it was the valuable works of art that were primarily taken.

The fate of Bosnian archives and books was especially drastic. Nothing is known of the archives of the lordly Kotromanić or Kosača families. The Pavlović records disappeared after they had been confiscated by Duke Stjepan in 1439. Part of the Hrvatinić papers were found in the library of the Hungarian Counts Bathyani. Some documents relating to the Franciscans of the Bosnian Vicariate are in Ljubljana. It is still today difficult to explain why in the Franciscan monasteries in Bosnia there is not a single document relating to the Middle Ages. The treasures of mediaeval Bosnian culture and its illuminated manuscripts are scattered throughout Europe. Traces can be found in libraries and museums in Leningrad, Moscow, the Vatican, Venice, Montepradone, Istanbul.

The last sparks of Bosnian mediaeval culture, extensive but decadent, from 1463 to 1528, can still be found in some towns and monasteries in the Jajce and Srebrenica banates. But when the Jajce banate finally fell in 1528, Bosnia became part of the Ottoman Empire and entered a completely new and different epoch of its cultural and political history.

OTTOMAN BOSNIA – ADMINISTRATIVE DIVISIONS (ca. 1606)

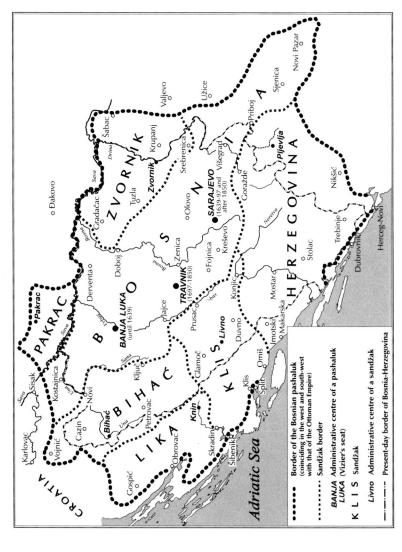

Border of the Bosnian pashaluk (coinciding in the west and south-west with that of the Ottoman Empire)

Sandžak border

BANJA Administrative centre of a pashaluk *LUKA* (Vizier's seat)

K L I S Sandžak

Livno Administrative centre of a sandžak

Present-day border of Bosnia-Herzegovina

CROATIA

Karlovac

Sisak

Obrovac

Gospić

Vojnić

Cazin

Novi

Petrovac

Bihać

Knin

Skradin

Šibenik

Klis

Split

Omiš

Makarska

Adriatic Sea

Kostajnica

Ključ

PAKRAC

Pakrac

B

BANJA LUKA (until 1639)

Jajce

Prusac

Glamoč

Duvno

Livno

K L I S

Imotski

Mostar

Stolac

H E R Z E G O V I N A

Trebinje

Nikšić

Dubrovnik

Herceg-Novi

Pljevlja

Goražde

Priboj

Sjenica

Novi Pazar

Užice

Valjevo

Krupanj

Srebrenica

Tuzla

Olovo

Zenica

Fojnica

Kreševo

SARAJEVO (1639-97 and after 1850)

Konjic

Višegrad

Derventa

Doboj

TRAVNIK (1697-1850)

Zvornik

Gradačac

Đakovo

Šabac

Z V O R N I K

B O S N A

Nerenva

LIKA

BIHAĆ

Una

Sava

Sava

Sava

Vrbas

Bosna

Bosna

Drina

Neretva

SIX

A Century and a Half of Turkish Conquest

Neither the last six to seven decades of Bosnian independence, nor the last years of the fifteenth century after the fall of the kingdom and state, nor the sixteenth century following the incorporation of the whole of Bosnia-Herzegovina into the Ottoman Empire, can be fully understood if the 140 years that it took the Turks to conquer Bosnia – from the battle of Bileća in 1388 to the fall of Jajce in 1528 – are not taken into account. Thus the assault by Mehmed II Fatih, the fall of Bosnia and the death of King Stjepan Tomašević in 1463 should be seen as a single scene in this protracted drama: not an isolated tragic episode, but in logical continuity with what came before and what followed afterwards. Bosnia did not fall 'šaptom' [with a whisper, i.e. at one fell swoop], in the course of a few days. This is a misleading interpretation of events, the product of a romanticized narrative historiography that has still lost none of its potency. It took Bosnia a full 140 years to fall, almost a century and a half, eroded by dissension from within and weakened and worn down by well-planned Turkish military, political, cultural and religious infiltration. The Turks demonstrated their special method of gradual conquest, and exploited to the full all the disagreements that developed within Bosnia's waning feudalism. The final invasion came in 1463, but it had been preceded by years of preparation, years moreover in which the Western European powers did nothing to strengthen this first line of their own defence.

The first meeting between the Turkish scimitar and the Bosnian sword was in 1386 during a casual raid by a small Turkish unit in the Neretva valley, which was easily repulsed. Two years later in 1388 the military commander Murat I Šahin-pasha, leading a stronger force, was defeated at Bileća. But the success of the Turkish army at the battle of Kosovo in 1389, and the conquest of Skopje in 1392 with the organization there of a typical Ottoman military administrative district, established an important base for further conquests to the north and west. By 1396 there was a Turkish unit permanently stationed in Zvečan in Old Serbia. Two years later the Turks mounted another strong attack on Bosnia, only defeated by the onset of a harsh winter. But from that time onward the Turkish presence became a permanent feature of life in Bosnia, both politically and as part of the daily psychological climate.

In the next fifteen to twenty years the Turks were occupied with their own internal problems, arising from Tamerlane's defeat of Bayezid in 1402 and the power struggle between Bayezid's sons. But in 1411 the Bosnian nobleman Sandalj made a pact with Prince Suleyman to maintain a Turkish mercenary army (about 7,000 strong!) in Hum; while his rival Hrvoje, who was out of favour with King Sigismund of Hungary, found an ally in Ishakbeg, commander of the Skopje district, who at Hrvoje's request attacked Bosnia in 1414 and demanded that King Ostoja and Sandalj pay tribute to the Sultan.

In the following year, 1415, the Turks won a great victory over the Hungarian army in the battle of Doboj. From that time on the balance of power in Bosnia between the Ottomans and Hungary perceptibly changed in favour of the Ottomans. The Bosnian nobility now began with increasing frequency to call on Turkish support in their own internal power struggles. Such alliances were temporary and unstable, but their effect was to weaken still further an already frayed national cohesion. Thus in 1415 the Pavlović lords of Podrinje, helped by the Turks, raided Sandalj's lands; but in 1418 Sandalj acknowledged Turkish supremacy, and in 1420 to aid him Ishakbeg killed Petar Pavlović. From that time onwards the Turks were equal players in all important political developments in Bosnia. Raids, robbery and all kinds of military involvement became commonplace and protracted; lightning attacks became frequent, right across to the Croatian lands and beyond, like that of Ishakbeg in 1432. The Turks now began to occupy Bosnian fortified places such as Hodidjed and Vrhbosna, and strengthened their position in the east of the country. The 'Turkish threat' had become a 'Turkish presence' in the political, economic, social and finally religious life of Bosnia.

Isabeg Ishaković, who had succeeded his father Ishakbeg as commander of the Skopje district, was in 1439 appointed by the Sultan as 'guardian and administrator' of Bosnia. In 1448 Isabeg organized a strong two-pronged attack. One army advanced down the Neretva valley as far as the old market town of Drijeva, which was thoroughly plundered and gutted; the other again occupied Hodidjed and Vrhbosna, both of which from that time onwards remained firmly in Turkish hands. Administrative units were now set up in Bosnia. In 1453 Bosansko Krajište is first mentioned, and in 1455 'Vilayet Hodided' and 'Vilayet Sarayovasi'. What is today Sarajevo was founded by Isabeg Ishaković with his first pious endowments in 1457. That same year in Dubrovnik he is referred to in a letter as 'the true ruler of Bosnia'. When in 1459 the Serbian despotate too fell to the Turks, the next logical goal of the Ottoman Empire in its expansion towards the heart of Europe was Bosnia.

King Stjepan Tomašević, now definitely turning to the West for help, wrote in panic to the Pope and to Western rulers setting out what would inevitably follow if Bosnia fell to the Turks:

> If it were only my kingdom that Mehmed wanted to take and he did not intend to advance farther, then you might leave me to my fate and there would be no need to disturb other Christian lands to defend me. But his insatiable hunger for power knows no ends. After me he will attack Hungary and Dalmatia, subdue the Venetians, and through Carniola and Istria seek to conquer Italy. He often declares that his heart longs for Rome. If as a result of the indifference of other Christians he takes my kingdom, he will

find the most suitable country and the best way to fulfil his dream. I shall be the first to experience the storm and after me the Hungarians, Venetians and other nations will meet their fate.

(from Stjepan Tomašević's appeal to Pope Pius II)

Stjepan Tomašević, placing too much faith in the solidarity of the Christian powers, in 1462 refused to pay tribute to the Sultan. His illusions were quickly shattered, and in alarm he tried to negotiate a fifteen year peace pact with the Turks, of course in vain. Sultan Mehmed II Fatih left nothing to chance. With the Hungarian army tied down by apparently important operations on the Sava and Danube, he dispatched Isabeg to Herzegovina to prevent help coming from that quarter and, in May 1463, led a new attack himself. Easily conquering the Pavlović and Kovačević lands, he surrounded Bobovac, the strongest Bosnian town, which surrendered after three days. He then marched his army across the chaotic and panic stricken land through Visoko and Travnik to Jajce, which surrendered to him. He dispatched Mahmut Paša to Ključ to capture the king, who had escaped there – and who some days later was brought to Jajce and executed.

The Turks now created the sandžak of Bosnia from the conquered lands of the king, the territories of the Pavlović and Kovačević families, and parts of the lands of Herceg Stjepan. Thus the feudal Bosnian state ceased to exist, but the entire territory of Bosnia was not to be under the Turks for a long time yet.

In the devastated country food for the huge Turkish army soon began to run out, which forced the Turks to withdraw, making a counter-attack possible. That same year, the Hungaro-Croatian armies of King Matthias Corvinus attacked from the north via Ključ to Jajce, while Vladislav and Vlatko, sons of Herceg Stjepan, moved into south-western Bosnia and the Drina valley. Jajce was retaken and though it was again besieged by the Sultan the following year, 1464, this time he was unsuccessful. For more than half a century Jajce was a dramatic focus of interest for the whole of Europe, right down to its final fall in 1528. Hungary now formed parts of northern Bosnia into the banovinas of Jajce and Srebrenik, which constituted a constantly troubled military frontier (*limes*) against the Turks. Herzegovina on the other hand, though continually weakened and depleted, managed to hold out until 1482, when after the fall of Herceg Novi it was entirely subjugated, so that what had once been the Bosnian state was now divided between the two old adversaries, Turkey and Hungary.

Bosnia was to have a rather different development from other Turkish frontier territories. One difference was seen from the start. In 1465 the Turks proclaimed a Bosnian kingdom in the conquered territories and nominated a 'king' (Matija, son of Radivoje), even taking care that he should come from the traditional Kotromanić dynasty. This looked like a concession but was in fact a diplomatic trick. Even so the very fact that it was an unknown precedent in Turkish practice showed the exceptional importance Bosnia had in the overall Turkish plans; also the acceptance – and, of course, use – of certain rooted traditions which they found there. Doubtless as a counter to this move, the Hungarians too produced a Bosnian 'king', in this case Nikola of Ilok. This double farce of the 'kingdom' and its 'kings' did not last long, only till 1476 on the Turkish side and 1477 on the Hungarian. The following year Katarina, last queen of Bosnia, died in exile in Rome, and there was no further talk of royalty.

The sad fate of Queen Katarina is variously told in numerous historical – and even more numerous pseudo-historical – accounts. But even if we ignore all the stories and legends that have gathered round her name, she really did fuse in the most sublimely dramatic way the personal with the collective tragedy, in the bizarre (in civilizational terms) Bosnian situation of the second half of the fifteenth century. It is worth giving at least a summary of the known facts about her life.

Katarina was the daughter of Herceg Stjepan Vukčić Kosača and Jelena, daughter of the Zeta nobleman Balša III. In 1466 she married King Stjepan Tomaš and became queen of Bosnia. She had nobility of both blood and nature, and under the influence of her two chaplains, who were ardent Franciscans, she became a devout Catholic and spread about her a benign atmosphere. She bore two children, Sigismund and Katarina, and was on good terms with her step-son Stjepan, the heir to the throne; he was Tomaš's son by a previous irregular marriage to Vojača, who had been expelled from the palace after Tomaš began to incline towards the Pope and of whose later fate nothing is known.

King Tomaš died in 1461 in suspicious circumstances: natural causes? or a murderous court conspiracy in which his son Stjepan played a part? – there is still no accepted answer. According to Turkish sources (Christian ones are silent), Queen Katarina turned for help to Ishak-pasha, governer of Bosansko Krajište, 'to give a ruling on the succession and prevent civil war'. At all events, Tomaš's son Stjepan Tomašević, who had married Jelena-Mara daughter of the Serbian despot Lazar Branković, became king and immediately gave Katarina official recognition as Queen Mother.

When two years later in 1463 the Turks took the chief Bosnian towns, ended the kingdom of Bosnia and killed Stjepan Tomašević, Katarina is said to have been staying at the time with her brother Vladislav in Herzegovina. From there she escaped with an escort to Dubrovnik and thence to Rome. Christian sources say her children were seized by the Turks, taken into slavery and converted to Islam. Parts of the account are somewhat unconvincing. Would Katarina in those uncertain times have gone to her brother and left her children behind? And if so, where? In Bobovac? Jajce? No one knows. Turkish sources suggest that Sigismund and Katarina had already in 1461 been taken – as hostages, or in some other capacity – by Ishak-pasha to Sarajevo, already an Islamic town, had there converted to Islam, and had then been taken to Istanbul. No one knows what happened to Katarina's daughter, but Sigismund, under the name of Ishakbeg Kralj-oglu (sic.), held the office of sandžak-beg of Karasi in Asia Minor.

In Rome Katarina devoted herself to a religious life, but continually tried to discover how she could see her children again. We know of the contacts she made to this end with the Porte itself and with prominent Italian notables. An intriguing detail is that while

Katarina's children were in Istanbul in the emperor's palace and she was pining for them in Rome, her half-brother Stjepan, youngest son of Herceg Stjepan from his marriage to Barbara daughter of the Duke of Bavaria, was also at the palace. He probably went there of his own accord, after quarrelling with his brothers. He converted to Islam, and after an extensive education became as Ahmed-pasha Hercegović one of the most distinguished men in the Ottoman empire. Five times Grand Vizier, he was a poet, built towns and made endowments. People from Bosnia-Herzegovina, both Moslems and Christians, lived in his court, and it was as a result of his intervention that Turkish military expansion side-stepped Dubrovnik.

Katarina's destiny and person and entire life-story were marked by the ruptures and unifications and dissensions and reintegrations – through countless inner experiences, illuminations and obscurities – of all those worlds that nonetheless had but a single name: Bosnia.

Never realizing any of her hopes or ambitions, Katarina died on 25 October 1478. In her will she entrusted the Kingdom of Bosnia to the Pope until such time as her children should be freed from captivity and return to Catholicism. She was buried in the Franciscan church of Ara Coeli and her name was inscribed on her gravestone in her own language, written in the Bosančica script. We only know this because it was recorded and published in 1547 by the Roman calligrapher Giovanni Battista Palatino. For when the church was renovated in 1590, the original gravestone and the earthly remains of Katarina disappeared, and a new memorial tablet was put up with an inscription in Latin.

Katarina is honoured by the Franciscans as a Tertiary Franciscan and 'blessed'. Round Bobovac and Kraljeva Sutjeska 25 October, the day of her death, is still commemorated, and Catholic women still wear a black head-scarf in memory of 'their queen'.

In 1503 Turkey and Hungary made a shortlived peace; for just under ten years there were no military operations of any size. But in 1512 the new sultan Selim took Srebrenica and the whole of northeast Bosnia. This marked a new stage in the Turkish conquest and proved to be an overture to the overwhelming Turkish expansion that was to continue unabated until halted just short of Vienna at the end of the seventeenth century.

The Turks advanced on a wide front towards their goal in central Europe. In 1521 Belgrade and Šabac fell, in 1522 Knin and Skradin, in 1523 Ostrovica on the Una, in 1526 Mohács, in 1527 Obrovac and Udbina, by which time Hungary had become seriously imperilled. Finally in 1528, after holding out for 65 years of bloodshed, Jajce fell and with it all the other strongholds of the Jajce banovina. The 140 years of conquest were over, and what is today Bosnia-Herzegovina found itself within the Ottoman Empire.

SEVEN

Four Centuries of Turkish Rule

General overview

In the sixteenth century an outstanding individual came to power in Turkey – Suleyman the Lawgiver, known in the West as Suleyman the Magnificent. His reign from 1520 to 1566 was a period of internal stability and external expansion. The Ottoman Empire consolidated its domains on three continents. In Europe its frontiers were already established far to the north and north-west, even Vienna was not far from its grasp.

One of Suleyman's successes was to curb the power of his great feudal lords, which allowed him to organize a centralized state with stable laws and to create a well-developed administrative apparatus with the military support of a large number of minor warlords.

Territorially, administratively and in social, economic and cultural life, Bosnia-Herzegovina in the sixteenth century to all intents and purposes became a province of the Ottoman Empire. The first administrative unit, the sandžak of Bosnia, was founded in 1463, to be followed by a whole series of other sandžaks as organized administration followed conquest, culminating in 1580 in the establishment of the Bosnian *pashaluk*, *beglerbegluk* or *eyalet*, with its religious centre first in Banja Luka till 1639, then in Sarajevo till 1697, in Travnik till 1850, then again in Sarajevo. Its territory originally extended far beyond the frontiers of today's Bosnia-Herzegovina, but later con-

OTTOMAN BOSNIA:
MOSQUES, MONASTERIES AND BRIDGES

tracted as Turkish power contracted, until it finally coincided more
or less with today's borders.

With Turkish rule came the social and economic organization
typical of the Ottoman military-feudal system. The primary aims of
this system were to make it impossible for any large body of independent feudal lords to arise and become independent, and to develop
and maintain a state control of land whose basic form was the *timar*
and *zijamet* holdings of feudal lords or spahis whose main duty was
to fight for the empire. The situation of the peasants in this first
period, influenced by the importance accorded to them within overall imperial policy, was much more favourable and stable than that
of peasants in feudal Europe. Peasants were not tied to the land,
taxes were bearable and precise, and the power of the spahis was
limited by effective laws.

In Bosnia-Herzegovina certain modifications in the workings of
the overall system were made from the beginning to appease local
tradition, more marked than in other conquered countries. Faced
with a nobility with a deep rooted sense of its own heritage, the
Turks, when introducing the *timar* land holding system, recognized
the position of lesser feudal lords who had remained after the fall of
the monarchy and managed to create the illusion that the traditional
system was being upheld. On both the practical and psychological
level this was an incentive to accept Islam. Thus a local feudal class
developed with a special relationship with Islam and imperial power,
yet at the same time conscious of its own native identity.

One of the most characteristic forms of such modification was
the creation of kapetanijas. Administered by members of the pre-
Turkish feudal class and hereditary, these when originally formed
served to ensure safe frontiers and internal stability; but they became
focal points around which a military class developed unknown in
other parts of Turkey. In later centuries, as Turkish power weakened, these kapetanijas developed aspirations to autonomy and
expansionism which the central administration in Istanbul found it
increasingly difficult to handle.

Although historians have not yet succeeded in putting together a
complete picture of the life of ordinary people at this time, it is clear

that significant social differentiation was taking place. The most numerous group were the peasants of all religions and ethnicities, but
alongside these a whole social spectrum emerged, in which a special
place was taken by so-called *martolosi*, non-Islamized groups of Vlachs
serving on the frontier and exempt from tolls and taxes.

In the inaccessible forested mountains patriarchal communities
and family groups raised stock and cultivated the land, practically
beyond the reach of government administration. These small autonomous units were tacitly tolerated by the Turks. They continued to
exist right down to the nineteenth century and even caused a problem for Austro-Hungary: small oases which refused to fit into their
administrative scheme or ownership laws. One well known example
is the Korićani region on Mount Vlašić.

An intense process of urbanization began. Urban trades, commerce and crafts developed. People increasingly gravitated to the
towns, producing an urban and suburban *raya* with little in the way
of land or possessions and unable to pay much in the way of taxes.

The building of more towns required the provision of more trans-
port between them. Some developed where there had already been
mediaeval towns, but others were built on new locations. The majority of present-day Bosnia-Herzegovina's towns began to develop
at this time. In this development the Turkish and Islamic religious
and charitable institutions of *vakuf* and *zadužbina* were important.
Most of the construction of the religious and public buildings was
financed through *vakuf* endowments: mosques, *medresas*, *hamams*,
bezistans, bridges, *česmas*, *hans*, *caravanserai*. Whole new towns were
built whose names still reveal their origin – Skender-Vakuf, Varcar-
Vakuf, Kulen-Vakuf, Gornji-Vakuf, Donji-Vakuf.

Banja Luka, Mostar and many other towns, above all Sarajevo,
flourished and expanded, and the names of the people, mostly locals,
who financed and organized their building are still remembered. The
scope of their imagination is impressive. They did not confine themselves to the construction of individual buildings, nor did their interest
end when construction was finished. They had long-term perspectives based on elaborate and precise plans. They left endowments

with clear instructions to ensure growth and provide lasting financial support. Documents show that they were concerned in financing all aspects of life: trade, crafts, education, communal installations, social welfare.

Thus Bosnia at the end of the fifteenth century and during the sixteenth underwent deep and far reaching structural changes, the most obvious and lasting being the influx of oriental civilization and Islamization, the intensity and extent of which have still not been satisfactorily explained and evaluated. We are too often fobbed off with stereotyped views that fit the purposes of national ideologies and do not satisfy serious historiography. The two most widely known – and mutually contradictory – legends speak of mass forcible Islamization and a 'Bogomil nation' supposed to have opted voluntarily for mass conversion to Islam. So far as the former is concerned, even if we ignore the Koranic principle expressly forbidding the use of force in conversion, and even if we give full weight to the civilizational shock of the Turkish invasion, the fact remains that the Ottoman Empire used various methods to achieve the integration of the countries it conquered, but did not force them into linguistic, religious and ethnic assimilation. As for the latter legend, we have seen that no 'Bogomil nation' existed in Bosnia. People called themselves *Bošnjani* in national terms and in religion simply 'Christians'. In the fifteenth century the Bosnian Church diverged entirely from its hypothetical authenticity and grew weaker, losing ground and members alike. So in religious terms the Bosnians who at the end of the fifteenth and during the sixteenth centuries converted to Islam were doubtless overwhelmingly Catholics, with a small number of Orthodox on the eastern borders of both Herzegovina and Bosnia, the only parts where there were Orthodox congregations in this early period.

In no other country conquered by the Turks was there anywhere near such a wholesale conversion to Islam as in Bosnia; not, for example, in Serbia, which they conquered earlier and ruled longer. Conversion among those who saw in it a way of keeping their estates is not difficult to explain. But in the sixteenth century the peasants too were converted in great numbers. It was a far reaching movement that cannot simply be attributed to economic reasons. To explain it we need to reconstruct the complex economic, political, social, cultural and religious context in the midst of whose contradictory and conflicting currents Bosnia found itself in the last days of feudal independence.

The religious situation in Ottoman Bosnia arose from the theocratic nature of the Empire, in which Islam and shariat law embraced all aspects of life. A certain amount of tolerance was shown to followers of other religions (*ahl- al-kitab*, 'people of the book'), to a degree that allowed them to preserve their identity; but they were still second-class citizens. Because of Bosnia's religious complexity a new political and spiritual order emerged, in which religion was the only criterion for the establishment of group identity and from which all its national specificities and divergences later developed.

As we have seen, after the removal in the thirteenth century of the Bishop of Bosnia to Đakovo in Croatia, the Catholic Church did not operate in Bosnia through its regular structure and hierarchy, but through a monastic institution, the Franciscan Vicariate of Bosnia. With the fall of the kingdom and conquest by the Turks in 1463, and thereafter because of warfare, insecurity, frontier changes, and periods of increased persecution, the Church suffered enormous destruction and devastation. Churches and monasteries were destroyed; their congregations were scattered or enslaved, some wiped out, some converted to Islam; property and estates were seized. The Franciscans feared that they and the remnants of their followers faced complete extinction. This was the situation when an important event took place: the famous meeting between the Franciscan *custos* Brother Anđeo Zvizdović and Sultan Mehmed the Conqueror on Milodraž Field in the early summer of 1463.

This meeting has developed all the aura of a historical legend, and is a very good demonstration of the mentality of both participants. Zvizdović was in a terrible dilemma. Should he and the other brothers lead their flock out of the country, end the Vicariate (the only institution that had withstood the eclipse of the Kingdom of Bosnia), and flee to a foreign land in which, ideologically speaking, they should find themselves at home; or should they remain faithful

to their roots and calling, and in an unknown situation try to find a
modus vivendi with the new rulers. The Turkish Sultan was probably the most powerful man in the world at the time. The choice he
faced was whether simply to ignore the negligible power represented
by the impoverished friar standing before him and deny him any
kind of recognition; or, since what he represented was so marginal
and unimportant, to acknowledge and even support him. The result
of this somewhat mythical meeting was an Imperial Grant of Privi-
lege that gave Bosnian Franciscans and Catholics the right to their
faith and, *eo ipso*, to civilizational, political and ethnic identity and
life. The document reads:

> Mehmed son of Murad-khan, forever victorious! The decree of
> the honourable and sublime Sultanic seal and serene edict of the
> Conqueror of Worlds is as follows:
>
> I Sultan Mehmed-khan [proclaim] to the whole world, both
> lords and commons, that the Bosnian Clerics are recipients of my
> great grace and I therefore command that nobody shall molest or
> trouble them nor their church. They shall peaceably exist in my
> empire, and those who have fled may feel free to return and with-
> out fear live in their monasteries in the lands of my empire. Neither
> my high majesty, nor my viziers, nor my servants, nor my sub-
> jects, nor any of the inhabitants of my empire shall cause them
> offence or harass them. Nobody shall attack or threaten them, or
> their life, or their property, or their church. And if from abroad
> they bring someone to my empire, this is allowed.
>
> I have extended the above grace by imperial decree and I swear
> the following oath:
>
> By the Creator of earth and heaven, He who sustains all crea-
> tion, and by the Seven Holy Books, and by the Great Prophet,
> and by the sword with which I gird myself, no one shall act in
> opposition to what is written here as long as they are in my serv-
> ice and true to my commands.
>
> *Written 28 May in Milodraž*

This imperial decree was the basis on which, in spite of many later infringements, the legal status of the Franciscans and the Catholic Croats of Bosnia rested. It has for centuries been the basis of their political existence in Bosnia.

The position of the Serbian Orthodox Church was regulated by the general attitude of the Turkish authorities towards the Eastern Church as decreed by Mehmed II the Conqueror after the fall of Istanbul in 1453, when he personally performed the ceremony of the investiture of Patriarch Genardi Skolaris as previously performed by the Byzantine emperor. The church retained the same internal autonomy and structure that it enjoyed under the Byzantine Empire, and was thus incorporated into the structures of the Ottoman Empire. The church elders were recognized as elders of the people – *milet-basha*. Although the Catholic Church in principle had a status similar to that of the Orthodox, in practice the Serbian Orthodox Church had greater privileges, especially in the earlier centuries, since the centre of Catholicism was outside the Ottoman Empire and this was the source of continuous tension and mistrust. The representatives of the Serbian Orthodox Church continually did their best to get the Catholics under their spiritual, political and material jurisdiction, so that the Catholics at great sacrifice and expense had continually to prove their identity.

The stable position enjoyed by the Serbian Orthodox Church was of long duration. It was renewed in 1557 by Patriarch Makari, a near relative of Grand Vizier Mehmed-pasha Sokolović. The Peć patriarchate, the centre of the Serbian Orthodox Church, was a powerful guarantee of smooth relations with the Porte.

After the downfall of mediaeval Bosnia the jurisdiction of the Orthodox Church easily and swiftly spread into Bosnia-Herzegovina. Until that time it had been confined to the border areas of eastern Herzegovina and the Drina valley. With the consolidation of Turkish power came a systematic settlement of nomadic Balkan Vlachs in the ravaged and depopulated areas of western and north-western Bosnia, Lika, Dalmatia and central Croatia. These areas were under the religious jurisdiction of the Serbian Orthodox Church, leading to their gradual Serbianization.

Bosnia underwent a dynamic transformation in the sixteenth century, as a result of the social stability and great prosperity associated with the rule of Sultan Suleyman and Grand Vizier Mehmed-pasha Sokolović. Any hopes of regaining Bosnian independence were relinquished after the chaos of Mehmed II's invasion in 1463, and in the atmosphere of insecurity caused by the conflicts between Turkey and Hungary and the frontier fighting that continued down to the fall of Jajce in 1528. In compensation, Bosnia embarked upon a period of peace and became part of a legally regulated state. Urban life increased all over the country, and with it increased economic activity, especially trade and diversification of crafts. Connections between town and country improved and Islamization opened up career possibilities for gifted Bosnians. All this played a part in the adoption of Islam and an oriental culture and civilization. The great monuments of Islamic culture in Bosnia date from this period: the Mostar bridge, the Ferhad-pasha mosque in Banja Luka, the great covered market in Sarajevo.

Towards the end of the sixteenth century early symptoms of internal crisis and a beginning of the weakening of the Ottoman Empire began to make themselves felt. The Turks suffered their first serious defeat by the European powers at the battle of Lepanto in 1571, in which the greater part of the Turkish navy was lost. The next setback was the battle of Sisak in Croatia in 1593, in which Hasan-pasha Predojević, commander of the Turkish army, was defeated and killed. The battle of Sisak is a paradigm of the tragic history of the people of these parts. The war was between Vienna and Istanbul, Austria and Turkey, West and East. But our people fought on both sides. It was our heads that fell. Vienna and Istanbul were equally indifferent; we were useful as frontier guards and soldiers, as cannon fodder, and we produced an inexhaustible supply of candidates for death to fill in the great overall plans drawn on military maps in supreme headquarters far away.

The battle of Sisak began the Turkish-Austrian war of 1593–1606 which, though it did not result in any significant frontier changes, was successful in blunting the Turkish strike power. In Bosnia it triggered off a whole series of revolts and uprisings, all caused by the complex (and barren) games of the great European powers for which we had to pay the price.

In the seventeenth century the powerful centralized government of Suleyman's time began to fall apart. Successful liberation movements arose, especially in Africa. The empire was riven by disorder. The corrosion of anarchy and corruption affected its military, social and economic systems. This made possible the ruthless manipulation and exploitation of the peasants through the *čiftluk* system of land holding.

From 1618 to 1649 Europe was torn by the Thirty Years War, following which the European powers, especially Austria, began to review plans for a campaign against Turkey, which, though torn by internal crises, now began the long and crippling Candian war with Venice for the island of Crete (1645–69).

Military obligations became heavier and more frequent. Nobility and janissaries, hitherto the main military power base, became increasingly unreliable, rebellious and demanding. One of their main demands was recognition of rights of private ownership, which the central authorities were forced to concede. Thus estates were privatized and became inheritable; but peasants became serfs, increasingly dependent on their lords, who could make almost unlimited demands on them. One aspect of this retrograde social and economic process was the beginning of a gradually increasing antagonism between Christians and Muslims, an antagonism fanned by foreign interference. There was increasing pressure from Austria, Russia and Venice to recruit the Christians of Bosnia-Herzegovina, both Catholic and Orthodox, for their anti-Turkish policies. The inevitable result was increasing suspicion of Christians among the local Muslim population.

In this climate of general stagnation and social anarchy, the great constructive and cultural impetus of the sixteenth century petered out. The main feature became a climate of rebellion, manifested in diverse forms among the various social strata and religious or ethnic groupings. The most typical products of this anarchic situation were the *hajduks* [brigands]. There had been *hajduks* in earlier times, but in the seventeenth century they increased enormously in numbers. The general picture was one of ferment, which came to a head in rebellion against the central government by janissaries and spahis, and a revolt among lesser merchants and craftsmen – mostly Muslim – against both rich merchants and imperial officials. In 1683 a major revolt developed in Sarajevo and spread beyond the city. It was in this revolt that the Sarajevo poet Hasan Kaimija showed himself an outstanding popular leader.

A general atmosphere of fear and uncertainty reigned during the Candian war, especially in western Bosnia-Herzegovina. After defeating a Turkish attempt to conquer Venice's possessions in Dalmatia, the Venetians managed to take many more places. In 1647 they took Zemunik, Novigrad, Obrovac, Karin, Nadin, Ostrovica and Solin, and in 1668 Klis above Split. The defence of these towns, indeed of their Dalmatian possessions in general, became an increasing burden for the Venetians, and in various ways – mainly with hollow promises – they encouraged refugees from Bosnia-Herzegovina to settle in them, with the intention of organizing them into a frontier force to fight against the Turks. There were bloody transfers of population, which assumed the character of a massive exodus. In this way the demographic picture of the whole region changed on both sides of the frontier. The Venetians inspired and organized a form of 'special warfare' against the Turks, in which *uskoks* [raiders] attacked Bosnia-Herzegovina, plundering, enslaving and burning. This caused only indirect difficulties for Turkey – it was the local population that suffered. It also inflamed antagonism between Christians and Muslims, which erupted in acts of vengence. There is an exceptional poetic record of this tragic period of history in the epic ballads of Christian *uskoks* and Muslim frontiersmen, which can be fully understood only if you see their anthropological and literary unity as mirror images, two sides of the same coin.

In the turbulence of this unsettled period it was the peasants and ordinary townspeople of all ethnic groups who suffered most. They were constantly under economic pressure and defenceless against robbery, revenge and violence. In that religious and ethnic mosaic, which provided such fertile ground for intense antagonism, there also developed, perhaps as a natural reaction thrown up by the need for survival, a cult of good neighbourliness, with its own traditional terms such as *komšiluk* [neighbourhood, neighbours] and *dosluk* [friendship] of which there are many examples in folk memory, in poetry, in written chronicles and in records of bequests: a ground-roots negation of division and particularization.

Events at the end of the seventeenth century fundamentally altered the magnetic field of the Balkans. In 1683 war between Austria and Turkey finally broke out, with the catastrophic defeat of the Turkish army before Vienna. The war lasted until 1699. As a result the Turks lost the land they had conquered to the north-west on the Sava and Danube. From now onwards Turkey was on the defensive in this part of Europe and faced an ever growing anti-Turkish policy among the European powers. The aim of what came to be known as 'the Eastern question' was to drive Turkey out of the Balkans, to be followed by a division of spheres of interest among the great powers. It went on being an aim for the next two centuries and involved political and economic alignments, manoeuvres, intrigues and a series of cruel wars.

The Ottoman-Vienna war ended with the Treaty of Karlowitz (1699), which marked the beginning of a long, hard political period in Bosnia-Herzegovina. The north and north-west frontiers of the Bosnian *pašaluk* now became the frontier of the Ottoman Empire, beyond which lay the increasingly aggressive powers of Europe – Vienna and Venice. Military and political conditions in the *pashaluk* were already a mixture of stagnation and anarchy, made worse by an influx of Muslims from the areas Austria had conquered in the war. Thus Bosnia became the outpost of a declining empire. Another result was an increase of ideological tension on the Austrian-Ottoman frontier after two centuries of co-existent toleration between European Christianity and Oriental Islam. In this new constellation, Bosnia-Herzegovina became increasingly polarized, backward and provincial in its social, economic and cultural structure. The tendency of the population was to withdraw into an isolation that had strongly divisive currents within it. One area in which this was manifested was demographic movement and change, which often attained catastrophic proportions.

The wars that the Turks had been forced to wage against Austria, Venice and Russia continued into the eighteenth century with shorter or longer intervals of relative peace and stabilization. These wars had a fatal effect in Bosnia-Herzegovina, and the incessant fighting on all European fronts accelerated its decay.

Spahis and janissaries ceased to obey the Porte and became deaf to the orders of the military, a situation reflected in self-seeking rebellions. The distancing of the janissary from the centre was dangerous for the common people of both village and town. The families of *kapetans* and the high nobility had become so strong and independent that they had almost unlimited power on their own huge estates. Their defiant attitude towards the power of the authorities is well shown in the Muslim poem in which Alija Bojičić, a frontiersman, when asked whom he fears replies, 'God a little, emperor not at all, and vizier no more than my own bay [horse]'.

Taxes and fines multiplied beyond any kind of governmental control. They often developed into a caricature of legality, choking even the minimal existence of ordinary townsmen and peasants alike. Heavy taxes were imposed to meet the needs of the Empire, added to which was the insatiable appetite of government representatives, which impoverished Muslim and non-Muslim, peasant and merchant alike. A chaotic society with no proper system of justice was a seedbed for the unscrupulous banditry of *hajduks* who, in their own way, were a sign of social revolt. They were in direct confrontation with authority and its institutions, as a result of which not only that authority but the common people suffered.

A series of rebellions among the Muslims, especially in the towns, was directed against economic tyranny and the arbitrary demands of government officials, merchants and feudal lords.

And all this was played out against a background of war or the fear of war. There were the wars that the Turks waged against Russia, in whose marshes and below the walls of whose castles many generations of Muslims from Bosnia-Herzegovina left their bones. There were wars waged against Austria and Venice, which took place in Bosnia itself. Fighting, raids, attacks and looting in the frontier zone between Bosnia and Austria and Venice were continuous occurrences, and from them developed a frontier world, a frontier mentality. Frontier wars were waged in 1716–18, 1737–9, and 1788–91.

This constant state of warfare allowed nothing to develop in Bosnia-Herzegovina other than a slow and anachronistic economic life by which intolerance and distrust were constantly reinforced and intensified. This became worse at the end of the eighteenth century, when Austria and Russia began to camouflage their interests in the Balkans with a religious veneer of being the protectors of Catholics or Orthodox. In Bosnia, where three religious groups were so inextricably mixed, and largely territorially mixed as well, this was an added element of divergence. Yet another complicating element was that after each war there was a mass population movement, especially in the frontier zone. When the Austrian army retreated it drew in its wake a whole train of Christian people fearful of reprisals. In the regions which the Turks were forced to cede to the Austrians, the Muslims withdrew from the frontiers of the *pashaluk*. All these were factors contributing to feelings of insecurity and were inimical to development.

A short-lived period of relative stability and apparent reinstatement of government and legality followed the war of 1737–9, when Turkey (to be more precise, an army of Bosnian Muslims who were little more than reservists, since the main Bosnian army was at the time shedding its blood on distant Eastern battlefields) with unexpected efficiency threw the Austrians out of Serbia and Bosnia and in the Treaty of Belgrade realized many of its demands. This war was also the scene for an event that illustrated the historical paradox of Bosnia's situation, especially with regard to the position of the Bosnian Muslims, in the context of a continually intensifying 'Eastern Question': the famous battle of Banja Luka (1737), in which the Muslims on their own initiative and with scant help from the Turkish troops catastrophically defeated the Austrians, marking the beginning of Austria's defeat in the war. Objectively considered, this was a typical case of people defending an occupying power and thereby prolonging its rule. Subjectively, however, as in other such situations, it was above all a case of defending their own existence and homeland. And that other power coming from across the Sava, with its different insignia and flags, was in fact coming with the same aim of conquest and occupation – and differentiating the Bosnian population in a purely demagogic way according to the classic imperial principle of divide and rule.

The period of peace following the Treaty of Belgrade was reflected in Bosnia, especially in the towns, in an expansion of commerce and crafts – but it did not last for long. The Russo-Turkish war of 1768–74 had a two-fold effect on life here. On the one hand, a large number of Bosnian janissaries never came back from the war. On the other, many young men ignored the call-up, and attempts by the authorities to arrest them led to a series of janissary rebellions which usually ended in destruction and bloodshed, worrying the authorities and devastating the land.

It was not long before Austria and Russia were again at war against the Turks (1787–91), with ambitious plans to redraw the map of the Balkans, plans enthusiastically supported in Serbia and Montenegro, where there was an upsurge of insurrectionary activity. In this explosive climate and surrounded on all sides by war, the *pashaluk* of Bosnia, immobilized by its feudal and ethnic problems, remained largely passive. But the war was a prolongation of its historic calvary: from Novi, Gradiška and Dubica (subjected to such a bloody Austrian siege that the whole conflict was remembered as the Dubica war) to Russian Khotyn, Bosnians and Herzegovinians bled for various foreign interests and policies, while their own land sank into increasing backwardness and disunity.

The political and military upheavals, the industrial and social revolutions and the great cultural sea-change that marked the end of the eighteenth and the beginning of the nineteenth century and heralded the beginning of the modern world by-passed Bosnia-Herzegovina.

It remained isolated from the outside world, sunk in anachronistic feudalism and racked by social and religious discord. The faint sounds of what was happening came like echoes from some other, unintelligible world. Its own social structure, its deep-rooted religious differences, a frontier position between two totally opposite worlds and the accretion of centuries of negative historical experience had formed a Bosnian psychology of hardened defensive reflexes: conservatism, deep-seated distrust and caution, a contemplative and static approach, xenophobia and an inherent stubbornness. All this meant that Bosnia could not provide fertile ground for modern ideas, either for the enlightened absolutism of Joseph II or for the attempts of Selim III to move in a similar direction (attempts frustrated in any case throughout Turkey). Nor was it open to the new spirit of secular education and culture introduced by Napoleonic France in the short episode (1805–14) of its rule over parts of neighbouring Croatia. But there was a further circumstance casting a different light on the opposition to all these new European ideas. They all embodied a strong tendency to cultural and linguistic denationalization, so that resistance to them was at the same time a way of preserving one's own essential being.

In the early nineteenth century the Belgrade *pashaluk* revolted against the janissaries, a revolt that culminated in the Serbian rising of 1804–13. This first Serbian rising stirred the Orthodox population of Bosnia to political action, and they too organized a series of risings, some small, some large. In 1804 a revolt broke out in Herzegovina and among the Drobnjaks in Montenegro; in 1807 another in Bosansko Podrinje; and in 1809 the largest of all in Bosanska Krajina.

At the beginning of the century there appeared in acute form a very specific form of insurgence, contradictory and as yet insufficiently understood, whose roots lay in the many centuries Bosnia had spent under the Turks – an insurgence that had always existed in latent form and often came to the surface. This was the increasing autonomy of the powerful Bosnian feudal families (*begs, kapetans* and *ayans*). By the early nineteenth century they had achieved a position that was practically independent of the vizier, the representative of the Istanbul government. This was especially true of the families whose family seats were on the fringes of the *pashaluk*, and who in defending their lands had for centuries defended the frontiers of the empire. Among these a proud, cruel, warlike mentality gradually emerged. The *kapetans* of Livno, Banja Luka, Prijedor, Kulen-Vakuf, Bihać, Novi Zvornik, Počitelj, Stolac, Dubica, Cazin – the Kulenović, Stojčević, Rizvanbegović, Fidahić, Dadić, Gavrankapetanović and Firduh families – became famous as guardians of the frontiers, feared by Austrian, Venetian and French generals. They were on the one hand arrogant and disobedient subjects caring little for Istanbul, on the other oppressive feudal lords under whom the impoverished peasants groaned, Christians and Muslims alike.

While Turkey, torn by internal crises and foreign wars, was in a state of disorder compounded by the unsuccessful attempts at reform of Selim III (1789–1808) – continued on a lesser scale and more cautiously by Mahmut II (1808–39) – the demands of the Bosnian *kapetans* and *ayans* began to take the form of an armed movement of ever-increasing dimensions. In 1814 the infamous vizier Ali-pasha Derendeli managed only with difficulty to put down a rising under the Herzegovinian *ayan* Ali-aga Dadić. In 1831 came the great revolt led by *kapetan* Huseinbeg Gradaščević, the 'Dragon of Bosnia'. In 1850–51 a new wave of rebellion was evenually put down in blood by Omer-pasha Latas. The autonomist aspirations of the Bosnian lords continually increased, to the point where it took the dangerous form for the Empire of an explicit separatism – of which Husein Gradaščević's revolt was a striking example. Husein had far-reaching ambitions and managed to achieve at least temporary agreement and unanimity among the majority of the most powerful Bosnian nobles. He also had a mass following among the people. His revolt was unique in that the Bosnian army marched far from home to meet the Sultan's troops in Kosovo, and actually managed to defeat them there, posing a threat to Istanbul itself. But unable to reach an agreement with the pasha of Skadar and betrayed by the other feudal lords, Husein returned to Bosnia, lost the next battle and saved his own life only by escaping across the Sava to Austria.

Although an important and perhaps crucial motive in the Bosnian nobility's resistance to central Turkish authority was its hostility to reform, in the name of preserving traditional feudal rights and possessions, but it cannot be reduced to that alone. It was also a natural result of the great mosaic of centrifugal forces then at work in opposition to the outdated political structure that the Ottoman Empire had become. At their highest points, moreover, these movements of resistance seemed to suggest, in however rudimentary and incomplete a manner, the possibility of Bosnia as an autonomous political entity. In the mid nineteenth century Europe was the scene of great social movements for national emancipation and liberty. The revolution of 1848 was crushed by guns and money, but the ground-swell that it created spread irresistibly across political and other frontiers into the furthest corners of the continent.

In the Balkan lands the effect was most visible in programmes for cultural and national unification and freedom. The most outstanding champions of such ideas were Ljudevit Gaj and others involved in the Illyrian movement in Croatia, Vuk Stefanović Karadžić and his followers in Serbia, and Petar Petrović Njegoš in Montenegro. All of their programmes presupposed the inclusion of Bosnia-Herzegovina, but not one of them seriously considered Bosnia's specific historical traditions, cultural identity, national structure or political needs. They nevertheless had a powerful secularizing effect on Bosnia-Herzegovina's traditional confessionalism and on the process of national identification – first among the Serbs and later also among the Croats – in Bosnia. The process of national identification among the Bosnian Muslims was to take a different path and develop at a different tempo, for various historical reasons but also as a result of assimilationist tendencies on the part of both Serbs and Croats, especially after the withdrawal of Turkey from Bosnia.

The idea of cultural and national renaissance found eminent champions in Bosnia-Herzegovina. But whatever their various points of departure and differences, they all tended to strike a more explicit political and social note and one more coloured by Bosnian realities than is to be found in the programmes for Croatian renaissance with which they were associated. This is well illustrated by the Bosnian variant of Illyrism espoused by Ivan Frane Jukić.

After Omar-pasha Latas had formally introduced the *tanzimat* (reform), with unscrupulous cunning and such terrible repression that it culminated in the death or expulsion in chains to the Middle East of endless processions of rebels, giving him such a reputation for cruelty that his name among the common people has never been forgotten to this day, Bosnia-Herzegovina entered the last stage of its rule by Turkey. The new vizier was Sherif Osman-pasha (1861–69), an educated man, a level-headed politician whose policies in education, culture, economics and administrative life were influenced by European developments. The construction of modern roads began, telegraph lines were installed, capitalist industry became possible. There was freedom to trade with Europe, which allowed the expansion of such towns as Mostar and Banja Luka, and an urban business class developed, especially among the Serbs.

During the governorship of Topal Osman-pasha the first modern printing press was opened in Sarajevo (1866) and the first newspapers began to be printed: *Bosanski vjesnik, Bosna, Sarajevski cvjetnik, Neretva* – all, with the exception of *Bosanski vjesnik*, bilingual in Bosnian and Turkish. It was now that a very interesting personality made his appearance, Mehmed Šaćir Kurtćehajić (1844–72), probably the first professional journalist in Bosnia-Herzegovina. With his dynamic, flowing style and total commitment to enlightenment ideas, in his articles he unwaveringly championed the need to Europeanize life in Bosnia. He also clearly articulated the notion of tolerance among the various members of Bosnia-Herzegovina's community. He was both publisher and editor of *Sarajevski cvjetnik*.

But however serious the Turkish authorities' efforts at reform were, they could not bolster the old order, essentially because they did not touch the most burning problem of the time, agrarian reform. On the contrary, the Safer Decree of 1859 sanctioned the *čiftluk* system of private estates which was quite obviously against the interests of the greater part of the population of Bosnia – the peasants, both serfs and free peasants.

With the spread of modern methods of production to the towns the economy began to expand, enhancing the importance of urban communities that were increasingly in touch with national movements in the neighbouring South Slav countries.

'The most complicated country in Europe'

Bosnia-Herzegovina was part of the Ottoman Empire for four hundred years and, until its new occupation by Austro-Hungary in 1878, a border province permanently at the crossroads of opposing worlds and civilizations; the developments in and around it shaped the physiognomy of a country that, as Slovene writer Josip Vidmar put it in 1943 – at the first session of ZAVNOBIH [Anti-Fascist Council of Bosnia-Herzegovina] in Mrkonjić-grad – entered the twentieth century as 'the most complicated country in Europe'.

A complex religious picture had crystallized here, in which Islam and Orthodox and Catholic Christianity shaped the spiritual life of a population with close ethnic origins and a common language; a picture that in complex interaction with other historical factors – social, political and cultural – had by the nineteenth century produced the national identities of Bosniak-Muslims, Serbs and Croats. In the context of an all-embracing confessionalism, three cultural identities emerged: Muslim-Bosniak, in which Turkish-Islamic culture dominated; Serbian Orthodox, linked to the Byzantine religious tradition; and Catholic Croatian, shaped by western Christian traditions. After the expulsion of the Arabs and Jews from Spain and Portugal in the sixteenth century, these three components were joined by another, that of the Sephardic Jews. The result was an exceptionally complicated and ambivalent society, characterized on the one hand by cultural and spiritual isolationism, on the other by tolerance for difference as a normal aspect of life.

In its content, forms, range and lines of development, Bosnia's cultural life during the Ottoman period was the product above all of its position in the Empire. For centuries it was Turkey's military outpost against a continuous offensive by the European powers. Retarded by the fetters of conservative feudalism and poverty, it turned towards an oriental Islamic culture whose heights it could never hope to reach. Still less could it follow the profound changes that were changing the spirit and face of western Europe. Yet in spite of this Bosnia-Herzegovina did manage to maintain a cultural output of undoubted continuity, range and value, even though many aspects of this have not as yet been properly studied.

Urban architecture developed, as did calligraphy and fine craftsmanship. The towns acquired their own individual ambience and layout, and a distinctive Bosnian-oriental lifestyle. But this evolution did not affect the villages, which were left behind and in which a petrified, patriarchal way of life continued on a minimal level, in primitive houses that had scarcely changed over the centuries. In these villages the collective creative spirit could be expressed only in the archaic folklore of art, music, dance and songs.

One characteristic and widespread form of art that continued through these entire four centuries was oral folk literature. It took various forms, but reached its greatest heights in two: epic poetry and *sevdalinka* love songs.

Epic ballads were written and fostered by all three ethnic groups with equal intensity, exhibiting interesting nuances of style and subject on a common basis and within the framework of a single poetic, philosophic and patriarchal morality. For the great majority of people, these folk poems were the most important form of aesthetic expression, providing a cathartic release from the labour of everyday life. Embodying as they did a centuries-long crystallization of classic harmony and moving tragedy, they were actually the first cultural products through which Europe recognized the creative force of these regions. This happened two hundred years ago after the publication in Venice in 1774 of *Viaggio in Dalmazia* [Travels in Dalmatia] by Alberto Fortis, thanks to which the European literary world was excited by the moving Muslim ballad *Hasanaginica*, which immediately awakened wide interest and inspired numerous translations, the most famous being those by Johann Wolfgang Goethe, Gottfried Herder, Gérard de Nerval, Alexander Pushkin and Adam Mickiewicz. The Romantic movement in European literature in the first half of the nineteenth century stimulated a heightened interest in the exotic and in folk poetry. The discovery of *Hasanaginica* aroused interest in the large corpus of South Slav epic poetry, which led to the collection and recording of such poetry both in Bosnia and elsewhere in Europe; it is still of interest today to scholars and students of literature.

The most frequent subjects for such poetry are duels and battles, abductions and pursuits, horses and heroes, the oppressors of the poor and their protectors, mountain brigands and splendid knights, blood and death in its two starkest and cruellest forms: the coward's, by which his whole life is blighted; and the hero's, by which his life is redeemed and perpetuated in poetry. Just as themes are continually repeated in these ballads, so too are the figures that appear in them. Prince Marko, who is a hero in all South Slav epic traditions. Or the remarkable characters from the *hajduk* epic cycles, closely linked with Bosnia-Herzegovina: Starina Novak, Mijat Tomić, Stari Vujadin, and many others. The epic poetry of the Bosnian Muslims introduced certain special elements into this corpus, which come to distinctive expression in the frontier ballads composed in the endlessly troubled borderlands, among the Muslims of Bosanska krajina, Lika and Dalmatia (while these latter regions were still part of the Bosnian *pashaluk*). Here fights with *uskoks* and with Austrian or Venetian sailors – actually fights between men of the same blood and the same language – were daily occurrences, but the sense of kinship was never extinguished; and it was this specific existential counterpoint that to a large extent gave this poetry its tone. The figures in the Muslim epic poems are highly individual, the most famous of them being Ali Đerzelez and Tale of Orašac (or Budalina [clumsy lout] Tale), who with their instinctive sense of justice, expressly plebeian outlook and bohemian character are like no others in South Slav epic poetry.

Bosnia and the Islamic world – the Muslim-Bosniak cultural context

Islamization, which began in Bosnia in the second half of the fifteenth century, in the sixteenth and seventeenth centuries spread to all parts of our land and all layers of the population, from the highest nobility to the lowest peasants. This meant that a Turko-Islamic variant of oriental culture put down deep roots, imbuing with its spirit the everyday life and creativity even of non-Muslims and impacting strongly on the entire spiritual and material culture of the region.

Islamic culture flourished from the conquest until the end of the seventeenth century, as numerous fine buildings bear witness. It was during this time that primary and secondary schools, mektebs and medresas, were built throughout Bosnia-Herzegovina to teach the spiritual and scholarly disciplines of Islam.

In the eighteenth century, when Turkey began to decline and rapidly lose its expansionary power, and when the Bosnian *pashaluk* after the Vienna War, became a frontier zone of the Empire facing Austria and Venice, Islamic culture in Bosnia entered a period of decadence, borne witness to once again by the appearance of its buildings, now increasingly impoverished. At the same time, however, the weakening of intellectual and spiritual ties with the central authorities allowed a form of writing to develop that is very important in the Bosnian-Muslim literary tradition: *alhamijado* literature, written in the vernacular but using Arabic script.

Oriental culture in Bosnia came to its highest expression in the towns, which sprang up in large numbers and flourished after the establishment of Turkish rule. Sixteenth-century travellers were fond of comparing Sarajevo with Damascus, considered the most beautiful city of the East. Towns reflected the basic oriental urban plan – divided into a *čaršija* or market and business sector and *mahale* or residential areas – and the spirit of oriental domestic architecture. But in a creative symbiosis they also contained evident elements from other traditions, that of mediaeval Bosnia and a strong Mediterranean influence, so that in time Bosnian towns developed a physiognomy of their own, differing in many ways from the typical Turkish-oriental town though rooted in it. They exhibit a certain human scale, aesthetic proportion, refinement of composition and attention to small, intimate details that contribute to a special beauty still able to exercise its charm.

21. The Gazi Husrev-beg Mosque (1530–1) and the Kuršumlija Medresa (1537–8), Sarajevo.

22. The Ferhadija Mosque (1579–80), Banja Luka, endowed by Ferhat-paša Sokolović.

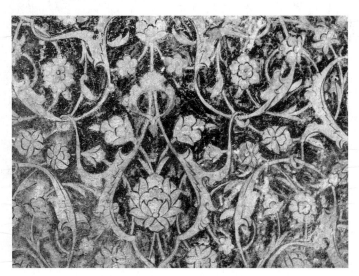

23. Detail of wall painting from the Aladža Mosque, Foča (1550–1).

24. The Aladža Mosque (1550–1) Foča, endowed by Hasan Nazir and built by Mimar Ramadan-aga.

25. Muslim graveyard, Jakir near Glamoć with the *mašet* of Omer-aga Bašić (1798).

Fine examples of public building, both sacred and secular, from the period are to be found in the shape of numerous mosques, fountains, gravestones, inns, caravanserai, schools, administrative and residential buildings, covered markets, baths, clock towers, drinking fountains and bridges. The finest and best known date from the sixteenth century and were the work of leading architects of the day like Master [Mimar] Sinan and Master Hajrudin; but many local builders too had a high reputation, such as Nedžar Hadži Ibrahim and another Sinan, both from Sarajevo.

The finest examples of religious architecture are Ferhad-pasha's mosque, the Ferhadija, in Banja Luka and Gazi Husrevbeg's in Sarajevo, buildings which in boldness of design and imagination can take their place among the best of their European counterparts. They belong to an early type, with an interior space covered by both dome and half-dome. Many more mosques were built with a single dome,

26. The *sahat-kula* (clock tower), Mostar, 17th century, endowed by Fatima Kaduna Šarić.

their outer form developing naturally from their inner spatial organization. Examples are the Aladža mosque in Foča, those of Karadozbeg and Koski Mehmed-pasha in Mostar, those of Ali-pasha and the Emperor in Sarajevo, Hadži Alija's in Počitelj, the Arnaudija (more properly Hasan Defterdar's mosque) in Banja Luka, Sinanbeg's mosque in Čajniča, the Jeni-mosque in Travnik and Krzlaragin's in Mrkonjić-grad. Mosques were completed by a polygonal or circular *šadrvan* or fountain, with a roof standing on columns. These are often delightfully conceived miniatures, spreading around them an atmosphere of peace and intimacy. Some are of particularly outstanding beauty, such as those at the mosques of Karadozbeg and Koski Mehmed-pasha in Mostar, at Esme Sultan's mosque in Jajce and at Gazi Husrevbeg's in Sarajevo.

Bosnian Muslim gravestones reflect a very specific spiritual and formal tradition, especially those of the fifteenth and sixteenth centuries: *nišani* and *bašluci*. Basically they are Islamic, but in many details they are an extension of the stećak tradition. They are tall straight stones, commonly called *šehitski* [*šehid* = martyr] or *gazijski* [*gazi* = hero] tombs; the graveyards are often sited near mediaeval necropolises, just as they have taken over many artistic elements from the stećci. The stone is cut in the same way with similar motifs, ranging from ornamental and symbolic to figurative ones that include animals and even human portraits, though this is not in the accepted Islamic tradition. Sometimes there are inscriptions in niches, written in the Bosnian Cyrillic script using the vernacular tongue, with the same style and formulas as on the stećci. Later on, Islamic inscriptions in Arabic script and oriental languages became widespread, providing a whole series of brilliant poetic miniatures. But throughout the centuries the Bosančica script and the vernacular language remained part of the everyday usage of the Bosnian Muslims. A characteristic architectural feature from Ottoman times is the clock-tower (*sahat kula*), its shape based on the Western European church belfry. Sometimes it stands beside the mosque (Gazi Husrevbeg's, Ferhadpasha's), sometimes in the market place or as part of a castle, or it may even be free-standing with an architectural form and function

27. The Arslanagić Bridge on the Trebišnjica, near Trebinje (1572–4).

of its own. Until 1992 clock-towers were to be found in Sarajevo, Banja Luka, Donji Vakuf, Prozor, Prusac, Tešanj, Livno, Počitelj, two in Travnik, Foča, Gornji Vakuf, Gračanica, Maglaj, Nevesinje, Trebinje and Mostar.

Bridges were outstanding architectural creations, some of breathtaking beauty and architectural daring. The best known are those financed by Mehmed-pasha Sokolović. These include the Bridge on the Drina at Višegrad and the famous Old Bridge at Mostar (the former the work of Master Sinan, the latter of his pupil Hajrudin the younger), and the Arslanagić bridge in Trebinja. But the same kind of beauty radiates from lesser known bridges, such as the Bridge on the Žepa, the Goat's Bridge on the Miljacka near Sarajevo, the Crooked Bridge on the Radobolja in Mostar, the bridge at Klepci on the Bregava near Čapljina, the one on the Duman in Livno, the one over the Šuica in Duvansko polje, the one on the Bosna in Blažuj near Sarajevo, and many more all over Bosnia-Herzegovina. The bridges over the Miljacka at Sarajevo were once famous, but their original form was not preserved; another irretrievable loss was the

28. The Mehmed-paša Sokolović Bridge on the Drina, Višegrad (1571–7).

destruction of the bridges in Konjic and over the Buna, destroyed by the Germans when they retreated in 1945.

These old bridges were functionally and aesthetically adapted to the rivers they spanned and the shores they linked. They had certain common stylistic elements, but there was no fixed pattern of construction and they were wonderfully varied, ranging from the powerful horizontal of the Višegrad bridge with its eleven arches to the wonderful arc of Mostar's fantastic bridge, held in place by sheer mathematical accuracy, and to the imaginative asymmetry of the Arslanagić bridge on the Trebišnjica.

Islamic art developed quite differently from that of western Europe. Anonymous perfection within the accepted canons of aesthetic experience and abstract ornamentation were more important than artistic individuality. Hence there was intense development in decoration and fine workmanship. This suited Bosnia very well, for fine applied craftsmanship had been a tradition from the Middle Ages. There were famous craft centres in Sarajevo, where about sixty different crafts were practised at a high level. But Sarajevo was not the only place where a high aesthetic level was achieved. Other important centres included Foča, Travnik and Fojnica, famous for the production and decoration of cold steel and firearms; engraving and embossing were developed to a fine art in Sarajevo, Travnik and Mostar; brasswork and filigree in Sarajevo, Mostar, Banja Luka, Foča,

Fojnica, Kreševa, Čajniče, and Livno; carpet-making in Stolac, Gacko, Foča, Livno, Sarajevo and Višegrad. Sarajevo was also famous for its *mudželiti* or bookbinders, skilled at working in leather. Other handicrafts such as embroidery and wood carving flourished as cottage industries. Many crafts crossed confessional and customary barriers to become a common tradition.

A special form of Muslim art was decorative calligraphy in inscriptions and manuscripts, on walls, and on articles for everyday use. Gravestones and niches bore intricate foliar and geometric patterning. Many local craftsmen were engaged in such work, among them Osman-baša and Mustafa Faginović from Sarajevo, whose work adorned even one mosque in Istanbul.

In somewhat the same way that the Franciscans in Croatia wrote literary works in Latin which became part of Croatia's literary tradi-

29. Calligraphic inscriptions on the Sinanova Tekke (1638–40) Sarajevo. The inscription dates from the 18th century.

tion, the Bosnian Muslims produced rich and varied literary, philo-sophical and scholarly writings in Arabic, Turkish and Persian. Just as many people originating from Bosnia reached high, even the high-est, military and political ranks in Turkey, so too many were counted among the intellectual élite, and some found a place among the lead-ing thinkers of the time, studying and working in the great centres of the Islamic world. Rather than forgetting the land of their origin, many returned home and carried out significant educational and crea-tive work there. It is characteristic that almost all who made a reputation for themselves in learning or literature retained in their names a mark of their origin: *Bosnevi, Bosnali*... Sarajevo, Mostar and Prusac were all at various times centres of intellectual activity and work that became a permanent part of Islamic theological and schol-arly thought. Among the most important names: Ahmed Sudi (b. in Sudić near Čajniče), Abdulah Bošnjak (died 1644), Muhamed Musić-Allamek from Sarajevo (1595–1637), Hasan Kafi Pruščak (1544–1616), Mustafa Ejubović (sheikh Jujo) from Mostar (1651–1707), and two famous Turkish historians of the sixteenth and seventeen centuries, Ibrahim Pečevi, born in Župa Lepenica, and Kodža Husein, born in Sarajevo.

There was writing of many kinds in oriental languages, above all various kinds of classical poetry, but also chronicles, travel accounts, biographies, letters etc. In their day these names were famous in the literary world: Dervish-pasha Mostarac, poet; Ibrahim Opijač (1678–1726), scholar and biographer of Mustafa Ejubović; Sabit Užičanin (d. 1712); Fevzi Mostarac, author of the famous *Bulbulistan* in eight-eenth-century Persian; Mula Mustafa Bašeski (1731–1809), author of a lively diary of Sarajevo life in the second half of the eighteenth and first years of the nineteenth century, written in the Turkish spoken in Sarajevo, with many elements of the vernacular; Mehmed Mejli (1713–1781), a well-known Sarajevo poet, composer of *tariha* and calligrapher; Salih Sidki Hadžihuseinović Muvekit (1825–1888), au-thor of a *History of Bosnia* in Turkish; Abdurahman Sirri (d. 1847). Some of these also wrote in Bosnian.

In the second half of the seventeenth century *alhamijado* literature flourished and expanded among the Muslims of Bosnia-Herzegovina and it went on being written even into the twentieth century. In language, subject matter and spirit (despite the obvious influence of oriental literary motifs) it tells us much more about the intellectual, political and social life of Bosnia and the spirit of folk oral poetry than does the literature written in oriental languages.

Some *alhamijado* writers, because of their nonconformist attitude, both personal and poetic, to the moral, social and political abuses of the time, were made to feel the brutal power of the rulers, so that they gained a popular reputation as defenders of the common folk. This was especially true of the poet Hasan Kaimija. In the year 1683 during the Vienna War, in a chaotic atmosphere of hunger and food speculation and when refugees were arriving en masse from across the Sava, he became the spokesman of the Sarajevo poor in their distress and was exiled to Zvornik, where he died. Abdulvehab Ilhamija from Žepče, who left a collection of *alhamijado* poems as well as writing in Turkish, Arabic and Persian, suffered an even worse fate. Because of his unsparing criticism of the hypocrisy and corruption of the religious and administrative hierarchy, he was imprisoned and strangled in Travnik castle in 1821 or 1822, at a time when a Muslim rising against the central government was being bloodily suppressed.

One of the first and most important *alhamijado* writers was Muhamed Hevaji Uskufi, born 1601 or 1602 near Tuzla. He was among other things the first Bosnian lexicographer; he composed a Turkish-Bosnian dictionary in verse – the *Makbuli arif* or *Potur-šahidija* (completed 1631) – an important source today for linguistic research. We should also mention Hadži Jusuf Livnjak and Mehmed-aga Pruščanin, authors of two *arzuhal* or protest-petitions in verse, vividly describing the autocratic behaviour of local authorities and the hardships of life on the military frontier; Ahmed Karahodža from Žepče; and the Sarajevo poetess Umihana Čuvidina (1794–1870), author of a number of poems resembling folk epics of which one, *Pogibija Muje Čamdži-barjaktara*, contained moving elements of autobiography.

The Bosnian lyric song or *sevdalinka* is the crown jewel of popular literature. It is the product of an urban environment, born in a materially stable middle-class milieu of merchants and craftsmen, predominantly Islamic and oriental. For this reason the *sevdalinka*, especially in its melodic structure, has obvious oriental elements. But its lyrical structure, sensibility, rules of versification, symbols, imagination and archetypes all have their cultural source in a traditional substratum common to the whole Bosnian folk heritage, as is shown by the fact that people all over the country were able to accept the *sevdalinka* as 'theirs'.

We are naturally thinking here of the authentic article, whose later 'orientalization' is mere kitsch, foreign to the true *sevdalinka*. The origin of this orientalization, paradoxical as it may seem, lies in Austro-Hungarian times and the Austrians' conception of a cultural policy for Bosnia; it is analogous to the 'Moorish' style they promoted in architecture. But the Moorish style disappeared with the Austrians, while the kitsch *sevdalinka* has lasted with variations to this day.

The Orthodox-Serb cultural context

In the political and cultural life of the Serbs of Bosnia-Herzegovina during the Ottoman period, membership of the Serbian Orthodox church was of particular importance. The high and low points of their cultural activity largely correspond to the relations at any given moment between that church and the Turkish authorities.

The sixteenth and seventeenth centuries were relatively fertile periods in religious life, church building, culture and education. New parishes were formed in which great importance was attached to literacy and elementary education. The number of churches and monasteries increased, and the free flow of priests and ecclesiastical artists led to increased literacy and a higher standard of church art. The first printing press, owned by Božidar Goraždanin, was set up in 1519 in Goražde. Though it lasted only until 1523 and printed just three religious books, even such a short life and small output made this a major cultural event. The next printing press was not opened in Bosnia until the second half of the nineteenth century, during the time of Topal Osman-paša.

In the nineteenth century, when Turkey became weaker on the international scene and Austria and Russia both began to get involved in Balkan affairs, the Peć patriarchs began to take an anti-Turkish line, forging links with both Austria and Russia. This led to abolition of the Patriarchate in 1766, after which the general position of the Serbs deteriorated.

After the Patriarchate was abolished, Phanariot Greek priests began to be appointed to all important ecclesiastical posts. Only the lowest level of parish priests were Serbs, and they often lacked even the most elementary education. The Phanariot priests were largely concerned with increasing their own wealth. They remained in Bosnia until the end of Turkish rule, richly contributing to the cultural stagnation of the Orthodox Church. It was a long time before the development of an urban middle class could act as a counterweight. Thus the most basic conditions for producing anything resembling the frescoes of the sixteenth and seventeenth century had ceased to exist among the Serbs of Bosnia-Herzegovina. The only outlet for their creative potential was the popular art of the *guslar* [fiddler] and folklore in general.

Not until the nineteenth century did individual writing begin to emerge from this unchanging background of archaic forms of collective creativity. It emerged as part of a Pan-Serb political and national programme powerfully stimulated by the first Serbian rising and Vuk Karadžić's concept of cultural and linguistic nationalism. More concretely, in Bosnia-Herzegovina such efforts were concentrated mainly in Mostar and Sarajevo, linked to the activity over many years of the Zadar *Srpsko-dalmatinski magazin*, under the editorship of Đorđe Nikolajević and Božidar Petranović, and to the powerful propaganda action of the Slavophile ideologue Aleksander Feodorovich Hilferding, the first Russian consul in Sarajevo (1857–59).

The work of these first writers was inspired by national needs and can hardly be treated as literary in the narrower sense. It consisted mostly of amateur historiography, historical memoirs, or ethnography-cum-travelogue. But it did mark the transition from collective and oral 'literature' to writing by individual authors.

Joanikije Pamučina (1810–70), a churchman, was the author of a quite large corpus ranging from national literature, folklore and historical memoirs to an effort with a more pronounced authorial stamp, in the story *Pobjedonosno mučenje Hristine Rajkovića Djevojčice* [Glorious Martyrdom of the Virgin Hristina Rajković].

Ato Marković Slomo wrote a description of Mostar's national customs in the *Srpsko-dalmatinski magazin*, accompanying them with an interesting commentary.

Staka Skenderova (1821–91) was the first woman among these writers. She had an unusual lifestyle, dressing and living as a man. Discovered by Hilferding, who was looking for someone to inform him about contemporary historical events in Bosnia-Herzegovina, she gave him the story of her life in epic decasyllabic poetry, and he included part of it in his travel book on the country, published in St Petersburg in 1859.

Prokopije Čokorilo (1802–66), rector of the Orthodox Church in Mostar, had personal and literary links with Hilferding. His *Ljetopis Hercegovine 1837–1857* [Chronicle of Herzegovina 1837–1857] was first published in Russian and not until 1908 in a Serbian translation. Čokorilo's diary has also come to light, in which he recorded eyewitness accounts of contemporary events.

Nićifor Dučić (1832–1900) was the most prolific writer of this literary group. He was a monk, but very active in politics and military activities, including skirmishes with the Turks in Herzegovina and Montenegro in the sixties. He had studied at the Bogoslovija and the Velika Škola in Belgrade, and also in Paris. He published nine volumes of historical works at his own expense, but they are of little literary or scholarly value. His memoirs are much more interesting as literature.

Gavro Vučković Krajišnik (1830–76) had a lively personality and led a dynamic and turbulent life. As a writer he stands out from the

30. The Old Orthodox Church of SS Michael and Gabriel,
Sarajevo, 16th century.

31. Gomionica Monastery, first half of the 16th century
but restored several times.

Mostar-Sarajevo circle. He was self-taught. His work is an expression of his political sufferings and his views on the political situation in Bosnia-Herzegovina in the last ten years of Turkish rule. His *Ropstvo u slobodi ili ogledalo pravde u Bosni* [Slavery in freedom or mirror of justice in Bosnia], published in 1872 in Novi Sad, was banned by the Turkish authorities in Bosnia as had been his *Krvava knjiga fra Ante Knežević* [The Bloody Book of Brother Ante Knežević] the previous year.

Vaso Pelagić – thinker, writer, rebel, tribune of his people and sufferer with it – was an outstanding literary and political figure, in every sense the most remarkable Serb writer of the nineteenth century in Bosnia-Herzegovina.

In artistic terms the finest work within the Serb tradition in Bosnia-Herzegovina was produced in churches and monasteries: exquisite examples of goldsmith's work, carving, painting, frescoes and icons.

A certain number of monasteries and churches, especially in Podrinja and Hum (Herzegovina), existed towards the end of the mediaeval Bosnian state: Dobrun, Panik, Srebrenica, and others. Their cultural contribution included the preservation of a number of mediaeval Bosnian illuminated manuscripts. Before the Peć Patriarchate was abolished a number of new churches and monasteries were built; the most important were in Sarajevo (the Old Orthodox Church), Trijebanj, Gomiljani, Srpevići, Dobrićevo, Aranđelovo, Žitomislići, Zavala, Mostaći, Rmanj, Tavna, Papraća, Lomnica, Ozren, Gomionica, Tvrdoš, Vozuća, Moštanica and elsewhere.

In quantity and in artistic level, fresco painting in the Serbian-Byzantine style was at its height at the end of the sixteenth and in the seventeenth century and, though constantly decreasing, was still widespread in the eighteenth century: it is among the most important cultural achievements in Bosnia-Herzegovina during Ottoman times. The late-sixteenth-century frescoes by probably the greatest Serbian painters of the whole four centuries of Ottoman rule – *Longin* and *Georgije Mitrofanović* – are particularly noteworthy. The former painted the monastery church at Lomnica, to which he also gave an iconostasis of exceptional artistic value. The latter painted the frescoes in the churches at Dobrićevo and Zavala. The work they did in Bosnia-Herzegovina represents the major part of their known opus.

There are remarkable frescoes also in the churches at Trijebanj, Papraća, Srpevići, Ozren, Žitomislić, Dobrun, Aranđelovo, Mostaći, Gomionica, and the names of some of the artists are recorded: Father Strahinja in Dobrun, two Jovans, Nikola and Georgije at Lomnica, Master Vasilje in Mostaći, Master Teodor in Dobrićevo, Konstantin in Gomionica . . .

A considerable number of icons have come down to us in Bosnia-Herzegovina, especially in Sarajevo, which was the richest religious centre and, from the eighteenth century, the seat of the bishopric. The Sarajevo icons demonstrate various styles of Byzantine iconography, with influences ranging from the Cretan to the Kotor school, and there are also many of the Dalmatian type produced in large numbers for both Orthodox and Catholic churches. Most of the artists are anonymous; we know only a few names: Todor Vuković Desisalić, (sixteenth century) MaksimTujković (eighteenth century), Simeun Lazović (nineteenth century), all master painters who came to work in Bosnia-Herzegovina. And we also know that some local artists painted icons, like Nenko Solak from Sarajevo (seventeenth century) and Sanko Daskal (eighteenth century), as well as Risto Čajkanović (second half of the nineteenth century) who was already painting secular portraits as well as icons.

The Catholic-Croat cultural context

The great catastrophe of 1463 and the process of Islamization that followed it did not destroy the middle class of merchants, craftsmen and miners, which indeed in the long period up to the Vienna War of 1683–99 continued to develop and provide an important basis for cultural life. During the sixteenth century and later, out of the once numerous mediaeval monasteries, the following Franciscan houses and monasteries continued to be active: Srebrenica (Argentina), Fojnica, Olovo (Plumbum), Visoko, Kreševo, Gradovrh (*Salinae*

1. Hrvoje's Missal (1405–7). Written for Hrvoje Vukčić Hrvatinić in Glagolitic script.

2. Chalice, of Bosnian production from a Fojnica goldsmith's workshop, late 15th–early 16th centuries.

3. Ottoman metalwork now in the collection of the Zemaljski Muzej.

4. The Old Bridge (Stari Most) over the Neretva River, Mostar, built by
Hajrudin the Younger (1566).

5. View of Počitelj with the Hadži Alija (or Šišman Ibrahim-paša) mosque (1562).

6. Turbe 'under the lime trees', Travnik (1748).

7. Astrological manuscript, 15th–16th centuries (detail).

8. Icon of St. George with Hagiography (1574) by an unknown local artist, the Old Orthodox Church, Čajnice.

9. The Sarajevo Haggadah, 14th century: The crossing of the Red Sea and Miriam and the women dancing.

10. Gabrijel Jurkić: High Meadow in Flower (1914).

11. Šišava on Mount Vlašić, central Bosnia.

32. The imperial
doors of the
iconostasis, Lomnica
Monastery, by an
unknown artist,
probably early 17th
century

Superiores, Gornja Tuzla) Donja Tuzla, (*Salinae Inferiores*), Modriča, Rama. There were concentrations of Catholics, some smaller some larger, in towns and villages all over Bosnia, especially in the commercial centres (though these were rather quickly orientalized and converted to Islam). Catholics were most numerous of all in the surviving mining centres, such as Fojnica, Kreševo, Kraljeva Sutjeska, Vareš, Varcar Vakuf. Bosnian Catholic merchants (the Brnjakovićes, Grgurevićes, Brajkovićes, etc) still at this time maintained important business contacts with Dubrovnik, Osijek, Dalmatia and Italy, and crop up as patrons of cultural life. Not only were works of art commissioned from abroad (paintings from Italy, Austria and Germany), but Bosnian painters too now made an appearance, like the well-trained and talented Stjepan Dragojlović; while the old traditions of fine craftsmanship in precious metals, wood-carving, book-binding and textiles continued to be nurtured. Finally, this was the period that gave birth to that unique product of Bosnian culture in the Ottoman period: the literature of the Bosnian Franciscans.

But the Vienna War was an absolute catastrophe for the Bosnian Catholics, especially the middle-class, and one from which they took a long time to recover. In 1697 the Austrian general Eugene of Savoy advanced along the valley of the Bosna right down to Sarajevo. Wherever the army went, looting, burning and wrecking went with it. Sarajevo itself was put to the torch. When Eugene withdrew he took with him a large proportion of the Catholics of central and northern Bosnia, fearful of reprisals. The depths of the tragedy can only be imagined, but the figures tell us something: after this, there were fewer than 30,000 Catholics left in all Bosnia, only 29 Franciscans and three of their monasteries, Kraljeva Sutjeska, Fojnica and Kreševo.

Thus the work of the Franciscans was of vital importance for the cultural life of Bosnia's Croats during the period of Turkish administration. In particular, as a result of complex historical events, the centre of their order in Bosna Srebrena came in time to have a unique position within the Catholic Church; it is the only institution in the history of Bosnia maintaining a continuity with the mediaeval Bosnian kingdom. It has been known as Bosna Srebrena [Silver Bosnia] since

1514, when the Franciscan Vicariate was raised to the level of a Province; the name was taken from one of the order's oldest monasteries, that in Srebrenica.

Without exception natives of the region, organically integrated with the people, filling the roles of priest, teacher, doctor, intellectual, and political representative, the Franciscans for long centuries were the most relevant authorities for their flock, not only in religion but in all aspects of life.

Their province once covered a huge area stretching from the Adriatic coast to Hungary, Rumania and Bulgaria. But after the Turks were defeated and withdrew from the lands across the Sava, the region in which the Franciscans had once been spiritually supreme was divided between three great powers – Turkey, Austria and Venice. This meant that the Bosnian Catholics were cut off from their coreligionists in areas ruled by Venice (Dalmatia) and Austria (North Croatia).

Bosna Srebrena thus became smaller, and as 'mother province' gave birth to others: in 1735 the Dalmatian province of St Caius, later renamed province of the Most Holy Redeemer; in 1757 the Croato-Hungarian province of St John Capistrano; and in the nineteenth century the Herzegovinian province. The formation of this last was a result of political events, relating first to the founding of the Herzegovinian *pašaluk* in 1832, after the crushing of Husein-kapetan Gradaščević and the Bosnian leaders and of Ali-paša Rizvanbegović's autonomist ambitions, and secondly to the so-called Barišić affair, in which the Herzegovinian Franciscans backed Bishop Rafo Barišić in his defiance of Bosna Srebrena, supported by the landowners of Herzegovina. Herzegovina was first given the status of a *custodia* in 1852 and became a province in 1890.

The regular hierarchy of the Catholic Church was introduced into Bosnia only in 1881, when Austro-Hungary took Bosnia from the Turks. The newly appointed archbishop Josip Stadler immediately tried to take over all parishes from the Franciscans and place his priests there, which would have had the result of dividing the Franciscans from the people. He was only partly successful, and the animosity created between these two religious organizations has still not entirely disappeared to this day, sometimes erupting into open conflict with adverse effect on the life of the people.

The Franciscans with great skill and much sacrifice managed to retain their position and carry out their work during four centuries of Turkish rule; but they were a constant source of irritation to the Turks, who saw in them – and Catholics in general – the danger of Austrian influence. This became still more the case as the Turks became weaker and began to be defeated in vital battles, like the one before Vienna in 1683. From then onwards Austria began to increase its political propaganda and intelligence activities in Bosnia-Herzegovina, in which it managed to make use of the Franciscans' and other Catholics' mistrust of the Turkish authorities. This weakened the Franciscans' position, and the records of their work in the eighteenth century are full of examples of reverses and overriding by the government.

The Franciscans were of the greatest importance for cultural life in Bosnia-Herzegovina during these centuries. They received an elementary education in the monasteries as novices and later went on to be educated abroad, mainly in Italy, Austria and Hungary. They were thus among the most highly educated people in Bosnia. Matija Divković (1563–1631) is considered the founder of a true literary tradition among the Bosnian Franciscans, though they had already left some writings from the Middle Ages. When we speak of Matija Divković as the founder, we are thinking primarily of literature in the vernacular language reflecting popular needs.

Of course the Franciscans also wrote in foreign languages, especially Latin. One of the best known names in European humanism writing in Latin was Georgius Benignus de Salviatis, born Juraj Dragišić. Fleeing from the Turks, he left Srebrenica in 1463 for Dubrovnik, whence he went on to study at the universities of Rome, Bologna, Florence, Padua and Oxford. He lectured on theology, philosophy, and philology at a number of Italian universities and was in contact with the most famous European humanists. He defended Savanarola and Reuchlin in the name of freedom of conscience and scientific thought. He was the author of a number of theological and philosophical works still of interest to scholars. Literature in Latin continued to be a living force among the Franciscans throughout this period, and in the nineteenth century Ambroža Matić and Blaž Josić, for example, were still writing Latin verses modelled on the Roman classics.

But of greater interest to us is literature in the tradition begun by Divković and still alive today. Naturally over this long period, which experienced such great historical and spiritual changes in Bosnia, literature too has changed in many respects, just as has the figure of the Franciscan writer and intellectual. We shall here confine ourselves to two very different periods.

The first of these covers the seventeenth and eighteenth centuries. These were the centuries when there began throughout Europe, on the initiative of the Council of Trent (1545–63), the great Counter-Reformation movement of the Catholic Church, aimed at strengthening the Catholic faith and the authority of the Pope in Rome, seriously eroded by the Reformation. In a formal sense Franciscan literature in Bosnia likewise drew its inspiration from the aims of the Counter-Reformation; but it expressed more strongly the specific needs and conditions of Bosnia. There was no special need here for counter-reformation activity, since the Reformation had never succeeded in reaching Bosnia as it did Slovenia and northern Croatia, where it had a serious cultural impact.

In this period Franciscan literature was basically subordinated to its religious and didactic aims, for which most suitable forms were sermons and moralistic works. It was not the intention of the religious teachers to be original: they reworked the huge European literature of this kind, and their literary talent and success can be measured only by the extent to which they did so in a lively and convincing way. Their great cultural contribution was to broaden Bosnian cultural and historical horizons, by introducing subjects, scenes and characters from European literature. Their books provided the only popular reading-matter of the day, going through numerous editions, undergoing many later reworkings and entering deeply into the collective memory. Important writers of this kind of literature were Stjepan Matijević (1580–1654), with his *Ispoviedaonik* [Confessor] (1630); Stjepan Margitić Markovac (?–1714), with his *Ispovid karstianska* [Christian confession] (1701) and *Fala od sveti* [Praise of the sacred] (1708); Ivan Bandulavić (17 c), with his *Pištole i evandelja* [Epistles and gospels] (1613); Ivan Ančić (1624–85), with his *Vrata nebesna i život vični* [The heavenly gate and life eternal] (1678), *Svitlost karstianska i slast duhovna* [Christian light and spiritual joy] (1679) and *Ogledalo misničko* [The priest's mirror] (1681); Pavao Posilović (?–1653), with his *Cvit kriposti* [Flower of virtue] (1647) and *Naslapenje duhovna* [Spiritual delight] (1639); Pavao Papić (1593– ?), with his *Sedam trublji za probudit grešnika na pokoru* [Seven trumpets to awaken sinners to repent] (1649); Jerolim Filipović (1688–1765), with his *Pripovijedanje nauka karstjanskoga* [Stories of Christian teaching] (1750) and *Put križa ili žalosno putovanje našeg izmučenoga Gospodina Isukarsta od kuće Pilatove do Kalvarie* [The way of the Cross, or the sad journey of our tortured Lord Jesus Christ from Pilate's house to Calvary] (1750). But the most productive of all, the most influential and in literary terms most successful, was Matija Divković.

The exceptional feature of Divković's work, especially in his collection of stories *Razlike besiede Divkovića svrhu evandelja nedieljnieh priko svega godišta* [Various of Divković's sermons for weekly preaching throughout the year], is its intimacy and warmth, with colourful, persuasive and self-contained narrative construction. Because of these literary qualities, many of Divković's stories have an authenticity that still impresses us, even outside the religious context in which they were originally written. He is important also as a writer who laid the basis for a literary tradition. From the beginning he tried his hand at almost every literary form. Unsurpassed as a writer of homilies, he also wrote verse and dialogues that were the beginning of dramatic discourse in Bosnian literature. His linguistic and orthographic activity was a landmark in Bosnian cultural history. From the first he had a clear understanding of the basic need to address people, in both speech and writing, in their own language and script. So the language he uses in his writing is pure Bosnian-Croatian speech,

33. 'Nauk karstianski' by fra Matija Divković, printed in Venice, 1611. The first
book by an author from Bosnia-Herzegovina and printed in Bosančica.

for which he had a finely attuned ear. But he did not leave this 'natural' speech at its raw level; he tried – successfully – with a highly developed sense of measure to ennoble and stretch it, integrating into his Bosnian tongue all the Croatian literary traditions: those of Slavonia, Dalmatia and Dubrovnik. Divković was thus a great forerunner of the attempt to standardize the literary language. He made a similar contribution in the field of orthography. His most important books apart from *Besiede* are *Nauk karstianski za narod slovinski* [Christian teaching for the Slav people] (1611), *Sto čudesa aliti zlamenia*

[One hundred miracles or signs] (1611), and *Život svete Katarine* [The Life of St Katarina] (1709). In writing and printing he used the ancient Bosančica script. As there was no printing press in Bosnia, he took his manuscripts to Venice and there made his own Bosnian Cyrillic font and printed his own books. He paid great attention to creating his own orthographic system, as closely adapted as possible to the speech of the people. In this too Divković showed himself to be the forerunner of an approach to orthography that was not to be widely accepted until two-and-a-half centuries later.

For all these reasons Divković was an example to all the Franciscan writers who came after him. For the next two hundred years his works were reprinted, read and well known throughout Bosnia-Herzegovina and Dalmatia.

In the eighteenth century religious and didactic literature continued to be published but other important kinds of writing also developed, including monastic records, chronicles and the first attempts to write historical works. The best known chronicles are those of the Sutješka monastery by Brother Bono Benić (1708–85) and of the Kreševo monastery by Brother Marijan Bogdanović (?-1772), the one by Brother Nikola Lašvanin (?-1750), and the yearbook of Brother Jakov Baltić in the nineteenth century. The main intention behind these chronicles was to record the history and work of the Franciscans; but they ranged far more widely and today constitute a very valuable historical and documentary source. At the same time many of them also have considerable literary value, providing as they do a direct portrayal of real life in all its multiplicity of colour and form. The writing is lively and addresses the reader directly, with a well-developed feeling for the historical continuity of life.

The earliest historians and chroniclers were imbued with similar ideas. The best known is Brother Filip Lastrić (1700–83), a learned and eminent Franciscan who spared no effort in defending the rights of Bosna Srebrena, travelled several times to Rome and Vienna and, by his depositions before the ecclesiastical authorities, managed to preserve Franciscan privileges and the integrity of the Province. Lastrić wrote a number of historical works; outstanding among them is his

Epitome vetustatum bosnensis provinciae [Survey of antiquities of the Bosnian Province] (1765). This was the first integral work on the history of Bosnia, and Lastrić may be considered the country's first scholarly historiographer. His importance is the greater in that his historical writing went beyond the framework of the Franciscan Province and was concerned with the history of Bosnia also from a 'civic' point of view, as he himself put it. As a historian Lastrić was important also for his contribution to the great church history *Illyricum sacrum* by the Italian monk Daniele Farlati. The description of Bosnia that Lastrić provided for the latter was so scholarly and comprehensive that Farlati used it as it was, simply printing it in a different script. Lastrić's work represented an indispensable source for all later historians. From the point of view of literary history, his works are distinguished by their lively style, expressive precision and organic composition. Some of his historical works are still read today as fine and even inspired examples of historical prose and travel writing. He also had a great reputation as a writer of homilies – e.g. *Svetnjak, to jest govorenja od svetie* [The saint, or discourse on sanctity] (1766), *Nediljnik dvostruk* [Priest twice over] (1766) or *Od' uzame* [Walk beside me] (1765) – and he left in manuscript form what was for his time an imposing synthetic manual of philosophical themes in Latin *Testimonium bilabium seu Sermones* (1755).

Among the eighteenth century Bosnian Franciscans there were also some who wrote poetry. Brother Vice Vicić (1734–96) wrote religious poems and, very interestingly for the period, composed music for them. Brother Lovro Sitović (?-1729) is remembered for his *Pisna od Pakla* [Songs of Hell], religious poems written in the decasyllabic metre of folk epic poetry.

The nineteenth century, as an age of immense social and intellectual changes in Europe, naturally did not leave Bosnia or the writings of the Franciscans untouched. In the first place the most progressive and active among them became very much involved in the political independence movement among the South Slavs, especially the Illyrian movement. Secondly, the Franciscans too were strongly influenced by the new spirit of secularism that swept through Europe after the French Revolution. They did not question their own spiritual calling, but in the cultural and political fields much of their work was wholly secular. This secular spirit was given notable expression by Ivan Frano Jukić in his polemical text *Samo za sada* [Only for now] (1842), in which he calls for literature to free itself from religion and criticizes those who 'mix religion into literature where it has no place'.

Under the influence of these ideas, especially those of national emancipation and renaissance, a number of significant creative writers and activists emerged. It is interesting to see how with individual variations they continued the basic Franciscan tradition of cultural action, literature with a national orientation, and Bosnian patriotism. Outstanding among such writers were Ivan Franjo Jukić (1818–57), Grgo Martić (1822–1905), Marijan Šunjić (1789–1860), Martin Nedić (1810–95), Petar Bakula (1816–73) and Anto Knežević (1834–99).

Franciscan writers now turned away almost completely from didactic and religious texts and began to write about cultural and political renaissance (Jukić) or political struggle (Knežević), or else espoused purely literary values (Martić).

Ivan Franjo Jukić (born Banja Luka 1818, died Vienna 1857) in the short thirty-nine years of his life developed from a Franciscan novice into an important figure in the cultural world, a master of many genres passionately committed to the struggle for cultural emancipation of his people.

Considering the contemporary Bosnian situation and traditions and the shortness of his active life, Jukić's opus is impressive indeed, not just in terms of quantity but for the new spirit that it breathes. All his writing is inspired by a love of his Bosnian homeland inherited in part from the long Franciscan tradition of which he was an organic descendant. His vision, sometimes mistily romantic but also passionate, with its origins in his youthful attempt to organize an uprising, was one of a Bosnia with political, national, cultural and personal freedom; with a well-organized secular education, a modern economy, a transparent legal system, a reformed taxation system and all the features of modern civilization – with special emphasis, only naturally, on printing and postal services. He summarized his beliefs for good governance under 28 heads in his *Želje i molbe kristjanah u Bosni i Hercegovini, koje ponizno prikazuju njegovom carskom veličanstvu sretnovladajućem sultanu Abdul-Medžidu* [Desires and requests of the Christians of Bosnia-Herzegovina, humbly addressed to His Imperial Highness the serene ruler Sultan Abdul-Medžid], a memorandum addressed to the sultan. In this document Jukić formulated the first constitutional demands in the history of Bosnia. At the time it reverberated like an explosion and for Jukić the consequences were permanent banishment, which in various forms lasted for the rest of his life. He died in a hospital in Vienna and was given an anonymous burial in a pauper's grave.

In the cultural and literary history of Bosnia-Herzegovina, Jukić has a permanent place as a pioneer. He founded one of the first secular schools, in Varcar-Vakuf (Mrkonjić-Grad) in 1849, and taught in it. He was active in the formation of the first cultural society (*Kolo bosansko*) [Bosnian Circle]. He wrote the first book on Bosnian geography and history (*Zemljopis i poviestnica Bosne)* [A geography and a history of Bosnia]; formulated the idea for the first national museum; founded and edited (largely alone) three volumes of the first literary periodical in Bosnia (*Bosanski prijatelj)*, which catered for very wide interests ranging from folk remedies and songs to travelogues, historical studies, political manifestoes and polemics. Finally he left a number of interesting fragmentary travel writings, especially one describing the early days of his exile *Putovanje iz Sarajeva u Carigrad godine 1852, mjeseca svibnja* [Journey from Sarajevo to Istanbul in 1852 in the month of May], that are full of dramatic power. These writings alone would have made him an irreplaceable figure in the literary history of Bosnia-Herzegovina.

Grgo Martić devoted his whole life to literature, with lofty artistic aspirations. His most ambitious work was the immensely long poem *Osvetnici* [The avengers], conceived as a national epic. As so often happens in the history of literature, this poem hailed as Homeric in its day is now seen as having no literary value, whereas

Martić's memoirs *Zapamćenja* are nowadays considered of greater interest. But whatever the final verdict on his work may be, Martić will continue to have a place as an interesting figure in Bosnian cultural and literary history, who had a significant influence in his day. He was the first writer, moreover, not just the first Franciscan, to devote himself entirely to literature. This option – to live from writing as a profession rather than as a way of achieving some other goal, political, national, religious or whatever – made him very much a man of our modern world.

Jukić's pupil Anto Knežević was the most characteristic writer in the Franciscan tradition of working for an integral Bosnia. In writings such as *Krvava knjiga* [Book of blood], he mercilessly attacked the monstrosities of feudal exploitation and advanced emancipatory ideas; at the same time he developed the idea of an autonomous Bosnia with state rights based on historical tradition and on tolerance and equality in matters of religion and nationality. His reward was to have a price put on his head. This book set him in direct confrontation with prevailing trends in Croatia and Serbia, both of whom claimed Bosnia. At first he welcomed the Austro-Hungarian occupation as a way of introducing civilized European standards into Bosnia-Herzegovina and a step towards the realization of his own goals. But he quickly saw his mistake and withdrew in disillusionment from public life. He also published historical works: *Kratka poviest Kralja bosanskih* [A short history of the kings of Bosnia] (1887), *Pad Bosne* [The fall of Bosnia] (1886), *Carsko-turski namjesnici u Bosni-Hercegovini – god, 1463–1878,* [Imperial-Turkish viceroys in Bosnia-Herzegovina 1463–1878].

From Divković at the beginning of the seventeenth century to Martić at the beginning of the twentieth there is thus a three-hundred-year span of rich literary tradition, passing through all the phases of the long evolution from literature in the service of religion to literature as individual creation. Yet through all that time, with all its changes, the tradition retained its vital link with the essential being of the people and with its own emphatic Bosnian patriotism.

The secular activities of the Franciscans were especially relevant

34. Baptismal record, written in Bosančica, 1641. From the Franciscan monastery at Kraljevska Sutjeska.

to people's everyday lives. They were always ready to help with advice and with their knowledge and skills, from crafts to agriculture and medicine. They did not confine their help to people of their own faith but always, so far as they could, offered their services to everyone and developed the idea and practice of religious and national tolerance and co-existence.

The historical and cultural importance of the Franciscans for their flock and for Bosnia itself has thus been enormous, influencing the country's entire development. Without them Bosnian history would lack one of its primary colours, the cultural process as a crucial yeast.

35. The Franciscan monastery at Fojnica, with the church designed by Josip
Vancaš (1889).

But for the sake of truth we must mention another view, according
to which the sway that the Franciscans exercised over all aspects of
the lives of their flock through so many centuries may have fostered
among the Catholic Croats of Bosnia a specific mind-set of depend-
ency and inconfidence.

The Franciscan monasteries, especially Sutjeska, Fojnica and
Kreševo, were not just centres of cultural activity; they were also
aware of the value of collecting and preserving works of art and other
cultural, historical and ethnographic materials. To this day they remain treasure houses of paintings, especially Italian; numerous
incunabulae (i.e. books from the earliest days of printing); precious
documents; ethnographic collections; articles of fine craftsmanship.
They are also the depositories of valuable paintings by local artists
schooled in the style of the Italian Renaissance. Some of the treasures
of the Bosnian monasteries were removed to Zagreb in the nineteenth century, under the direction of Bishop Strossmayer, and are
today in the Gallery of Old Masters of the Croatian Academy of
Sciences and Arts.

36. Woman with tattoos.

37. The Sephardic graveyard in the Kovačići district, Sarajevo, in use from the 16th
to the 20th centuries.

As with the Muslims and Serbs, the religious life of the Croats
contained a strong archaic folk substratum that survived despite all
the efforts of the Franciscans to root it out. In any case they were
themselves from the same stock and could not free themselves entirely from collective archetypes in their own thinking and behaviour.
These were present in many ethnographic practices and not just in
folk literature. One of the oldest and from the ethnological point of
view most interesting was tattooing on the hands, forehead or chest,
especially among women, which was very likely a relic of pre-Slav
times that in the Turkish period had come to include Christian symbols (crosses), and which can still be found today in sheltered locations.

Gravestones underwent an interesting transformation. As a kind
of counterpart to the *nišan*i, rounded vertical slabs appeared also

among the Croats, at one and the same time anthropomorphic and cross-shaped; certain features of their form and decoration show them to be a metamorphosis of one form of stećak.

The Sephardic Jewish cultural context

The Sephardic Jews came to Bosnia in 1492 as part of the great exodus of Spanish Jews, driven out by Ferdinand II and Isabella and allowed to settle by the Turks. They moved into Sarajevo, Travnik, Mostar and Banja Luka, and from then on, though their numbers were small, they made an interesting component in the ethnic mix of the Bosnian-Herzegovinian mosaic.

Retaining and developing their Hebrew-Spanish traditions while organized like the other millets into their own religious and political community within the Turkish confessional framework, over the centuries they developed a kind of dual life. On one hand they were a closed and compact group, but on the other they took an active part in everyday life in the business world as merchants and craftsmen, and were especially highly esteemed as doctors.

Living so long in the diaspora and being relatively few in number, it is amazing to what an extent the Bosnian Jews preserved their cultural and ethnic identity. They managed to do so from the eighteenth century onwards, always retaining contact with their fellow believers in other parts of the Balkans, in Palestine and elsewhere in Europe. One effect of this great concern for their traditions was that the Jews, in a time when this was not common, were almost one hundred per cent literate.

The foci of social life were the synagogue and the community centre; the latter organized the confessional schools where Hebrew was taught and the *Tora* and *Talmud* studied. In 1786 David Pardo came to be Rabbi in Sarajevo and founded a rabbinic high school.

In the academic and religious spheres the language of the Jews was classical Hebrew, the language of the Holy Books; but in everyday life a special Jewish-Spanish language called Ladino was in use.

The most famous authors of rabbinic literature were David Pardo (*Šošanim-le-David*, Split 1752), Jichak Pardo (*Toafotreem*, Thessalonica 1811), Moša Danon, Eliezer Sentov Papo and Eliezer Jichak Papo. The folk poems of the Shephardic Jews were among their most authentic cultural achievements: romances of polished form and calm, melancholy tonality. And in the Sephardic graveyards, such as the largest of them in Sarajevo, there are epitaphs of suggestive, meditative power.

One cultural treasure known the world over is the Sarajevo *haggada*, a precious illuminated codex that originated in Spain in the thirteenth or fourteenth century, was brought to Bosnia, and has been preserved through the centuries and through all historical upheavals to this day.

At the end of the nineteenth century a process of emancipation began among the Jewish community, leading them away from the confines of tradition and allowing them to play an important part in modern European life and thought. Hence the many Jewish scholars, intellectuals, writers, artists and politicians, and talented experts in the vital fields of economics, science and medicine.

EIGHT

The Austro-Hungarian Framework

General overview

The long period of Ottoman rule over Bosnia-Herzegovina ended with a mass uprising in 1875–8. At first this was a movement of peasants and serfs, whose demands were for agrarian and social reform. But the leadership was heterogeneous and within it the influence of the Serb urban middle class soon became predominant. The latter's interests coincided with those of the peasants only in so far as freeing and strengthening the peasantry would provide a stronger market and better opportunities for economic development. It began to steer the movement above all towards union with Serbia, turning it primarily into a national movement and obscuring its social component and Bosnian character.

The rising began in Herzegovina and quickly spread to Bosanska Krajina and the rest of Bosnia. It inflamed the whole South Slav population and was a signal for revolt in other parts of the Balkans ruled by Turkey. Because of their active support for the rising and their partnership in plans to divide Bosnia-Herzegovina, Serbia and Montenegro were soon at war with Turkey. Russia also went to war against the Ottoman Empire, and its successes in battle led to the Treaty of San Stefano (1878) which gave Russia a free hand to divide up the Balkans in its own interests. Since these did not coincide with those of the other great powers, however, the Treaty of San Stefano was revised that same year by the Congress of Berlin. There was a fresh division of the Balkans, by which Austro-Hungary satisfied its long-standing desire for Bosnia-Herzegovina, which it occupied in the name of a civilizing mission.

Austro-Hungary had special, indeed vital, interests in strengthening its position in Bosnia: Bosnia offered great economic and market possibilities, would be an effective counterweight to Russian influence in the Balkans, would make it much easier to monitor Serbia, and finally fitted in with important plans for expansion eastwards. In addition, a direct presence of Austria in Bosnia would put an end to the Austrian political nightmare: the formation of a sizeable South Slav state that might eventually jeopardize Austria's own political *raison d'être*. These considerations and interests guided Austro-Hungarian policy both in major matters and in detail. In the anachronistically feudal and generally backward Bosnia, the new administration had no difficulty in achieving significant progress and modernization quite quickly in many spheres of life – something which in no way conflicted with Austrian aims.

Bosnia was part of the Austro-Hungarian Empire for forty years. At first it was an occupied province under the formal suzerainty of the Turkish sultan, but in 1908 it was annexed and became a regular part of the monarchy. During this period Bosnia-Herzegovina made its entrance into modern history and underwent radical internal transformation. All the burdens and contradictions of its heritage came to the fore as never before, but the results of modernization and of becoming part of Europe ushered in a new era.

The most obvious change was in everyday life, especially in the towns. Central European ways of eating, dressing, living and behaving were adopted. These new ways were brought in by the many civil servants, mostly from the Slav countries of the Austro-Hungarian Empire. Besides civil servants and various kinds of specialists, the occupying powers resettled in certain areas of Bosnia-Herzegovina a significant number of peasants from their other European lands, while at the same time the emigration of Muslims took on mass proportions.

Socially and economically Bosnia under Austro-Hungary was a

bizarre conglomerate, unique in Europe at that time. The new administration left the backward, feudal agrarian relations between begs and serfs essentially as they found them, even though a solution of the agrarian problem was in fact the most obvious and crying need. But these relations had to coexist with the beginnings of modern industry, especially in timber, mining and metallurgy, accompanied by the building of roads and railways. The inevitable consequence was social diversification, with the appearance of a new class of industrial workers.

The situation of the peasants was the most acute social problem, as statistics show. In 1910 the rural population in Bosnian numbered 1,606,862, the urban population only 264,754. It was proclaimed legally possible for serfs to buy their freedom, but its price and the cost of land were so high and the interest on bank loans so crippling that this measure only made the peasants' position worse. One Viennese expert estimated that to end serfdom in Bosnia by this system would take until 2025.

When the Austrian army of occupation entered Bosnia, the process of threefold national identification – Croat, Muslim, Serb – had already begun. Though each national group experienced this new historical drama in its own way, all – situated as they were at a low level of national and political maturity – suffered the immensely negative fate of finding themselves once more occupied by a new power, once more unfree. Austro-Hungarian politicians judged from the start that the main hope for achieving stability was not to allow feelings of national separatism to take hold. This preoccupation was the basis for the political measures taken by the new authorities at every stage of their 'solution' to the nationalities problem in Bosnia.

The best and most consistent policy for creating a feeling of Bosnian nationhood was that formulated by Benjámin Kállay, who headed the administration in Bosnia for twenty years, from 1882 to 1902. He was a man of clear political vision, with an excellent understanding of South Slav history. He knew that there had been a traditional and spontaneous feeling for Bosnian identity, and that there had even been attempts to formulate it in national terms, so he calculated that his solution would be psychologically acceptable. From the Austrian point of view it was perfect. He left as specific and distinct only religion and church organization, but to a sufficient extent for these to act as factors of differentiation isolating and dividing the three groups and cutting Bosnia off from processes of political integration in the wider South Slav region. At first Kállay's policy was successful and met with co-operation. But this ambitious political planner had overlooked one factor of sufficient weight to prevent his policy from having any lasting effect. This was the fact that the tendencies towards separate national identification that had begun to take root before Bosnia-Herzegovina became part of Austro-Hungary could be neither halted nor reversed.

Cultural life

Among the Bosnian Serbs nationalism had been constantly on the increase ever since the Serbian uprising at the beginning of the century. It had been strengthened, moreover, by systematic Serbian government propaganda through its agents, especially after mid century when Ilija Garašanin's *Načertanije* set out a long-term national political strategy. It was supported after their own fashion by Russian agents, who attempted in every way to increase the Orthodox role in the structure of Bosnia-Herzegovina, this being an important criterion for international recognition of the right to establish a protectorate. The Bosnian-Herzegovinian rising of 1875–8 further strengthened a pan-Serb consciousness and desire for national integration. Under Austrian administration this came to a head in a Serb movement for freedom of religious education (1893–1903). The demand was based on the Ottoman millet system, under which the church authorities had represented their people politically. Serb church and school districts sought in the new circumstances to retain their powers and develop them towards a more complete political autonomy. The leading personalities in this movement were Gligorije Jeftanović, Vojislav Šola, Kosta Kujundžić and Vladimir Radović.

The movement had been built up over a long period, was well organized, and had very important national and political implications. It ended with its aims only half achieved, because of skilful Austro-Hungarian diplomacy, the action of the Patriarch in Istanbul, and the opportunism of the Serb *čaršija*.

The growth of national feeling among Bosnian Croats had also begun before the Austro-Hungarian period, but it developed in a more roundabout and sporadic fashion. This was because the new nationalist ideology conflicted with the tradition and heritage of the Franciscans, and the Catholics generally, as the ancient and autochthonous people of Bosnia, and because of the lasting influence of Illyrianism. The case of Brother Grgo Matić is typical. He went through all the phases in the course of his long life: from a traditional Franciscan identification with Bosnia, through Illyrianism to a Croatian identity. However, during the bitter and uncompromising conflict at the beginning of the century between the clerical Croatian Catholic Association of Josip Stadler, Bishop of Vrhbosna, and the liberal Croatian National Union, it became quite clear that Croatian national identity had become an accomplished fact, whatever it might cost.

When at the Congress of Berlin Turkey had to give Bosnia to Austro-Hungary across the green baize table, it was the turning of a new, and as it turned out dramatic, page of history for the Bosnian Muslims. For centuries they had had a sense of belonging almost equally to Bosnia, the Ottoman Empire and Islam; in other words, to a concrete regional and linguistic identity, to the political statehood of a huge cosmopolitan empire, and to a universal religious and civilizational system. Suddenly all three elements were called into question. Yesterday's picture of a stable and harmonious world was shattered. When the first shock had subsided they had to consider what their position was in this new world, in relation both to the new power structure and to the already formed national identities of the local Serbs and Croats, with their parallel assimilationist designs upon the Muslims. The main option for the latter was already articulated at the time by Mehmedbeg Kapetanović Ljubušak, who wrote in 1891,'We shall never deny that we belong to the South Slav family, but we shall remain Bosniaks like our forebears and nothing else.' How and why a whole century had to pass before the Bosnian Muslims were able to call themselves by that name (in 1993-4, in the middle of yet another war) is a story for a new book.

During the period of Austro-Hungarian rule fundamental changes took place in the cultural life of Bosnia-Herzegovina. Far more direct exposure to the intellectual life of western Europe; study in Vienna, Budapest, and other university towns of the Monarchy; a lively, many-sided circulation of cultural currents: all these factors combined – in conditions where a new middle class was being consolidated and culture was being secularized – to create dynamic cultural milieus and a local secular intelligentsia in Sarajevo, Mostar and Banja Luka, such as had never before been experienced in Bosnia. The activities of these circles were both cultural and political, with all the implications of the chaotic political life of a multi-traditional and multi-national occupied country, only yesterday a backward Turkish province and now an Austro-Hungarian colony. But it was a long time before any of this manifested itself in the spiritual life of the great majority of the people, who long remained firmly enmeshed in the paradigms and perceptions of folklore, myth and religion.

The new world of Europe and its modern sensibility began to penetrate chiefly through literature. An interesting addition to the cultural mosaic were the various art and cultural societies that began to be formed on religious and national lines, with the approval of the Austro-Hungarian authorities. In conjunction with these came the birth and relatively swift growth of theatrical and musical life of a kind previously unknown in Bosnia.

The first generation of all three nations to be educated abroad produced a considerable number of writers and intellectuals, and many periodicals and magazines now started up, of which the most influential on cultural and national political life were literary journals like *Behar*, *Nada* and *Bosanska vila* in Sarajevo or *Zora* in Mostar. In this context, conditions were favourable for the emergence of new Bosnian writers with a modern European outlook, such as Edhem

Mulabdić, Musa Ćazim Ćatić, Safet Beg Bašagić, Aleksa Šantić, Petar Kočić, Svetozar Ćorović. It was now that Ivo Andrić made his appearance, with formally innovatory early verse.

With Musa Ćazim Ćatić (1878–1915) – gifted poet of modern sensibility, translator, bohemian and victim of circumstance – Bosnian Muslim literature entered the sphere of European poetic concerns and techniques.

At the turn of the nineteenth century the Croatian poet Silvije Strahimir Kranjčević made a lengthy sojourn in Sarajevo. The visit was to be of great importance for the new upsurge of poetry in Bosnia-Herzegovina, particularly his activity as editor of the literary periodical *Nada* [Hope], for which he managed to get contributions from the leading South Slav writers of the day, and where with great discrimination he published key texts from contemporary European sources, thus enormously widening the literary and cultural horizons of the milieu. It is a little-known fact that the first work of Luigi Pirandello to be translated into a foreign language came out in Kranjčević's *Nada*.

Modern painting also began at this time in Bosnia-Herzegovina. Many artists came to the country and travelled round it in search of exotic genre subjects; some of them gave painting lessons. It was not long before a first generation of Bosnian artists appeared, after studying in the great academic centres of the Monarchy: Gabrijel Jurkić, Risto Vukanović, Petar Tiješić, Karlo Mijić, Roman Petrović, Đoko Mazalić, Todor Švrakić, Jovan Bijelić, Jelena Ber, Lujza Kuzmić, Špiro Bocarić, Vilko Šeferov, Lazar Drljača, Petar Šain. In 1917 a large and representative exhibition of artists from Bosnia-Herzegovina was mounted in Sarajevo, at which all the relevant movements in the visual arts of the period were on view.

The building work carried out during the Austro-Hungarian period greatly altered the oriental physiognomy of Bosnian towns. The introduction of European architecture produced an interesting and unexpected mix of the contrasting styles of two worlds. Most of the new construction was in public buildings. Schools, railway stations, administrative offices were built in the so-called 'Moorish style' that

38. The Vijećnica (Town Hall), Sarajevo. Designed in the pseudo-Moorish style by
Aleksander Wittek and Ćiril Iveković (1894–6). Later the National Library of
Bosnia-Herzegovina.

the government promoted as a superficial and misconceived expression of the continuity of oriental architecture in Bosnia. The archetypal building in this style was Sarajevo's Vijećnica [town hall – later the national library]. Contemporary European styles also featured in the architecture of this period: neo-romanesque, neo-gothic, neo-renaissance, and somewhat later that of the Viennese Secession.

Some gifted architects worked in Bosnia at this time. There was Ćiril Iveković, who built Sarajevo's Vijećnica, a number of commercial buildings and the Travnik municipal museum; Karl Panek, who built the Franciscan church and monastery of St Anthony in Bistrica and the offices of the central railways administration (today the Ministry of Foreign Affairs); Dionis Sunko, who left some valuable additions to Sarajevo (the *Napredak* building), as did Josip Pospišil, Franjo Blažek and Jan Koter. But the architects who expressed the

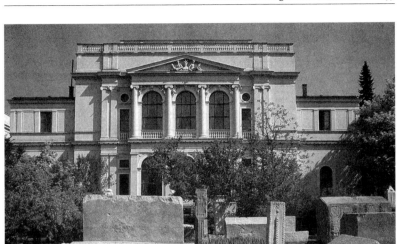

39. The Zemaljski Muzej (The National Museum of Bosnia-Hercegovina), in the pseudo-Renaissance style, Karel Pařik (1912).

spirit of the time most eloquently and left their stamp most unmistakably on Sarajevo were Karel Pařik and Josip Vancaš. The former was responsible for the new university building (today the Law Faculty), the National Museum and the Municipal Museum; the latter for the Cathedral, the National Government building (today the Presidency of Bosnia-Herzegovina), the main post office and Hotel Central.

The most valuable cultural legacy of Austro-Hungarian rule was certainly the National Museum in Sarajevo, and the scholarly work carried out within that institution through its research programmes and publications, which helped to form a new scientific and scholarly cadre for the entire country. It was especially well known for its work in archaeology, ethnography, and the natural sciences, establishing itself from the first decades of its existence as an institution of European status. The museum and its staff made a particularly important contribution to the understanding and presentation of Bosnia-Herzegovina's cultural history, especially with respect to prehistoric times, the Classical period and the Middle Ages. The research carried out in these domains within the framework of the Museum's programmes became the basis for scholarship and syntheses of significance for the whole South Slav and Balkan area.

* * *

When on 28 July 1914 Austro-Hungary declared war on Serbia, sparking a conflagration that was to reach world proportions and from which the world was to emerge with a considerably changed physiognomy, this was the climax of a process that had long been affecting the mutual relations of the great powers. Its main purpose was a new world division of colonies and spheres of interest, and in it the ambitions of the German and Austro-Hungarian military and political complex were very much to the fore.

Because of where this international catastrophe – the worst hitherto experienced – began, it remained historiographically and in popular perceptions linked to Bosnia: to Princip's assassination in Sarajevo of Archduke Franz Ferdinand and his pregnant wife Sophia. Accusing Serbia of being behind the assassination, Austro-Hungary exploited the event to put itself in an 'advantageous moral position' (the expression of an Austrian diplomat in Belgrade) to attack Serbia and move eastward.

In foreign uniforms, under foreign command, far from their homes and fields, on meagre military rations, with cheap army rum to inflame their courage, the people of Bosnia – Serbs, Croats, Bosniaks and Jews – began during the world war to discover Europe. They did not experience its academies, its galleries, its theatres, its temples or the glory of its thousands of years of culture, wisdom and science, but its bloody excesses, its barracks, its military hospitals, brothels and diseases, the mud of its front lines and pointless death in the anonymous mass graves of the Carpathians, Galicia, the Piave, Mount Meleta and other battlefields.

Before the war had ended the bitter and brutal experience of warfare had erupted into military rebellion in the lands of

Austro-Hungary and created a dramatic and unstable situation. In the forests of Croatia and Bosnia more than 50,000 armed men – the so-called 'Green Corps' [*zeleni kadar*] – began in spontaneous rebellion to attack police stations and large estates and factories. By autumn 1918 Austro-Hungary no longer existed; it had crumbled beneath the weight of its own anachronistic political and state structure. The desperate Green Corps units, until just yesterday Austro-Hungarian deserters and anti-Habsburg rebels, were mercilessly rooted out and killed in the name of a new order. The victor powers set about demolishing the tired old cosmopolitan central European empire, each with its own interests but without much farsighted political vision. So the Versailles Treaty turned the old Austro-Hungarian lands into new countries on the basis of the old social relations.

BOSNIA-HERZEGOVINA,1878–1945

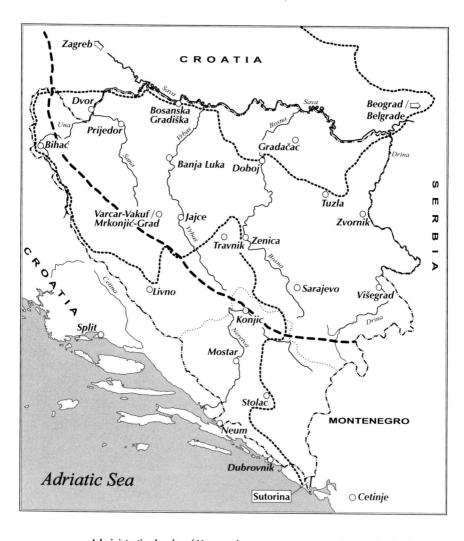

.... Administrative border of Herzegovina
(before 1918)

–––––––––––– Border between Croatian Banovina
and "Serb Lands" (1939-1941)

– – – – – 1941-3 line of demarcation between
Italian occupation zone in the south
and German in the north

–·–·–·– Present-day border
of Bosnia-Herzegovina

N.B. Sutorina: Bosnia-Herzegovina's
second outlet to the sea (along
with Neum), lost in 1945-6 when
republican borders were defined
for the post-war Yugoslav federation

NINE

In the Kingdom of Serbs, Croats and Slovenes / Yugoslavia

General overview

The South Slav lands became a unified state for the first time in 1918, at the end of the First World War, when they emerged from the ruins of the Habsburg Monarchy. The new state was a Babel of ethnicities, languages, political experiences and cultural identities. The fact that it was constituted as a state in that particular geo-political form, as a monarchy under the Serbian Karađorđević dynasty, was not so much a result of 'the centuries-old aspirations of our peoples', as the official historians of both Yugoslavias were to assert, but rather the outcome of arrangements made in the chancelleries of the victor powers, while other possible ways of redrawing the post-Habsburg political map of the Balkans were completely ignored.

The official name of the new state until 1929 was the Kingdom of Serbs, Croats and Slovenes. Bosnia-Herzegovina entered it with a decimated population, poisoned confessional and ethnic relations, and the difficult social, political and economic heritage of forty years of Austro-Hungarian. The weightiest ballast that it carried was the agrarian question, which Austro-Hungary had never even seriously tackled, even though this had precisely been its main argument at Berlin in 1878 for ever being granted the right to occupy Bosnia. In the next two decades, which is how long the first Yugoslavia lasted, the situation only got worse.

The newly formed state, based on merciless exploitation of the land and the people, with huge inputs of foreign capital, at a time of world economic crisis, was incapable of – and uninterested in – tackling its basic national and agrarian problems. The country was subservient in international relations and its internal political life was chaotic, prey to continuous inter-party conflicts, parliamentary crises, court intrigues and vendettas, and to assassinations and violence as weapons of political struggle. It fell deeper and deeper into corruption, national antagonism, political and economic criminality, general poverty and backwardness.

The poor, inequitable, extensive economy of the Kingdom was a particular tragedy for Bosnia-Herzegovina. A single statistic may be enough to indicate its position: by 1938, only 7% of all industrial companies in the country were located in it. The picture was the same in all other areas of life. There was a very shallow layer of nouveaux riches, mainly merchants, money lenders, a tiny number of industrialists and a few begs who had managed to survive the cataclysm. Meanwhile the majority – the petty bourgeoisie, workers, peasants – were pauperized to an extent that in many cases endangered their lives. The structure of land ownership now changed radically. The big landowners had previously been mainly Muslims, but land was now taken from them by the state and redistributed 'for services rendered' to the so-called *solunaši* [veterans of the Salonika front], who were naturally of Serbian nationality. There was a mass exodus of Muslims to Turkey, as there had been after the Austro-Hungarian occupation. Social advance was minimal, the old patriarchal and traditional social structure was consolidated. The population was overwhelmingly rural; immediately before the outbreak of the Second World War, the ratio of rural to urban population was 70:30, with the preservation of almost mediaeval ways of life. The petty bourgoisie continued to live off the old-fashioned combination of small cottage plots and numerous traditional craft shops somehow surviving. The gulf, and to an extent latent antagonism, between town and country was manifest – an antagonism that was basically social, but with a complicating ethno-religious component.

No new roads or railways were built. Illiteracy reached 70%. There were primary schools (state and confessional), and a small number of secondary schools in the main towns, but practically no possibility of further education: the only college – the agricultural college, later to develop into Bosnia's first faculty – was founded in Sarajevo only just before the Second World War. Two excellent Catholic high schools – the Franciscan one at Visoko, founded in 1900, and the Jesuit one at Travnik – should be mentioned as something of an exception; they were accredited by the state and open to non-Catholic pupils. Any kind of developed or dynamic social or cultural life was confined to the small number of larger towns – Sarajevo, Banja Luka, Tuzla and Mostar. Anyone who wanted or was suited to higher education had to go elsewhere, mainly Belgrade and Zagreb – or abroad. Such a Bosnia-Herzegovina could only in exceptional cases be influenced by the powerful social and ideological movements that were shaking the cultural and political life of the Kingdom.

Before the creation of the Kingdom of Serbs, Croats and Slovenes, Bosnia-Herzegovina had been part of two great empires, the Ottoman for four centuries and the Habsburg for four decades, but it had never completely lost its political and cultural identity. This was now seriously endangered by the rigid centralist conception of King Aleksandar, according to which the whole country should be divided into regions, thus erasing or down-grading the traditional historical, national and political particularities and rights of the lands that had come together. Aleksandar's ideology of Yugoslav unitarism was conceived as a means to further this. But whether considered from a political and administrative or from an ideological standpoint, his policy in fact simply mimicked the 'Greater Serbia' project for subjecting the entire territory of the new state.

It is important to understand how Bosnia-Herzegovina became part of the newly created Kingdom of Serbs, Croats and Slovenes. Just before the end of the First World War and the disintegration of the Austro-Hungarian Empire, at the end of October 1918, a 'State of Slovenes, Croats and Serbs' was formed in Zagreb out of what had been historic provinces of the Austro-Hungarian Empire. Bosnia-

Herzegovina, with its multinational government, joined this as an equal entity. Thus when the new country was proclaimed on 1 December of the same year an integral Bosnia-Herzegovina participated in the event, as a constituent part of the state of Slovenes, Croats and Serbs that united with Serbia and Montenegro to form the Kingdom of Serbs, Croats and Slovenes.

At first, because of the need to reach a compromise with Mehmed Spaho's powerful Yugoslav Muslim Organization, the new regime was inclined to make concessions. Bosnia was indeed divided into six districts – Sarajevo, Travnik, Bihać, Banja Luka, Tuzla and Mostar – that were subjected to the overall centralizing model; but its historic frontiers were preserved. This was regulated by the so-called 'Turkish Paragraph' (Article 135) of the Vidovdan Constitution.

Following a series of parliamentary crises, the assassination on 20 June 1928 in the Belgrade parliament of the Croatian political leader Stjepan Radić, and the inability of the party leaders to offer any way out of the political crisis, King Aleksandar took the pretext to dissolve parliament, abolish the constitution and declare what has come to be known as the 6 January Dictatorship. The name of the state was changed to the Kingdom of Yugoslavia and the doctrine of Yugoslav unitarism was consistently applied, to the extent of proclaiming the existence of a single Yugoslav nation. There was a new territorial and administrative division of the country into banovinas, districts and municipalities, completely obliterating the historic territories. There were nine banovinas, of which six were so constructed as to have a Serb ethnic majority. Bosnia-Herzegovina was divided between four banovinas – the Vrbaska, Drinska, Primorska and Zetska – which spilled over into neighbouring Croatian, Serbian and Montenegrin administrative and ethnic territory. Under the new disposition the integrity even of Serbian territory was impaired, that of Croatian territory even more, and that of the Muslim territories most drastically of all, so that the Muslims found themselves everywhere divided and in a minority.

In 1934 King Aleksandar was assassinated in Marseilles, which brought a new political climate to Yugoslavia. Centralism was weakened, and Croatian opposition politicians, the heirs of Radić, most explicitly and effectively articulated the idea of a federal system. But they took account of no relationships other than those between Zagreb and Belgrade, i.e. between Croats and Serbs. Vladko Maček, leader of the Croatian Peasant Party, was particularly successful in out-manoeuvring the Serbian politicians. In 1939 a regulation was passed concerning the banovina of Croatia, according to which it should consist of the Savska and Primorjska banovinas and the districts of Dubrovnik, Šid, Ilok, Brčko, Gradačac, Derventa, Travnik, Bugojno, Duvno, Konjic, Livno, Ljubuški, Mostar, Prozor, Stolac, and Fojnica. By this Croat-Serb agreement the Croatian banovina – though without Istria, Cres, Lošinj, Zadar, Lastovo, Boka Kotorska or Baranja – was rounded out and extended into a grotesque ring shape, while Belgrade was left with the effective right to administer as Serb all the rest of Yugoslavia (except, of course, Slovenia).

Discussions took place between the Zagreb and Belgrade politicians about national representation and the territorial political units. The people of Bosnia-Herzegovina, even the Serbs and Croats, had no opportunity to express themselves. The Muslims were totally ignored. Mehmed Spaho died while the discussions were going on, but even he would probably not have been able to change anything. Comment was confined to the despairing wails of individuals aware of what it meant and where it would lead. One such was the distinguished Franciscan Brother Josip Markušić, who wrote to his friends the politicians Mehmed Spaho and Tugomir Alaupović: 'Do not let Bosnia be divided or truncated by a single foot of land or a single herdsman – not for any expectations, possibilities, markets, promises. To do so would be a betrayal of history, of our soul.'

The law establishing the Banovina of Croatia marked the beginning of an administrative reorganization of the whole state. It did not get very far, because in April 1941 Yugoslavia ceased to exist.

Cultural life

Not even the most basic conditions existed for any vigorous development of cultural life in Bosnia-Herzegovina during this period.

Indeed certain not insignificant advances made under Austro-Hungary, which had promised to bring the country closer to Central European cultural and scholarly standards, now stagnated and withered. One example is the National Museum in Sarajevo, which had reached a European level both as a museum and as a centre of serious research, but which soon deteriorated into a neglected provincial institution with no programme, no money and no prospects.

The cultural climate was formed in a number of different domains, of which two were most important. The first was that of pedagogy and entertainment, traditionalist in content, fostered daily by cultural or educational associations and their reading rooms. The second was a more individual, artistic and intellectual domain, which although not at the level of other such milieux did register some vigorous creative qualities and some interesting developments.

Educational and cultural societies had begun in Austro-Hungarian times and now continued and even expanded into national institutions. The most outstanding were the Croat *Napredak,* the Muslim-Bosniak *Gajret* and later *Narodna uzdanica,* the Serb *Prosveta* and the Jewish *La Benevolencia.* The scope of their activities was very broad, including as it did the organization of everyday cultural life and entertainments; the provision of popular reading rooms; supplementary classes in literacy and general education; the building of student hostels; provision of scholarships for high-school pupils and students; the publication of calendars and almanacs that provided an outlet also for literary or scientific texts. From time to time they also published books. And so on. Although these societies had a national character, it is important to stress that forms of communication and cooperation did exist among them; although these were sometimes merely conventional, they were never broken off, nor were the associations walled round with rigid ethnic or religious barriers.

All this mainly applies only to the urban milieux – large, small and sometimes tiny – that were numerous in traditional Bosnia-Herzegovina, with a long and multi-layered cultural past of which their inhabitants were highly conscious: e.g. Stolac, Tešanj, Jajce,

Travnik, Fojnica or Bihać. The villages, as we have said, retained extremely archaic forms of life and folk culture, sometimes quite alien and unknown to people from the towns.

Writing and painting were the two most important fields in which individual intellectual and artistic life developed. The destiny of so backward an environment ensured that the most important writers and artists lived and worked wholly or in part outside Bosnia-Herzegovina; but thematically they never broke their links with it.

In painting – apart from those who had emerged in the previous period, like Gabrijel Jurkić, Roman Petrović, Petar Tiješić, Jovan Bijelić, Petar Šain, Todor Švrakić, Vilko Šeferov or Karlo Mijić, and were only now beginning to fulfil their vocation – Ivo Šeremet, Nedjeljko Gvozdenović, Milivoj Uzelac, Hakija Kulenović, Karlo Afan de Rivera, Omer Mujadžić, Kosta Hakman, Sigo Summerecker, Rizah Štetić, Kamilo Ružička, Mica Todorović and of younger artists Ismet Mujezinović, Vojo Dimitrijević, Danijel Ozmo, Branko Šotra and others now made their appearance.

All of these artists gained their knowledge and skills from well established European art centres (Munich, Cracow, Vienna, Paris, Budapest, etc.) and were in close touch with the most modern trends and explorations – from impressionism and symbolism at the turn of the century via Cézanne and expressionism to abstract art, surrealism, magical realism and politically committed art (especially in graphics).

In the first years of this period artistic life was very dynamic, numerous individual and group exhibitions were organized in all the larger towns of the country including Sarajevo, and art schools were started up. During his stay in Blažuj near Sarajevo, Vladimir Becić organized a painters' colony there together with Karlo Mijić and Vilko Šeferov. After 1924 this vitality flagged somewhat, only to pick up again in 1929 when the Group of Four was founded (Mijić, Petrović, Đoko Mazalić, Summerecker). In the years prior to the Second World War a group of young artists founded the *Collegium artisticum* association, at whose exhibitions in 1939 and 1940 Ozmo, Štetić, Dimitrijević, Mujezinović, Todorović and other painters and graphic artists displayed their work. The concept behind the association was an attempted synthesis of art and left-wing ideology.

In terms of their artistic freedom, their professional skill, and the seriousness with which they introduced the experience and concerns of modernity into our environment, painters and painting were perhaps the best and most important contribution of the period in Bosnia; and that probably also explains the splendid new flowering of the visual arts that occurred here from the fifties on.

Literature worked several different looms. The most common Bosnian literary form was the short story, which favoured traditional realistic narrative only slightly coloured – for the most capable and cultivated – by the techniques and discoveries of modernism. This led Jovan Kršić, the important interwar critic and editor of the renowned *Pregled* [Review], to formulate the idea of 'story-telling Bosnia'.

Ivo Andrić – after a lyrical and meditative phase coinciding with the First World War and his own internment and illness – by the period we are considering had reached his full literary power and was producing some of his most important work. Isak Samokovlija, who was to write some of our most accomplished short stories subtly observing the life of the Jewish urban poor, now entered literary life. So to did Hamza Humo, a poet and prose-writer with a powerful vocation and rich sensibility, lyrical and modernist, one of those who transcends Kršić's formula of 'story-telling Bosnia', at once contradicting and confirming it. In 1925, at the age of twenty-six, Antun Branko Šimić died in Zagreb: a wonderfully talented poet and theorist whose poems and essays were part of the modernist movement. The first efforts and mature poems alike of Nikola Šop belong to this period, a writer who lived his whole life out of the public eye, creating a great and individual lyrical opus. He is also renowned for excellent translations of the early Croatian Latinists, on which he concentrated after the Second World War. The names of a number of other writers will also be remembered: Borivoj Jevtić, Zvonimir Šubić, Abdurezak Hifzi Bjelevac, and Ahmed Muradbegović. It should also be noted that critical and theoretical works on literature, philosophical and aesthetic works on art, were already making an appearance. In different fields and with even more different theoretical stances, the following wrote texts of this kind: Jovan Kršić, Kalmi Baruh, Marcel Šnajder, Eli Finci, Safet Krupić, Akif Šeremet, Đorđe Jovanović, Arpad Lebl and others. Quite a number of women writers also now appeared: Štefa Jurkić, Ljerka Premužić, Verka Škurla-Ilijić, Laura Papo-Bohoreta – the author of a play in Ladino, the Jewish-Spanish idiom – Milica Miron and others.

Just as during the Austro-Hungarian period chance had brought the great Croatian poet Silvije Strahimir Kranjčević to Sarajevo, so now between 1930 and 1937 another important writer came to reside in Sarajevo: the erudite lyricist Tin Ujević, one of the founding figures of Croatian poetry. He published interesting literary and philosophical essays in Krišić's *Pregled*, and during those seven years his inimitable bohemian presence enriched Sarajevo literary life.

The Serbian playwright Branislav Nušić too resided in Sarajevo in the twenties as manager of the National Theatre, to whose repertoire he brought considerable freshness and variety. But this lasted for only a few seasons, after which the Sarajevo theatre stagnated.

However modestly, Bosnian literary life too in these years was caught up in a discussion of the nature of literature, the dichotomy between its social role and complete aesthetic autonomy. Such discussions did not achieve any great results, but they had a significant side-effect. The traditional – and to some extent the ideological – separation of the national literary currents was neutralized; a united (and certainly more elevated) level and context of debate, confrontation, and checking of criteria and values, was established. From this sprang also certain initiatives that are worth recording.

One of these was the establishment in 1927 of the journal *Pregled*, already mentioned; another was the foundation in 1928 of the Sarajevo Writers' Group. Apart from Jovan Kršić, names associated with this initiative include Borivoj Jevtić, Jakša Kušan, Hamza Humo, Isak Samokovlija, Marko Marković and others.

A different kind of literary collaboration saw the light in 1929 with the publication of *Knjiga drugova* [The comrades' book], an anthology edited by Novak Simić. The authors were young left-wing writers, expressionist in literary style and with a passionate concern for society. Besides Simić this group included Hasan Kikić, Hamid Dizdar, Eli Finci, and later Zija Dizdarević, Mak Dizdar, Džemo Krvavac and others.

This left-wing orientation influenced by Krleža also engendered the very important journal *Putokaz* [Signpost], launched in Zagreb by young Muslim intellectuals. It came out from 1937 to 1939, under the editorship and with the collaboration of Hasan Kikić, Safet Krupić, Skender Kulenović and others. *Putokaz* provided a forum from which for the first time it was possible to speak out publicly, and in terms of up-to-date sociological and political understanding, about the acute economic, social, cultural and national problems of Bosnia-Herzegovina and its future.

TEN

Temporary Disappearance of Bosnia: the 'Independent State of Croatia', 1941–5

At the outbreak of the Second World War the Kingdom of Yugoslavia tried for a while to remain neutral, but on 25 March 1941, under strong pressure from the Axis powers, it signed the Tripartite Pact. This triggered an army coup in Belgrade on 27 March and the Cvetković-Maček government was overthrown. German reaction was immediate. On 6 April 1941 they bombed Belgrade. The government and the Court fled abroad and the Yugoslav army was defeated in a little less than two weeks. Now came the occupation and dismemberment of the country. Some parts were given to existing Axis satellites: Albania got part of western Macedonia and part of Kosovo, Bulgaria got eastern Macedonia and parts of Serbia, Hungary got Prekomurje and Medimurje, Baranja and Bačka. Parts were annexed by Italy: southern Slovenia, a large part of the Croatian littoral, Dalmatia and Boka Kotorska. Montenegro got pro-Italian puppet status, and a species of higher control was exercised by the Germans over most of Slovenia, Banat and Serbia.

On 10 April, in Zagreb, an 'Independent State of Croatia' (known as NDH after its Croatian initials) was set up – organized by the Germans and headed by the Italian protegé Ante Pavelić, leader of the emigré Ustashe – after the Peasant Party's Vladko Maček, leader of the strongest Croatian party, had refused a German invitation to cooperate. Bosnia-Herzegovina was incorporated in this new arrangement with no specific status. The whole new political territory was divided, however, by a line of demarcation into German and Italian zones of interest. This line went right through the middle of Bosnia from north-west to south-east, from Bosanski Novi through Sanski Most, Varcar-Vakuf (Mrkonjić Grad), Donji Vakuf, south of Sarajevo, across Ustiprača to Rudo. Everything between that line and the Adriatic was in the Italian zone.

A new administration was speedily put in place on the basis of *velike župe* [provinces] with mediaeval names, *kotari* [districts] and *općine* [municipalities]. At the same time a parallel Ustaša military and political system was created. Infamous laws followed immediately, targeting racially or ethnically undesirable elements and all those seen to be in any way against the regime. Thus state terror was legalized to achieve the desired ethnic structure – a purely Croatian state without Jews, Serbs or ideological opponents of whatever nationality.

The 'Serbian question' was a nightmare for Pavelić. The NDH had about 6,300,00 inhabitants of whom 1,900,000 were Serbs. The formula devised was: drive a third into Serbia, make a third become Catholics (i.e. Croatize them) and kill a third. The new regime very quickly began to put the formula into action. The use of Cyrillic was banned, and a considerable number of Serbian Orthodox churches were destroyed. It is a bizarre fact, which must be recorded, that at one point the German military complained to Berlin of the brutality of what was being done; they did not wish to have an ethnic rebellion on their hands. One aspect of Ustaša terror that the Germans did not object to, however, was persecution of the Jews. All the synagogues in Bosnia were looted, and many burned to the ground. Of almost 14,000 Jews in Bosnia-Herzegovina 12,000 were liquidated. Thus one of the old and formative components of the Bosnian pattern was torn out, one that had shaped its urban culture and entire ambience.

The fact that Bosnia was included in NDH without even being consulted shows to what a low level it had sunk under the Karađorđević Monarchy. It was simply ignored and degraded. During the whole centralist period its position had been peripheral, and with the formation of the Banovina of Croatia and the handover of the rest of the country to Serbia, Bosnia-Herzegovina had politically ceased to exist: there was no institution left to offer even symbolic resistance to the takeover. Now fear re-emerged in the life of this ethnically varied country, the chief victim of a retrograde political move; and with fear came collective distrust and a withdrawal into isolationism. This was to have consequences of its own.

The fall of the Yugoslav monarchy and the creation of NDH was a terrible shock for the Bosnian Serbs. Till yesterday they had felt themselves to be in 'their' land with 'their' army and 'their' dynasty, holders of the dominant pieces in the game. Overnight they found themselves amid the ruins of all that they had taken for granted, part of a new setup which did not bode well for them. Many were prepared to overturn heaven and earth in their struggle against the new regime. The clash over the question of Bosnia-Herzegovina was particularly violent. The extreme Serbian nationalist ideology of the Chetniks only took to its logical conclusion the conception of Bosnia-Herzegovina as a Serbian land. It was very clearly stated in the writings of two ideologists who stood behind Draža Mihailović: Dragiša Vasić and Stevan Moljević.

Vasić was a gifted novelist from the period after the First World War, who from the thirties on devoted himself entirely to national politics. Moljević was a Banja Luka lawyer, author of the memorandum *Homogeneous Serbia* (1941), which had one basic idea – the creation of a Serbia 'which must include all places where Serbs live'. This was the basis of General Draža Mihailović's declaration that 'wherever there is a Serbian grave there is Serbian land'. Moljević wrote that the expansion of Serbia would be followed by a stage of homogenization: the 'cleansing of the country of all non-Serb elements. The course to follow would be to send those who had crossed over back where they belonged – Croats should be sent to Croatia, Muslims to Turkey or Albania.' In Bosnia-Herzegovina, Croats and particularly Muslims became the victims of this murderous policy.

It is very interesting that two such apparently opposite extremist national organizations, the Chetniks and the Ustashe, very soon found a common language in Bosnia-Herzegovina and already in April 1942 had a formal written agreement to cooperate.

The new state's propaganda offer to the Bosnian Croats was 'the achievement of their centuries-long dream'. In their political poverty people believed the offer, and so did those who were for them the highest authorities – the Catholic Church. But the mass atrocities against Serbs and Jews and innocent people of other religions (including Croats) carried out by Pavelić's vicious regime opened the eyes and troubled the consciences of many Croats. Some in the Church reacted in a similar way, and some even dared to come out openly and say so. Alozije Mišić, Bishop of Mostar, was among them, as was Andeo Kaić, head of the Bosnian Franciscan Province.

The position of the Muslims was the most complicated. The new regime flatteringly offered them the status of 'racial Croats', with the right to practise the Islamic religion. But they felt that Bosnia was disappearing from beneath their feet. The bloodily executed racial policy could elicit nothing but horror and revolt. The Muslims issued resolutions in several Bosnian towns against the persecution of both Serbs and Jews. After the death of Mehmed Spaho and the disappearance of the political climate in which the Muslim organization had been a respectable force, the Bosnian Muslims had splintered into a number of factions, all equally impotent and unarticulated. The desire for an autonomous Bosnia-Herzegovina was still their aim, and they tried to realize it in a number of different ways – from taking part more or less voluntarily in Pavelić's government and military forces to turning to the Germans to discuss the creation of an independent Bosnia-Herzegovina under the direct control of Berlin. One result was the formation of a Muslim division within the German army, the SS 'Handžar' [dagger] Division. The political results were nil. What those who joined had been expecting was the creation of local units to defend Muslim villages against attackers of any kind. But the recruits of the Handžar Division were sent to France for basic training, where they were joined by some Croatian engineers already there. What happened afterwards has never yet been fully explained. Under the leadership of Ferid Džanić a rebellion broke out in which the rebels captured their German officers, tried them and killed them. They then attempted to join the French resistance, but did not succeed. German troops attacked them and the rebellion was suppressed. Either then or later over 150 rebels were killed. All this happened in Villefranche-de-Rouergue near Toulouse.

From 1941–5 Bosnia-Herzegovina was the stage of a phantasmagorical war with politics to match. Officially a new state had been formed, with its twofold military organization – the Ustashe and the Domobrans or regular Croatian Army – its government organs, its state administration and accompanying infrastructure. At the same time and in the same area two other states were operating with their own armies: Germans and Italians, who made their own agreements about delimitation of zones. Then there were the Chetnik forces under the command of Draža Mihailović, plus all kinds of local units and militias, Serbian, Muslim and Croatian. From the end of 1941, after the unsuccessful rebellion in Serbia, another group of players entered this complicated drama – Tito's Partisans.

The first of a cycle of bloody battles began in early summer 1941, after the first Ustasha atrocities against the Serbs in Herzegovina. There was a rising in the Nevesinje region. The rebels consolidated and successfully defended their own district and then, in bloody revenge, turned on the local Muslim population and the small number of Croats whom they held responsible for the killings. This continued with large-scale massacres of Muslims by Chetniks in Foča and on the Drina.

The official historiographers of Tito's Yugoslavia turned the Partisan warfare in Bosnia into a national epic. In reality it consisted of little more than tactical manoeuvring, going round in circles, in search of temporarily safe areas. There were battles of course, those against the Chetniks being especially fierce and successful; and there were tragic Partisan defeats, such as the one on the Sutjeska. But the fact remains that Tito and the Partisans were in Bosnia the whole time, where especially from 1943 on the Partisan movement offered a real political alternative to inter-ethnic extermination, provided a credible platform for Bosnian-Herzegovinian autonomy, and played its own small part in the worldwide war against Fascism. The best proof of this is the fact that people of all nationalities and religions in Bosnia-Herzegovina joined it.

Of course, the Partisan movement was also associated with persecutions and pogroms. These happened throughout the war and there was not one ethnic or religious group that did not suffer. At the beginning came the 'uprising' of what we might call guerrillas, whom the Communists later claimed as 'theirs' even to the extent of dubbing 27 July the Day of the People's Uprising in Bosnia-Herzegovina. The rebels themselves, however, had felt themselves to be waging a Serb struggle for revenge, thus for example mercilessly wiping out the entire Catholic parish of Krnjeuša near Bosanski Petrovac. There was an action of tragic proportions in the so-called Chetnik putsches within the Partisan army in 1941–2, when large numbers of Muslims in eastern and part of central Bosnia were slaughtered in terrible ways. Worst of all was the work of Tito's army at the end of the war (indeed several days after it had formally ended), involving the fate of a very large and varied mass of people trying to escape across the Yugoslav frontier into Austria. Among them there were members of the quisling armies, mostly Ustashe and Croatian home guards, but also Slovene home guards, Serbian and Montenegrin Chetniks etc. But very many were Croat civilians, including women, old people and even children, urged to escape by Ustasha propaganda of a criminally cowardly sort that had incited a mass exodus which Pavelić used as a shield to allow him to escape himself together with his fortune. The intention of those trying to escape had been to give themselves up to the British army, but thanks to the dishonourable conduct of the British military authorities they were tragically handed back to the Partisans. Many were massacred within a few hours of being handed over, while an unknown but large number were marched back into Yugoslavia, and moved from camp to camp for months in a 'death march' all over the country. In inhuman conditions – hungry, thirsty, sick, exhausted, suffering all kinds of ill treatment – many were killed and many died. Those who managed to survive lived in fear for the rest of their lives and kept silent, afraid to talk about it even to those nearest to them.

* * *

Not all parts of Bosnia-Herzegovina suffered equally in the war. There were towns which lived for the whole four years in relative peace and did not feel the crescendo of hostilities until the end, when they were bombed by Allied aircraft after global military operations had begun to drive the Germans out of south-east Europe and back to where they started from. Until then the post worked and so did the telephone, trains ran and travel by road was possible. The fighting took place in forests and isolated places and over communications centres, seldom in the towns.

But there was neither the climate nor conditions for cultural life. Many artists and writers left Bosnia; those who stayed could do nothing but endure in this new corrosive atmosphere. A few young people with creative talent, like the writers Hasan Kikić (who already had a reputation) and Zija Dizdarević or the painter Danijel Ozmo, paid early in their lives for their left-wing sympathies: the first was killed by the Chetniks the other two by the Ustashe.

On the other hand, 'in the woods' among the Partisans a lot of emphasis was laid on education and culture. It was conducted in the spirit of Soviet ideology, the function of culture and art being to act as a means of creating the New Man. But political intentions are one thing and life is another. Yet even in those circumstances, in totally unpromising conditions both human and technical, some forms of art and creative work did nevertheless flourish and need to be remembered today. For example, at Tito's 1942 partisan HQ in the middle of nowhere, in the centuries-old forests of Mlinište on the road between Mrkonjić-Grad and Glamoč, a Peoples' Theatre was formed. Its members were some of the best actors and actresses of the Zagreb National Theatre, such as Vjekoslav Afrić and others. Žorž Skrigin, film producer and photographer, made a world-famous photographic record of war, which includes a number of fine works of art. In the deep shade of a cliff above Livno the perfect verses of *Jama* [The Pit] were written, a poem of Dantesque strength and inspiration which after the 1943 meeting in Topusko of the Anti-Fascist Council for the People's Liberation of Croatia was to become a poem of European relevance – while the bones of its author Ivan Goran Kovačić, prey to a Chetnik knife, lay on the heights between Zelengora and Sutjeska. The old poet Vladimir Nazor, apart from pathetic Partisan poems, kept a diary entitled *S Partizanima* [With the Partisans] which became an important literary document of the times.

Jure Kaštelan wrote some of the most beautiful and metaphysical verses in our language on the basis of the Bosnian Partisan experience, including *Jezero na Zelengori* [The lake at Zelengora] and *Tifusari* [The typhus sufferers]. Branko Šotra, Ismet Mujezinović, Vojo Dimitrijević, Đorđe Andrejević Kun, Đuro Tiljak, Marijan Detoni, Božidar Jakac and Stojan Ćelić produced graphic art of a high quality. Skender Kulenović wrote and published the poem *Stojanka majka Knežopoljka*, which later became a propaganda icon; it has long since been re-evaluated, but undoubtedly remains the literary document of an extraordinary linguistic eruption and virtuosity. Branko Ćopić, an expressive and successful writer of popular vocation, wrote humorous fragments of prose about the war, laying the basis for the subsequent novels and short stories in his characteristic style.

* * *

Bosnians of all religions and nationalities ended the war as victims and victors, cowards and heroes, torturers and tortured, traitors and loyalists – on all possible sides. That is this country's history; that was the kind of war it was. It is no exaggeration to say that there was not a single Bosnian family, urban or rural, that was not in some way touched by the war. Tito's army was raw, ideologically fanatical, full of the vengeful feelings of the frustrated rural poor. In terms of numbers, especially among the officers, the majority was Serb; some had even defected from the defeated Chetniks. This should not be forgotten. But an equally important fact is that the 'Tito option', both military and political, was the only one with which people could identify without any ethnic barriers.

At the beginning of May 1945, when the Axis had lost the war, the NDH disappeared from Bosnia just as it had appeared – overnight. Like the government of the Kingdom of Yugoslavia in 1941, Ante Pavelić and his supporters ran from the country, but this time in an unprecedented manner – they took hundreds of thousands of people with them to death and misery. But there is more even than that on their criminal debit account. Even worse and in the long run more fatal was the legacy of Nazism and the crimes the Nazi regime had carried out. The ominous dark shadow of these has lain across the Croat name ever since, nor has even the Muslim name been spared. In various ways many people have had to atone for what they did, even some who were born after it all happened.

When the 'uprising' began in 1941 Tito had only a few thousand people behind him. By the end of the war, when he had skilfully managed to get help from Stalin, Churchill and Roosevelt and had come out the winner, he had an army of 800,000 plus his fanatical Communist Party. He then managed to get aid from many sources, national and international, to enable Yugoslavia to rise from the ashes.

A number of political events organized by the wartime Partisan authorities in the autumn of 1943 were of prime importance for the reaffirmation and continuity of Bosnia-Herzegovina as a state. The first was the meeting of ZAVNOBiH [Antifascist Council for the National Liberation of Bosnia-Herzegovina] on 25–6 November in Mrkonjić-Grad, and three days later the meeting of AVNOJ [Antifascist Council for the National Liberation of Yugoslavia] in nearby Jajce. The final resolution of ZAVNOBiH precisely defined the character, political-administrative individuality and intergrity of Bosnia-Herzegovina in relation to the other Yugoslav republics, and the complete equality of all its nations based on the 'Equality of Serbs, Muslims and Croats of Bosnia-Herzegovina, which is their common and indivisible homeland.'

BOSNIA-HERZEGOVINA SINCE 1945

POSAVINA   Region

●   Regional centre

📖   University

—·—·—·—   Present-day border
of Bosnia-Herzegovina

ELEVEN

In Socialist Yugoslavia, 1945–92

General overview

Among the leading Yugoslav communists there was considerable disagreement about the political and territorial status of Bosnia-Herzegovina in the new federal Yugoslavia. Among them the spirit of the Serbian-Croatian Agreement was still very much alive, according to which Bosnia was supposed to be divided between Serbia and Croatia and the Muslim-Bosniak population regarded as a religious group which should declare itself Serb or Croat or remain nationally undetermined. This classification, 'nationally undeclared', was even offered to them officially as a category in the population census. It was an approach to Bosnia that has never completely died, as later events have shown.

Among the very top Party leaders, however, the first decisions taken by the new state at the ZAVNOBiH meeting in Mrkonjić-Grad and the AVNOJ meeting in Jajce were honoured, and the promise that Bosnia-Herzegovina should in all internal matters be a republic on the same level as the others held firm. The question of Muslim nationhood took some time to resolve, and there were many delays and fierce opposition, especially among the Serbian communists and, in a different way, among the Macedonians. It was achieved by comprehending and recognizing their separate ethnic, cultural and national affiliation.

Generally speaking, the history of Bosnia-Herzegovina in socialist Yugoslavia, which lasted almost half a century, can be divided into two very different periods. In the first, in spite of agreement in principle about equal status, in the context of the centralist and unitarist course stemming from Belgrade and the almost absolute domination of Serbian cadres in the political, party, administrative, and police apparatus Bosnia-Herzegovina was subjected to a form of colonialism. This included the exploitation of its industrial resources – heavy industry, mining, hydro-electricity, forests – without any attention to the development of infrastructure, technology and the standard of living.

In this first period in Bosnia-Herzegovina, as in the whole country, there was much organized enthusiasm for the ideal of 'renewal and rebuilding'. The other side of the coin was various forms of revolutionary terror. This was worst in those cases, of which there were many in Bosnia-Herzegovina, in which it was not obvious what was uppermost – revolutionary and 'proletarian' rights, or an obscure, ancient, atavistic social frustration reinforced by religious and ethnic resentment growing out of a war that was hardly over. A wave of social cleansing affected many families, especially in the towns. Various fictitious accusations were levelled against them (reactionary remnants of the old society, property-owners, kulaks, quislings etc.); anything that had its roots in pre-war institutions was a target for this social cleansing. Thus all national cultural and educational organizations dating from before the war were banned. There was also persecution of religious organizations, especially Catholic ones and in particular the Franciscan Order and the episcopate, accused of having been loyal to the NDH and collaborated with the Ustashe. But Muslim and Orthodox institutions were not spared either. The worst prisons were filled with priests and intellectuals. Then, after Tito's break with Stalin in 1948, there was a mass cleansing of all who had remained loyal to Stalin, of whom there were many especially among the Montenegrins and Serbs, though not only among them. Anyone was endangered on whom suspicion fell. There was a time when the prisons and forced labour camps of Tito's Yugoslavia were full of a most heterogeneous collection of people.

This first period of post-war Bosnian history began to come to an end in the mid sixties, with the fall of the second most important man in the state, security chief Aleksandar Ranković, and the resignation of Đuro Pucar Stari, a pre-war communist (a Serb from Bosansko Grahovo) who from 1945 on had completely controlled the Bosnian Party. The fact that the change was heralded by an important Party conference in Mostar in 1966 at which the main subject of discussion was the crisis in relations among the Yugoslav nations, and in particular the flagrant examples of marginalization and harassment of Croats especially in western Herzegovina, was significant and not devoid of symbolic importance. The conclusions of the conference, and later of all other official bodies, were that the most important political imperative was to establish the national equality of Muslims, Serbs and Croats and to strengthen the republic of Bosnia-Herzegovina. The result was a systematic 'entry' of the Party into western Herzegovina and a systematic inclusion of Herzegovinians in the Party power-structure at all levels. This was a time when a number of young politicians from all three nations headed both the republic and the Party: politicians such as Džemal Bijedić, Branko Mikulić, Hamdija Pozderac and some others, who followed the Tito line and were loyal members of the Party but who identified themselves with Bosnia-Herzegovina and sought to improve its position.

In the following years, from about 1966 to 1968, political self-confidence strengthened and a completely new Bosnia-Herzegovina began to emerge. This was the beginning of the second period of Bosnian history in post-war Yugoslavia. It was the result of a deliberate policy and brought about a kind of national renaissance, built upon the negative experience of the earlier period.

It is paradoxical, and hinders a proper understanding of the course they took, that the leaders of this renaissance were firm and ideologically conservative Communists, completely committed to Tito – even when in 1971 and 1972 he crushed the 'Croatian Spring' and the 'Serbian liberals' and, in a historical sense, pulled Yugoslavia backwards again. The period was one of general ideological and socio-political change in Yugoslavia, coinciding to a great extent with the protracted period of Brezhnev's attempts to re-Stalinize the USSR. Bosnian-Herzegovinian Communists could not support either the Croatian or the Serbian reformers and still remain true to their Bosnian course. For although those involved in the Croatian Spring were, in the widest economic and social sense, for reform and greater freedom, their heated nationalistic rhetoric and speeches in Bosnia and about Bosnia made it easy to see that they were not sworn supporters of its political autonomy and would very quickly have destabilized its national balance. This was equally true of the 'Serbian Liberals': however much their economic programme was designed to bring a breath of fresh air into the sluggish and spurious empire of the Tito-Kardelj idyll, they did not indicate that they would make any particular effort to prevent Bosnia becoming the prey of the traditional ideologues of a 'Serbian Bosnia'.

In Bosnia-Herzegovina itself there was nevertheless a true renaissance at that time. It gripped the whole republic, and it is no exaggeration to say that in a short time it completely altered the way people lived.

Many examples could be given, but the road system is one of the most outstanding, and there are many reasons to give it first place. For centuries the word 'Bosnia' had been almost synonymous with 'impenetrable country'. In Austro-Hungarian times a number of roads and narrow-gauge railway lines had been built, mainly to make the produce of the mines and forests accessible; but stagnation set in again during the Yugoslav Monarchy. At the end of the Second World War there were only 56 kilometres of asphalted roads, including urban streets. This is probably why there was such an enormous popular response in 1968 when a National Roads Loan was launched, the aim of which was to connect every town to an asphalt road. This was so successful that in a few years 3,000 km of asphalt roads had been built, and the target was almost 100% achieved. The drive to build a thousand schools and a thousand public libraries was almost equally successful.

This last was partly financed by the Ivo Andrić Donation. Ivo Andrić won the Nobel Prize for literature in 1961 – the first and so far only Bosnian writer to have done so. Somewhat later he donated half his prize money – the then huge sum of fifteen million dinars – to buy books for Bosnian libraries. Later he donated also the other half. The entire sum was made into a special republican fund for the buying of books, which lasted right down to the outbreak of war in 1992.

Primary schools were opened in most villages and secondary ones in all the larger towns, with colleges and faculties not only within the framework of the Sarajevo University but in Banja Luka, Tuzla, Mostar, Doboj, Zenica and elsewhere. Large numbers of towns had electricity, water and telephone-connections laid on, often as a result of local initiative. The economy was diversified, and in addition to the old, polluting heavy industries new factories were built for food, textiles etc. The old crafts tradition was now found to have new commercial outlets and many crafts were revitalized.

New urban development was a particularly visible and interesting phenomenon. Post-war socialist housing and functional construction destroyed the ambience of many Bosnian cities and small towns through their depressing uniformity and poor quality. Now series of new hotels, housing complexes and official and functional buildings created a new and more pleasant ambience.

A much larger proportion of young people received a school education. Travel became possible and first-hand knowledge of the wider world and its ways of life became ever more usual, almost commonplace. In its own way the renewal and construction of new places of worship by members of all religions bears witness to the change of climate. This was largely due to the many people who were forced into economic emigration 'temporary work abroad' as it was termed – and the financial strengthening of their households, traditionally ready to make donations to the church or mosque. It also demonstrates that a certain degree of tolerance had been reached between the (party) state and the religious communities.

Cultural life

Cultural life followed the pattern of political and economic life: repression up to the mid-sixties, an upsurge afterwards. But one thing that ran counter to this pattern must not be forgotten; Tito's break with Stalin. The 1948 political break between Yugoslavia and Russia offered a unique opportunity to make a fundamental break with ideological control of intellectual, literary and artistic life at the same time. The beginning of artistic freedom is usually dated to 1952, with the epoch-making speech of Miroslav Krleža, the leading Croatian literary figure, at the Alliance of Writers of Yugoslavia in Ljubljana. In one sense this is true. But some writers did not wait for Krleža's speech to free themselves from the suffocating demands of socialist realism, nor did socialist realism and Party-inspired lyrics cease after his speech. In Bosnia-Herzegovina there was not much chance at that time for anything to surface of high literary quality. But politically, culturally and historically Krleža's speech, resulting from the break with Russia, did indirectly have considerable impact in Bosnia, on account of his grandiose (if not in every sense sustainable) concept of 'our' South Slav cultural identity through the centuries. He saw this culture as standing erect, in sovereign equality and independence, between West and East. Its loftiest spiritual and aesthetic achievements, in Krleža's eyes, were Old Croatian church architecture, Serbian and Macedonian frescoes, and – supremely – mediaeval Bosnian stećci. Not only did Krleža write some brilliant essays and articles elaborating his idea, but with his enormous energy he also provided practical backing. One of the main ways he did this was by founding the Lexicographical Institute in Zagreb and beginning the great work of producing a Yugoslav Encyclopedia; another was by organizing an exhibition of mediaeval art, which opened in Paris in 1950, at which in illustration of Krleža's belief the central element and the greatest revelation were the Bosnian stećci. This coincided with advances in Bosnia itself in archaeological field-work, scholarly research and the training of a new generation of mediaevalists, mostly grouped round the National Museum in Sarajevo and building on the foundations laid by their predecessors at the beginning of the century.

It is probably here that we should look for the first changes in the cultural climate. During the next ten years there were all kinds of interesting transpositions of the ancient art of the stećak; they provided inspiration for poetry, painting, the graphic arts, sculpture, documentary films and even music. There is probably a link between this search for roots and the fact that the struggle for identity in Bosnia-Herzegovina, when it began in the sixties, was from the first most openly waged in the cultural field.

Every area had to be conquered: the right for Bosnia to have its own Academy of Sciences and Arts, its own TV programme, and a full range of university chairs; the legitimacy of a great research and publishing project on the cultural heritage of Bosnia-Herzegovina; the right to include the Muslim cultural heritage specifically in anthologies (and by the same principle others as well). Those opposed to this and other initiatives that in any way emphasized the particularity of Bosnia-Herzegovina fell into one of two categories: Serb nationalists, whether from Bosnia or Belgrade, masquerading under the guise of Party loyalism; and old Communist upholders of dogmatic unitarism, for whom the new course was 'destructive of the brotherhood and unity of Yugoslavia'. The latter included Muslims and the occasional Croat.

Conflict was relentless and waged according to the standard ideological Manichaean model. As always among the Communists it was a struggle to establish a final verdict, after which there would be no mercy for the losers. That is why this period will be remembered not only for the awakening of Bosnian identity, but also for the persecution of political opponents and the emigration from Bosnia of outstanding individuals, usually to Belgrade. The most famous of such cases, and for Bosnia the most traumatic, was the emigration to Belgrade of Meša Selimović, charismatic author of the novels *Derviš i smrt* and *Tvrdava* [Death and the Dervish, The Fortress].

All Yugoslav interpretations of that period in Bosnia lacked balance. No attention was paid to the importance of belief in an autonomous and cosmopolitan Bosnia. The emphasis was always on one-sided acceptance of some partial truth by people who had to face the political consequences of opposition, and who were not treated kindly. It was part of the ideological technique of the Party that if members of one ethnic group were accused of nationalism, then similar cases should be found in the other groups so as to 'keep the balance'.

At all levels of the conflict a constant theme was the question of language. During the first period the Serbian language was almost completely dominant at all levels. The historian of language Alija Isaković has convincingly shown how the language of journalism and public communication was from 1947–8 on systematically Serbianized. This policy was enshrined in the 1954 Novi Sad Language Agreement. This agreement was drawn up under great pressure from Belgrade; no one from Sarajevo or anywhere else in Bosnia-Herzegovina was present at the meeting. But in 1970 an important meeting in Sarajevo on 'The Croato-Serbian/Serbo-Croatian Language' marked the inauguration in Party circles of a new policy towards a Bosnian-Herzegovinian literary language. Experts in sociolinguistics were consulted in order to establish a scholarly basis for a Bosnian-Herzegovinian linguistic standard, which would have the same status as the Eastern and Western 'variants', as Croatian and Serbian were euphemistically called.

A similar conflict arose over the definition of our literature. Was it something which could be studied only as part of a Croatian or Serbian corpus (in which case the position of Muslim writers was unclear, since they were not to be allowed a national literature, it being always assumed that they had opted to be Croats or Serbs)? Or was there a body of Bosnian-Herzegovinian literature whose dual character in no way diminished its value? In 1970 the publishing house Svjetlost organized a symposium in Sarajevo to consider the question. Professor Midhat Begić, the essayist and theoretician, gave a lucid lecture on the idea of Bosnian literature as a single unified corpus characterized by dynamic complexity. Unfortunately his rich suggestions were never systematically explored.

In spite of various set-backs and all the difficulties of a slow emergence from colonial and provincial backwardness, from the sixties onwards the cultural life of Bosnia-Herzegovina began to flourish, especially at the institutional and organizational level, and to become comparable with that of other countries. It was manifested in radio, television (from the late sixties), the press, films, art exhibitions, theatre, and a rich range of publications including translations. From the seventies various forms of popular culture became part of the lives of a great number of people. Various institutions, public meetings and projects, all well above average, helped to raise the general standard. This can be seen in galleries such as the Art Gallery of Bosnia-Herzegovina, the Portrait Gallery in Tuzla, the Autumn Salon in Banja Luka, the *Collegium Artisticum* and other galleries in Sarajevo, where, especially from the mid-seventies, the most recent trends in the international art world could be seen. There were other forms of cultural life in Sarajevo, such as the small-stage MESS which was for years one of the chief theatrical festivals in Yugoslavia. *Izraz* [Expression], a literary periodical, began to appear with articles on art, literary criticism and theory, reaching an especially high level in the sixties under the editorship of Midhat Begić and Kasim Prohić. On film there was the periodical *Sineast.*

Literature and painting had already established themselves; now they were joined by film and TV, architecture and stagecraft, and in later years by lively and varied output in all aspects of mass and popular culture: graphic design, video production, pop music etc.

The example of Ivo Andrić had since the twenties been a kind of benchmark for Bosnian prose and literature in general, even though Andrić belonged to another literary milieu, that of Belgrade. This became the case even more strongly after 1945, when he published one after the other the novels *Na Drini ćuprija* [The Bridge on the Drina], *Travnička hronika* [Bosnian Chronicle], *Gospodica* [The Woman from Sarajevo], which soon became best-sellers. Up until 1953 Andrić periodically stayed in or visited Sarajevo as a member of the Peoples' Assembly of Bosnia-Herzegovina. In 1954 with the historical novel *Prokleta avlija* [The Damned Yard] Andrić reaffirmed his status as a great modern Balkan writer, whose work was organically linked to the Bosnian land of his birth. When in 1961 he was awarded the Nobel Prize for literature, his Bosnian subjects, language and characters became a focus of worldwide literary interest, translation and study.

Andrić was important for post-war Bosnian literary practice in yet another way. During the years when efforts were made to enforce the stereotyped ideas, subjects and characters of socialist realism on all writers, the perfectionist aestheticism of Andrić, the poetic individuality of his writing and his 'historical pessimism', in their own quiet and unrevolutionary way provided a living demonstration to Bosnian writers of the possibility of a different kind of writing and of individual freedom as something a writer must hold as a basic principal.

In the short period from 1966–70 so many literary works in so many genres were written that those years stand out as perhaps the richest, and as marking the turning-point, of the entire century. In the best possible way they 'legitimized' Andrić's work, and at the same time ended his absolute supremacy. In 1966 two key books of modern Bosnian literature were published: Mak Dizdar's poetical synthesis *Kameni spavač* [The Stone Sleeper] and the novel *Derviš i Smrt* [Death and the Dervish] by Meša Selimović. In those years appeared also the novels *Ugursuz* by Nedžad Ibrišimović (1968) and *Album* by Vitomir Lukić (1968). Midhat Begić published the first (1967) followed by the second (1969) volume of his *Raskršća* [Intersections], enormously influential essays on literary theory. Derviš Sušić published his novels *Pobune* [Rebellions, 1967] and *Uhode* [Spices, 1969]; Skender Kulenović his first book of sonnets (1968), whose masterly verses were densely solipsistic; and Branko Ćopić his brilliant book of stories, *Bašta sljezove boje* [The Blue Mallow Garden, 1970]. These books represented a thorough break with the dominant tradition of realism, while at the same time reaching the high aesthetic level hitherto achieved only by Andrić. It is also characteristic that the subject of many of them was Bosnia itself and its historical destiny, with attempts to reinterpret what had until then been the predominant cliché of the 'dark vilayet', a country under a curse. Art also flourished after 1945. At first the artists from the previous period were the most important: Roman Petrović, Mica Todorović, Branko Šotra, Ismet Mujezinović, Vojo Dimitrijević, Ivo Šeremet, Hakija Kulenović, Rizah Štetić and others. Gabrijel Jurkić was at this time living in the Franciscan monastery in Livno, withdrawn from the world, and it was only later that the special, distinct value of his work would be recognized. In 1945 the State Art School was founded and played a highly important role in the training of a generation of exceptional Bosnian and Herzegovinian graphic artists.

Modern trends in art had already after 1954 begun to take over from the short lived period of socialist realism; besides Sarajevo there were art centres in Banja Luka, Tuzla and Mostar. There was soon a great diversity of genres and techniques in Bosnian painting and art in general (graphic art, sculpture etc.), and for the whole of its further development it continued to be wide open to the most contemporary influences in world art.

A large number of excellent artists, among the best in what was then Yugoslavia, developed naturally in these conditions; many of them made a name abroad for the vitality of their work. Behaudin Selmanović, Radenko Mišević, Franjo Likar, Ljubo Lah, Mario Mikulić, Mirko Ćurić are only the leading names among the first post-war generation. They were followed by Afan Ramić, Mevludin Ekmečić, Milorad Ćorović, Nada Pivac, Tomislav Dugonjić, Viktor Majdandžić, Borislav Aleksić, Alojz Ćurić, Bekir Misirlić, Ibrahim Ljubović, Mehmed Zaimović, Seid Hasanefendić, Kemal Širbegović, Mersad Berber, Ismar Mujezinović, Ljubomir Perčinlić, Milivoje Unković, Salim Obralić, Ratko Lalić, Sead Musić, Safet Zec, Edin Numankadić, Braco Dimitrijević, Nusret Pašić, Mustafa Skopljak, Muradif Ćerimagić, Perica Vidić, and so on.

Bosnian graphic artists, venturing into the realm of painting, not only achieved results of the greatest value at the individual level but gave rise to an entirely recognizable authentic Bosnian school. The first stimulus to this development was given by the reorganization of the school of applied art, which in 1949 gained a graphic-art department. A true vitality, supreme virtuosity and ceaselessly creative search characterizes the 1970s generation of graphic artists, who returned from training in Zagreb, Ljubljana or Belgrade (while others remained behind in these places or went abroad): Memnuna Vila-Bogdanić, Halil Tikveša, Dževad Hozo, Radovan Kragulj, Mersad Berber, Kemal Širbegović, Emir Dragulj, Virgilije Nevjestić, Borislav Aleksić, Enes Mundžić, Radmila Jovandić, Petar Waldegg.

In the realm of sculpture Zdenko Grgić, Arfan Hozić, Mirko Ostoja, Boško Kućanski, Ibrahim Bilajac and Alija Kučukalić created a range of valuable artistic works.

In 1949 an architectural department was opened in the technical faculty in Sarajevo, from which generations of architects emerged who with their modern approach affected both architecture and urban planning in Bosnia-Herzegovina. They built on the foundations laid by the two founders of theoretical and practical work in this field, Dušan Grabrijan and Juraj Neidhardt. Outstanding practitioners of the Sarajevo School of architecture were Zlatko Ugljen, Ivan Štraus, Živorad Janković, David Finci, Mirko Ovadia, Halid Muhasilović and Branko Bulić.

Although there were some film studios, film production never became a major activity capable of production on any scale. However, some successful films were made. In the sixties in Sarajevo the climate was favourable for exploring the possibility of extending the language of film; such exploration usually found an outlet in documentaries. A rare freshness of ideas and experimental daring were shown by the gifted director Ivica Matić, who died prematurely. In this period a whole series of characteristically Sarajevan documentary films were made by Bakir Tanović, Midhat Mutapčić, Bato Čengić, Vlatko Filipović, Mirza Idrizović and their younger contemporaries Vefik Hadžismajlović, Zlatko Lavanić and Suad Mrkonjić.

Bato Čengić stands out in this whole period because of the seriousness and completeness of his authorial personality and film poetics.

Hajrudin Šiba Krvavac made some extremely skilful and commercially successful action films set in the war. The most innovative director of the more recent period, however, was Emir Kusturica with *Sjećaš li se Doli Bel* [Do you remember Dolly Bell?] and *Otac na službenom putu* [Father is away on official business], whose scenarios were written by the poet Abdulah Sidran.

The last ten years of this period, the years following Tito's death, were very dynamic. Ideological pressure in cultural and social life continued to make themselves felt during the first five years; from the end of the seventies Bosnia was continually a target for accusations of Islamic fundamentalism emanating from political, cultural and media centres in Belgrade. The effect of this was that in 1983 the ruling politicians in Bosnia-Herzegovina, baffled as to how to deal with these increasingly hostile and explicit accusations, carried out the last great political trials. Alija Izetbegović and a number of other prominent Muslims were given long prison sentences for fictional crimes. This was a time when it was still not possible to publish Solzhenitsyn's cult dissident work *The Gulag Archipelago*. The manuscript of the translation had been ready since 1985 in the hands of the Sarajevo publishing house Veselin Masleša, but publication had been stopped by the Central Committee of the Communist Party. The manuscript was then sent to Belgrade, where it was immediately published amidst great public attention.

The middle of the decade saw the start in the USSR of Gorbachev's policies of *glasnost* and *perestrojka*. Ideological interference in cultural life swiftly lost momentum, and communication with the outside world became completely open and unlimited. The faultless organization of the Winter Olympic Games in 1984 had a great propaganda and media effect; Sarajevo was seen as a city in complete accord with the contemporary world. This was most clearly seen in cultural life: in books published, exhibitions held, performances given and films shown; in texts published in periodicals, in public lectures and discussions, in vigorous, witty pop music; in graphics, in music, in alternative publications and youth magazines. All testified in one breath to a definitive escape from a leaden time and a leaden system.

TWELVE

The 1992–5 War and its Aftermath: Is There a Future?

The late eighties brought spectacular changes in the polarized ideological and political relations of East and West. After the destruction of the Berlin wall, with all its symbolic meaning, came the unification of East and West Germany and the quiet disintegration of the Soviet empire. Yugoslavia was at the crossroads and torn by multiple internal crises: in the economy, the move from a planned to a market economy; in the political sphere, the demands of the republics and provinces for greater freedom within the federal system; and as background to everything, Serbian attempts to stop these developments from taking place. All this came to a head in the crisis of the League of Communists of Yugoslavia, which fell apart at its Fourteenth Congress in January 1990, signalling the beginning of the demise of Tito's Yugoslavia. Serbia, through its president Slobodan Milošević, together with the commanders of the Yugoslav People's Army (JNA), issued a menacing threat that any attempt to found independent republics would not be allowed to take place without frontier changes, on the principle that everywhere Serbs lived was part of Serbia.

For the Serbian nationalists, Yugoslavia had in each of its variants been a metaphor for Greater Serbia. This had been so under the Karađorđević monarchy, and was so in a different way in socialist Yugoslavia. It had been very apparent in the fierce Serbian opposition to the 1974 Constitution, in which Tito had been forced to give in to pressure from the republics for greater autonomy. The Serb domination (sometimes absolute supremacy) in both Yugoslavias was made possible by the fact that they were from the start non-democratic, ideologically controlled states. In the first, the imposed ideology of Yugoslavism had been supposed to foster loyalty to a supra-national state, but it was based on Serbian national epics and the tradition of St Sava. In socialist Yugoslavia, the supposedly unifying role was taken over by a programme combining the ideologies of class and nation, encapsulated in the slogan 'brotherhood and unity'. In both versions, the ideological and political interests of those in control of the state were served by a repressive army and police. This explains why it was only Milošević among the Yugoslav leaders who stubbornly held on to the communist rhetoric and ritual. Only thus could he be sure of maintaining Serbian domination. But the time came when the whole empire, from Vladivostok to Vis, began to fall apart, and international class ideology was being erased from Europe. The arrival of democracy ended forever the conditions that permitted the maintenance of Yugoslavia as a metaphor for Greater Serbia. So now Greater Serbia had to be achieved in literal, physical fact, which meant gaining possession of as many of the key areas of Yugoslavia up to the Adriatic Sea as possible. These were parts of Croatia, almost the whole of Bosnia-Herzegovina and Montenegro, the latter having already been annexed.

During 1990 political parties were formed in Slovenia, Croatia and Bosnia-Herzegovina with a view to holding the first multi-party elections in Yugoslavia. In all these the communist Party, reformed and renamed as the Social Democratic party, lost its leading social and political position.

The elections in Bosnia-Herzegovina were held in the autumn of 1990 and were jointly won by three parties: the (Muslim) Party of Democratic Action (SDA) led by Alija Izetbegović; the Serb Democratic Party (SDS) led by Radovan Karadžić (which had the same name as the Serb party in Croatia led by Jovan Rašković, both parties being directly linked to Milošević); and the Croatian Democratic

Union (HDZ), which was a branch of the party of the same name led by Franjo Tudman that had won the elections in Croatia. Power in Bosnia-Herzegovina was divided between the three national parties. From the beginning serious analysts considered this arrangement unnatural, incompatible with democratic usage and non-functional. During the whole of 1991 and into 1992 the functioning of the republican parliament was blocked, mainly by the SDS. During the same period tension between Serbia on one hand and Slovenia and Croatia on the other reached a critical point. Open war began at the beginning of summer 1991, after first Slovenia and then Croatia had declared independence. The JNA waged a short but brutal thirteen-day assault on Slovenia, from which it withdrew only to mount an all-out attack on Croatia. Occupied regions were established in parts of the republic which had a Serb population, with the obvious intention of detaching these from Croatia. At the same time that open war was being waged against Slovenia and Croatia, the JNA with the complicity of Karadžić's SDS was secretly arming the Serb population throughout Bosnia-Herzegovina. These well-armed and well-indoctrinated Serbs were later to be presented as 'people who had organized themselves to protect their age-old hearths and homes'.

The JNA, which had hitherto included all Yugoslav nationalities, had been rapidly transformed into an army consisting, especially in all positions of command, almost exclusively of Serbs and Montenegrins. Members of other nations either left the army or did not answer their call-up papers.

The attack on Croatia by the JNA was largely conducted from Bosnian territory, where it had strong bases. Croatia put up fierce resistance, during which it suffered terrible destruction in Vukovar and other towns, while atrocities against the civilian population were carried out by the JNA and by Serb rebels. At the end of 1991, under the auspices of the United Nations, a ceasefire was declared. All the huge military might of the JNA now withdrew from Croatia to Bosnia.

Bosnia-Herzegovina now became the central focus of the crisis. Radovan Karadžić and his SDS, in full accord with Slobodan Milošević and the JNA generals, began a re-run of the drama that had just ended in Croatia and made preparations for declaring a separate Serb political entity. On 9 January 1992 the 'Serb republic in Bosnia-Herzegovina' was declared, renamed in August as simply Republika Srpska [Serb Republic]. All this was accompanied by daily doses of ideological propaganda designed to convince the Serbs that a common life with any other nation, especially the Muslims, was impossible; that the other nations had nothing but hate and enmity for the Serbs; that the only solution was territorial and political division, whatever the cost; and that any Serb who thought differently was a traitor to his nation.

The international community required a referendum on independence to be held, with the single question: 'Are you in favour of a sovereign and independent Bosnia-Herzegovina, a state of equal citizens and nations, of Muslims, Serbs, Croats and others who live in it?' Karadžić's party forbade Serbs to vote, though it is known that a considerable number did so, especially in the towns. The referendum was held on 29 February and 1 March 1992. 63.7 percent of the total electoral body voted and of these 99.4 per cent voted 'Yes'.

This was the signal for attack on the nascent state. There had in fact already been fighting: Ravno, a village in Herzegovina, had been destroyed, and savage battles and Chetnik atrocities had taken place around Bosansko Brdo, Bijeljina and elsewhere. The same day that the European Community recognized Bosnia-Herzegovina, the JNA and Serbian para-militaries attacked Sarajevo, an act which signalled the beginning of the war to destroy the republic, now a recognized member of the United Nations.

During the first months it was the JNA which tried attacking. It shortly became officially the army of the Bosnian Serbs, working with the para-military formations of the SDS and with para-militaries from Serbia led by Željko Ražnatović Arkan and Vojislav Šešelj. This whole force was concentrated on the conquest and ethnic cleansing of as much of Bosnia-Herzegovina as possible, with systematic crimes as its main weapon. Towns were subjected to protracted siege, shelled and deprived of food, water, medicines and electricity. Concentration camps were set up at Omarska and Keraterm near Prijedor, Ljubija, Luka in Brčko, and many other places. People were kept in sub-human conditions, tortured and killed, with mass rape of women and sexual harassment of men. Civilians were massacred, and the non-Serb population systematically driven out of towns, villages and entire regions.

During the spring, summer and autumn of 1992 a large part of Bosnia-Herzegovina was occupied by using these methods. Towns were pulverized, and many ancient churches, mosques and other cultural monuments were destroyed or burned, Catholic as well as Muslim. Eastern Bosnia and Podrinje – from Foča through Višegrad and Zvornik to Bijeljina and Brčko – and Bosanska Krajina, from Prijedor to Sanski Most, Ključ and Bosanski Novi, suffered most terribly. Thousands of Muslims were expelled or killed and many Croats suffered the same fate, wherever they had stood without defence in the path of this brutal aggression.

We need to see Serbia's attempt to conquer Bosnia in the same context as its attack on Croatia. From the beginning of 1993 Slobodan Milošević's Bosnian and Croatian puppets, Karadžić and Milan Martić, had given him military control of one-third of Croatia (Eastern Slavonia, a vital part of Western Slavonia, and what was called 'Srpska Krajina', which at Benkovac and Obrovac stretched down to the Adriatic coast) and of a huge area of Bosnia-Herzegovina: eastern Herzegovina, which with Trebinje extended to Dubrovnik; the whole of eastern Bosnia and Podrinje, except for Goražde and its immediate environs; Bosanska Posavina; and the whole of Bosanska Krajina, except for the Bihać-Cazin area. The Republic of Croatia was split in three. Bosnia-Herzegovina was almost 70 percent occupied, and all the occupied territories throughout the two republics were linked together. It now became clear that Milošević was going to begin replacing warfare with political moves to lay the foundations of a new Serbian state.

On the eve of the referendum, while public debate was going on about how the referendum question should be formulated, it had already become apparent that the HDZ in Bosnia-Herzegovina was totally subject to Tudman's policies and ideas, and was aiming at the ethno-territorial dismemberment of the country. These intentions had already begun to surface in the formation of what were termed the Croat Communities of Bosanska Posavina (in Bosanski Brod on 12 November 1992) and of Herceg-Bosna (in Grude on 18 November). What also made these intentions clear was the installation of the Herzegovinian Mate Boban as head of the party, a man unashamedly obedient to Zagreb, inclined to cooperate with the SDS, and explicitly hostile to Sarajevo, Bosniaks and even Bosnian Croats. At this point the HDZ of Bosnia-Herzegovina produced what was almost an ultimatum, requiring the referendum question to include a formula about organizing the state according to 'national cantons'; but it was forced to retreat in the face of opposition from the Bosnian Croat public, intellectuals and church leaders. At the last moment the Bosnian Croats were called upon to vote 'yes' to the referendum as presented. But it was obvious that the HDZ would not easily give up. This was publicly stated several times by Tudman himself, most clearly in his statement on the last day of 1991, when the cease-fire was signed in Croatia and the war definitively moved to Bosnia. The statement was published in all Croatian and many foreign newspapers:

'[Peace between Croatia and Serbia] *can be achieved in such a way that Serbia's national goals are achieved and it therefore has no further need of expansion, while Croatia would at the same time annex its lands, because Croatia's present croissant shape is unnatural. It is in Croatia's interest that the problem should be solved in the most natural way, in the way it was solved by the Banovina. There could be a little bit of Bosnian land left* [the idea of *horion Bosona*, as recorded in Constantine Porphyrogenitus' *De administrando imperio* in the 10th century: I.L.] *where Muslims would be in the majority, and the state of Bosnia would act as a buffer between Croatia and Serbia. In this way the colonial creation of Bosnia-Herzegovina would at the same time disappear.*'

Croatian interests, thus defined, would entail massive relocation of population to achieve ethnic purity, the break up of Bosnia-Herzegovina's political structure, and inevitable conflict with

Bosniaks. It would have to be prepared by media propaganda, similar to that of the Serbs, aimed at persuading the Bosnian Croats of the impossibility of a common life with Bosniaks. The tragedy involved was not difficult to predict when we remember that for centuries the Croats – 560,000 of them in the 1991 census in Bosnia alone, without counting Herzegovina – had lived intermingled with others, especially with the Bosniak Muslims, to form the ancient social structure of central Bosnia, Posavina, Bosanska Krajina and all Bosnia's towns.

At the beginning of the war in April 1992, a Croatian Defence Council (HVO) was formed. This was a military organization, and the explanation given by the HDZ was that it was intended to 'protect Croats against Serbian aggression'. The HVO immediately took over civil power in all those communes which had elected HDZ representatives. Thus, under orders from Zagreb, a form of military *putsch* had been carried out in Herzegovina and everywhere else where power was held by the HDZ or where the HVO was the preponderant military force.

At first the HVO, in whose ranks there were then many Bosniak Muslims, fought the Serbian Army fiercely in a number of places: Čapljina, Stolac, Popovo, Mostar, Kupres, Jajce, Posavina, Konjic and elsewhere. But in late spring 1992, after the Vienna Agreement between Radovan Karadžić and Mate Boban and the proclamation on 3 July of the 'Croat Community of Herceg-Bosna' as Croat territory in Bosnia-Herzegovina (president – Mate Boban, capital – Mostar, army – the HVO, language – Croatian), Croat relations with Sarajevo and the legal government of the republic became increasingly strained, and clashes with the Serbian army steadily decreased. On 28 August, at the height of the war between the HVO and the Army of Bosnia-Herzegovina, Herceg-Bosna was proclaimed the 'Croatian Republic of Herceg-Bosna', in an explicit demonstration of secessionist aspirations analogous to those of Republika Srpska.

After merciless shelling of the town and fierce fighting with HVO units, in which Bosniaks also took part, the Serbian army retreated from Mostar. For reasons never yet explained the Croatian army now withdrew from Posavina, allowing the Serbs control of the corridor at Brčko through which all Belgrade – Doboj – Banja Luka – Knin traffic had to pass. For equally unexplained reasons the HVO too withdrew – bringing in its wake the local Croatian population – from the front line that it and the Bosniaks had held against the Serbian army on Mount Vlašic above Travnik. Soon in similarly mysterious circumstances Jajce too fell, and there was a dramatic exodus of more than 30,000 Croats and Bosniaks. At other points of contact the front was stabilized: in the Dubrovnik hinterland (Popovo, Stolac), Kupres and elsewhere. At only a few local flashpoints was there still fighting (Gradačac, Orašje, Bihać, where the far larger Army of Bosnia-Herzegovinia was in action), but these were exceptions.

When all these movements and counter-movements are considered, all this secretive occupation of land and stabilization of lines, it is easy to hear beneath all the rhetoric about 'the struggle of the Croat people for their existence and their land' the voice of an HVO that was functioning as a second Croatian army, with the purpose of providing Croatia with a deeper hinterland for the long, vulnerable coastline of central and southern Dalmatia. It is also easy to see how the HDZ was working together with the HVO in relocating Bosnian Croats into the evacuated areas of Herzegovina, all with the same end in mind. During the autumn and early winter of 1992, relations between the HVO and the newly-formed army of the Republic of Bosnia-Herzegovina became increasingly tense. After a series of incidents beginning with the HVO's bloodily-conducted occupation of Prozor, and after the HDZ following orders from Zagreb had withdrawn from the legal state bodies in Sarajevo to which they had been elected, the tension developed by the spring of 1993 into a real war.

At the beginning of the war the Presidency of Bosnia-Herzegovina was still a legal body, even though its SDS members had withdrawn from it. It retained its statutory multi-national and elected legality by co-opting Serbs from other parties which had won some votes in the elections. As *primus inter pares*, and in terms of his personal standing, the strongest member of the Presidency was Alija Izetbegović, who was also president of the SDA and informal leader of the Bosniak-Muslim nation. Izetbegović did not manage to save Bosnia from war, though he tried every possible political move to do so. It was an illusion to believe that by declaring neutrality they might avoid having to fight; indeed it turned out to be fatal. The direction in which Bosnian politicians were attempting at that time to steer Bosnian policy was perhaps best outlined in the 'Decisions Concerning Sovereignty' which the parliament of Bosnia-Herzegovina enacted on 15 October 1991: 'Bosnia and Herzegovina will develop as a civil republic, sovereign and indivisible. It will remain neutral in conflicts between Serbia and Croatia and may remain in the Yugoslav community only if Serbia and Croatia do so.'

Equally fatal was the hope, fuelled in Sarajevo, of armed international involvement if Bosnia should be attacked. This possibility was still being discussed in the first weeks of the war, in spite of the fact that the main leaders of the Western powers, George Bush, then American president, François Mitterrand of France, and John Major of the UK, kept repeating that military involvement was out of the question. At the same time the absurd arms embargo was imposed, which Bosnia, given its geographical position, especially at the beginning of the war had no means of breaking.

The SDA of which Izetbegović was and remained the charismatic leader made declarations in favour of a democratically organized multinational state. But within its ranks there had never been any very clear discussion of the various aspects and goals of Bosnian-Herzegovinian state policy, of a distinct Bosniak-Muslim policy, or of the role of religious communities and the Islamic religion. It was understandably difficult to separate out these concerns, intertwined within the web of Bosnia, Bosniaks and their religion. But besides this difficulty there was often deliberate ambiguity. This always created difficulties and gave credibility to accusations of hypocrisy about the intention to create a Muslim state, accusations made from Belgrade against the SDA even before the war and later supported by

Zagreb and the HDZ. Such accusations had a very dangerous purpose: to throw doubt on the legitimacy of the state's institutions as having been usurped by one party and one people, thus calling into question the legality of Bosnia-Herzegovina's international status and political existence. It is unclear whether the SDA realized to what an extent their ambiguous stance produced a train of events that eventually did the greatest damage to the Bosniak people themselves.

Armed Bosnian resistance began in the very first months of the Serbian attack, at first on people's own initiative, later in an organized fashion. A certain amount of organization came from Bosniak Muslim political organizations, which early in the war gave rise to the 'Green Berets' and the Patriotic League. At the same time the state had begun to create an organized army from the territorial defence forces, with a few low-ranking officers and some weapons. But little had been left because the arms depots had been thoroughly stripped by the Yugoslav army, in spite of having been originally intended for local territorial defence. These motley, lightly armed small units of volunteers, operating locally, achieved surprisingly good results against the well-armed military machine which confronted them. Gradually the scattered, loosely organized local units were knitted together as the Army of the Republic of Bosnia-Herzegovina, which was eventually 200,000 strong. In the first phases, although most of the volunteers were Bosniaks (a fact that at first was purely statistical), the Bosnian army was truly multi-national. Later, through conflict with the HVO and as a result of the ambiguous stance of the SDA, it became more mono-national, as an army of the Bosniaks, sometimes with an explicit Islamic dimension.

At the end of 1992 Bosnia-Herzegovina was politically almost at its last gasp. It was divided between three armies. Two of these (the Army of Bosnia-Herzegovina and the HVO) had at one time operated together, but by this time it was clear that they were all three fighting each other. If we now add a fourth ingredient, UNPROFOR the United Nations peacekeeping force, we get an approximate picture of the highly complicated military position in Bosnia.

After having passively watched destruction and occupation in

Croatia, and after recognizing in the winter of 1992 the independence of the former Yugoslav republics and acknowledging that Yugoslavia had disintegrated by dissolution and not by the independent breakaway of individual republics; after UNPROFOR troops had been sent to Croatia and Bosnia to monitor the so-called lines of demarcation (which often in practice meant protecting the parts occupied by the Serbs); after authorizing UNHCR to supply the basic needs of the hungry populations of the towns and regions cut off by Serbian forces; the international community finally began the endless process of seeking a diplomatic solution to the crisis in Bosnia-Herzegovina and the rest of Yugoslavia, constantly declaring that it would respect the integrity of states and refuse to acknowledge frontiers that had been altered by violence, ethnic cleansing and conquest.

At the beginning of 1993 Cyrus Vance and David Owen, then the UN negotiators, proposed a plan for dividing Bosnia-Herzegovina into ten cantons. Like all others this plan was based on a tacit acknowledgement of Serbian gains. The boundaries of the cantons were drawn on the basis of military maps. They were drawn according to ethnicity, and all autonomy was concentrated in them. The central authorities had only symbolic significance. The plan further suggested that the cantonal boundaries had not yet been precisely fixed, with the direct result that the HVO and the Army of Bosnia-Herzegovina began to draw borders between Bosniaks and Bosnian Croats by armed conflict and the seizure of territory. It was at this moment that members of the HDZ in Bosnia received instructions from Zagreb to quit the Sarajevo government. This reinforced the feeling that Bosnia-Herzegovina was about to become an ethnically structured state. Moreover, the Vance-Owen Plan offered more territory for the Croats than had been foreseen by the HVO strategists, who had previously organized defensively in parts of central Bosnia with a considerable Croat population. It was at this time that the Bosnian-Herzegovinan Army was becoming increasingly mono-national, and was developing a specific ideology connected on the one hand to Islam and on the other to the idea that, although all nations in Bosnia-

Herzegovina were in principle equal, the Bosniak-Muslim population was the 'basic nation'.

In the end the Vance-Owen Plan was not accepted, but it had brought about war between the HVO and the Army of Bosnia-Herzegovina. This changed the nature of the conflict in Bosnia. Until then it had been the aggression of one country (Serbia) against another (Bosnia-Herzegovina); now it took on elements of a civil war within Bosnia, with fighting between 'three warring parties'.

The HVO engaged in this war with a wrong assessment of the strength of the Army of Bosnia-Herzegovina, of the level of disorientation in Sarajevo, and of the readiness of the international community to back the partition of Bosnia. In their attack on Mostar on 9 May 1993 (the eastern part of the city was inhabited largely by Bosniak Muslims); in the long period of siege and shelling of that city; in the brutal expulsion of Bosniak Muslims from Čapljina, Stolac and the whole region and their imprisonment in concentration camps in Gabela, Dretelj, the Mostar helidrome, etc; and in their systematic destruction of mosques and other architectural monuments in the Bosniak-Moslem tradition (on 9 November 1993 the Old Bridge at Mostar was destroyed), the HVO and the Herceg-Bosna leadership used similar methods to those used by the Serbian aggressors at the beginning of the war. They also used exactly the same kind of rhetoric in their propaganda in the media and in political speeches. They denied the value of the Bosnian tradition of a common life, ridiculed the idea of Bosnia as a state and community, derided the Bosniak Muslims and their culture and challenged the notion of their separate identity.

This war was not confined to Mostar; there was fierce fighting in the valley of the Lašva (Vitez, Novi Travnik), around Žepče, Bugojno and Gornji Vakuf, in the Fojnica-Kreševo-Kiseljak area, at Neretvica and Prozor. The front line was sometimes fantastically tangled, resulting in tiny enclaves completely cut off from anywhere else. Widespread crimes against the civil population began, such as those perpetrated by local HVO units against the Bosniaks in Ahmići, Vitez and Stupni Dol near Vareš. There was systematic destruction of mosques, graveyards and other religious and cultural monuments. A flagrant example was that of the ancient and renowned monastery of the Naksibendi Dervish Order at Oglavak near Fojnica.

The propaganda on both sides presented the war as being between two nations (often with a religious note being struck), not two political elites or ideas. The part of the country centred on Sarajevo, defended by the Army of Bosnia-Herzegovina but completely encircled by the Serbian Army, was cut off on all sides. Any aid that came from outside had to run a blockade in western Herzegovina involving great difficulty and large-scale theft and extortion. Although the part of Bosnia thus surrounded did still manage to be multinational, because a large proportion of the native population both Croats and Serbs resisted the nationalist call to arms, the Army of Bosnia-Herzegovina had in practice become a Bosniak-Muslim national army, fighting bitterly at first for sheer survival and later for the aim which had from the first been imposed on it – to gain control of as large a piece of territory as possible. The end result was that it too carried out war crimes: murders and attacks on the civil population, as at Neretvica, Grabovica, Doljani, Uzdol and Bugojno, including the murder of two Franciscans in the monastery at Fojnica. There was destruction of property, vandalizing of religious objects, threats and persecution on a mass scale. Kakanj, Kraljeva Sutjeska and Vareš in the heart of central Bosnia became practically denuded of their old Croat Catholic population. Their tragedy is not diminished by the fact that their removal to Herzegovina (Čapljina, Stolac) and Croatia (to what had been Serb villages in Lika, Banija, etc) was to a great extent the result of Croatian policy and the deliberate actions of the HVO.

Fighting between the Army of Bosnia-Herzegovina and the HVO lasted until the spring of 1994. Then for the first time the United States became directly involved in the conflict in Bosnia and former Yugoslavia, and on American initiative the negotiations were held which on 18 March 1994 resulted in the signing of the Washington Agreement. Before this a general assembly of the Croats of Bosnia-Herzegovina was held in Sarajevo, on 6 February, organized by a number of Croat institutions and individuals trying to extricate themselves from the destructive politics of the HDZ. This assembly issued a Declaration proposing a cantonal organization while demonstrating their firm belief in a unified, multi-ethnic Bosnia-Herzegovina. The Washington Agreement put an end to fighting between the HVO and the Army of Bosnia-Herzegovina; the Federation of Bosnia-Herzegovina was established in the parts of the country under the control of the two armies, and Mostar came under European Union administration. A Contact Group was formed consisting of the USA, Russia, Germany, France and the United Kingdom, representatives of which were to monitor the peace process. A division of the republic's territory was determined, with 51 percent going to the Federation of Bosnia-Herzegovina and 49% being left to the Serbian entity.

War between the HVO and the Army of Bosnia-Herzegovina was ended, but the two armies retained their positions on the front line. On the long front between the Serbian forces and the Army of Bosnia-Herzegovina (and still sometimes the HVO, as in the tiny section of Posavina at Orašja) fighting never stopped. In the period after the Washington Agreement the Serbian offensive actually increased, especially in three areas: Bihać and its surroundings, Žepa and Srebrenica, and Goražde. Sarajevo was completely besieged, and being systematically strangled. Throughout the whole war these areas had been besieged by the Serbian army, which had nevertheless never managed to take them. Throughout 1994 and 1995 the attacks were intensified and the sufferings of the civil population were dire. Pressure on the governments of Western Europe by media and public opinion increased. The international community tried to lessen the crisis by proclaiming 'safe areas' and increasing humanitarian aid. This proved to be a counter-productive policy, since it merely made it easier for the Serbian army to tighten its grip on certain areas and develop military operations unhindered.

Crisis point was reached in the summer of 1995. The army of Radovan Karadžić and General Ratko Mladić, before the very eyes of the world and with UNPROFOR soldiers observing passively, carried out the systematic massacre of many of the people of

Srebrenica and refugees in Srebrenica from other parts of Bosnia, so that the town was at last in Serbian hands. At the same time a fierce Serbian offensive against Bihać began, clearly intended to take that important communications centre on the Una at any price. The open brutality and blatant commission of some of the worst war crimes to date at last stung the international community into action. President Clinton took an active role from now on, having won a second term in office, while François Mitterrand ceased to be President of France. NATO aircraft were sent on a warning mission to bomb some Serbian objectives, and at the same time the Croatian army was briefly encouraged to start an important operation to defeat the Serb forces occupying what they called the 'Serb Krajina' in Croatia. This operation was coordinated with operations of the HVO and the Army of Bosnia-Herzegovina in western Bosnia and around Bihać. Faced with the liberation of Bihać and the loss of the Serb Krajina and large swathes of territory in western Bosnia, Slobodan Milošević remained wholly mute and passive.

In November 1995, as a result of US political initiatives, peace talks began in the American army base of Dayton, Ohio. All the chief actors on the political scene from Sarajevo, Zagreb and Belgrade took part, including Alija Izetbegović, Franjo Tudman and Slobodan Milošević. The latter was authorized to speak in the name of the Karadžić Serbs, this being an indirect acknowledgement by the international community that it had known all along of the territorial claims of Bosnia-Herzegovina's neighbours and that proxy local military forces were the means for achieving these. Negotiations lasted for a month, and the signing ceremony was held on 14 December in Paris.

The Dayton Agreement was an exhaustive and complicated document. It confirmed the statehood of Bosnia-Herzegovina, within its internationally recognized frontiers but divided internally into the Federation of Bosnia-Herzegovina and Republika Srpska. Territorially the ratio between the two was 51:49 per cent as previously determined. Some important changes were made. The four-year-long blockade of Sarajevo was ended, with the result that practically the whole town and the surrounding country, which had been under Serb occupation, became part of the Federation. In the same way Goražde and its corridor went to the Federation, as did the territory in western Bosnia taken by the HVO and the Army of Bosnia-Herzegovina (Glamoč, Drvar, Grahovo, Petrovac, Ključ, Jajce, Donji Vakuf, Kupres). Almost the whole of Bosanska Posavina, with the Brčko corridor, went to Republika Srpska. The status of Brčko itself was not solved at Dayton, but left for one further year to an arbitration commission.

The Dayton Agreement invested the Federation of Bosnia-Herzegovina and Republika Srpska with many attributes of state autonomy, but they did not have international status. This was vested in Bosnia-Herzegovina, and was to be exercised through the state institutions of a three-member Presidency, a council of ministers with the function of a government, an Assembly of Bosnia-Herzegovina, and a central bank with a single currency. The Dayton Agreement stressed the right of all refugees and displaced persons to return to their homes, and the need for all those accused of war crimes to appear before the International Court of Justice in the Hague. One of the most important requirements was the holding of elections for the new governing bodies at all levels throughout Bosnia-Herzegovina.

Elections were held in September 1996, but only at federal and canton level. Local elections had to be postponed because of the danger that in Republika Srpska, because the Agreement had been insufficiently implemented, elections might legitimize conditions achieved by ethnic cleansing and by the prevention of return of refugees and displaced persons. The results of the elections showed that after Dayton, government was again shared between three ethnic parties and their leaders. In Republika Srpska the election was won by the SDS (with the provision that Radovan Karadžić, who was indicted as a war criminal, should not have the right to take part in public or political life), while in the Federation it was won by the SDA and the HDZ.

***

The Dayton Agreement, paradoxical as it was, saved Bosnia from further war but not from exhausting political contradictions and tensions. The country was in ruins, and conditions continued to deteriorate although hostilities had ended; it was physically, functionally and organizationally shattered. The human loss was terrible: thousands incapacitated by injury, more than two hundred thousand killed, almost one and a half million refugees, emigrés and displaced persons, some within the country, some abroad. Hundreds of thousands of Bosnians and Herzegovinans, mostly Bosniak Moslems but also Croats and even Serbs, had been killed, tortured, exiled and terrorized; people had been moved from one place to another; suffered the loss of everything; were desperate with suffering; were victims of crime, fear and despair; had lost hope and purpose; had become dehumanized and had their personal fate marginalized for the sake of the new order now imposed upon them: the new, criminally based, ethnically structured Bosnia-Herzegovina supposedly created in the interests of these same Bosniaks, Serbs and Croats!

Seen in the long term, the degree to which the ethno-territorial ideology of this war was accompanied by crime (as the weapon) and suffering (as the result) – two sides of the same reality, the thorough destruction of the cultural and moral fibre of Bosnia and its people – is surely the most terrible outcome of the war and one whose burden will be carried by generations to come. The question of crimes and the responsibility for them will for a long time to come certainly be the most difficult aspect of the Bosnian moral recovery.

Ruined, gutted, plundered and desecrated churches and mosques – this is one of the faces of contemporary Bosnia. Especially terrible was the systematic, organized destruction of religious buildings in areas outside the war zone and under the absolute control of a particular national party and army. In Republika Srpska all sixteen of the historic mosques of Banja Luka were totally destroyed, beginning with the wonderful Ferhadija and Arnaudija. The incomparable Aladža in Foča was burned down, and mosques destroyed from Trebinje to Mrkonjić-Grad and Jajce, from Prijedor to Zvornik. The Franciscan monastery and church of Plehan, with its priceless works of art, suffered the same fate, as did those in Jajce and Petrićevac near

Banja Luka, and the legendary shrine at Podmilačje near Jajce with its unique, partly-preserved mediaeval Gothic chapel.

In the parts of the country under the control of the HDZ and the HVO, the centuries-long Islamic heritage has been destroyed, including not only religious buildings but many precious features of the urban ambiences of Stolac, Mostar, Počitelj and elsewhere. The marvellous ecological and architectural complex of the Orthodox monastery of Žitomislić below Mostar has also been destroyed.

The crowning glories of Bosnian social history and the achievement of the Bosnian experience and way of life have been deeply shaken. To be Bosnian was to have a feeling for otherness, for the different as part of the daily reality of one's most personal environment. It was this experience of the different that made it possible to be Bosnian. In the new territorialization, grown from the poison of chauvinism, Bosnians have ceased to be Bosnian and become just Bosniak Muslims, Serbs and Croats.

Three conflicting images of history have reached the final stage of crystallization. The danger was always latent, for the Serbian version was too long dominant, and people did not notice to what extent the other two histories, voiceless and repressed, were themselves based on pseudo-historical premises, popular fabrications and ideological myths. War equalized them and allowed each to dominate its own territory.

In order to recognize and understand Bosnian cultural identity, it was always crucially important to realize that composite integration was its essence: the parallel existence of three separate traditions (four if we include the Sephardic Jewish). Looked at diachronically we can see in the period of modern political history (i.e. the last 200 years) a constant tendency to shift the emphasis from the composite to the integral. It is a tendency linked to secularization and to the end of identification with religious civilization. In both Yugoslavias this was often combined with the forcible suppression of certain elements, usually non-Serbian. Yet there was an underlying process that could not be checked, because it had developed out of living experience. The modern sociological approach recognizes a common frame of reference, in which the way we communicate determines us more deeply than what we are; it is this that provides the basis for defining culture. In the eighties, in Sarajevo and Bosnia, an unusually rich simultaneous existence of cultures and sub-cultures of the most varied kinds evolved. In it, and this needs to be stressed, there was increasing freedom for a new affirmation and valorization of ethno-confessional traditions. This vibrant reality was experienced as an integral cultural ambience.

It is a tragic illusion that war, ethnic ideologies and the fixing of boundaries are necessary for the realization of self, through the production of a pure culture and a return to roots. It has always been known that this approach leads only to the use of force and a falsification of history, past and present. Its advocates and propagandists do not realize how dangerous it is to their own pure culture and much loved nation, for it is a process that leads nowhere except to a ghetto mentality, to cultural stagnation and eventually death.

The fine Bosnian multiplicity of perspectives has been reduced today to the crude sway of three cultural paradigms. Each thinks it must turn to its own pure separate history, its own pure separate literature, its own pure separate language. However this may develop, one thing is certain: it can give rise only to mediocrity, for in regimes of exclusivity it is the most gifted individuals and richest values that find no place.

One of the most unmistakable signs of the destructive regression of Bosnian society is the degree and mode of activity by religious institutions in everyday public life. The comeback began before the war, during the short period after the democratic elections, and from the first it was apparent that this religious revival showed some signs of replacing the fallen Communist ideology and its rituals. But it was the war, with all its horror and destruction, its imperilling of human existence, that created the full psychological, social and politically inescapable ethno-religious framework for a kind of re-clericalization or de-secularization. It was a process present in all the religions – Catholic, Orthodox and Islamic. Each had its specific form of the process and any mechanical equalization would be a mistake. The essential thing is to recognize that the process is an anachronism in the context of modern, secular civilization.

The old cultural societies, which the communists had in their early years so violently suppressed with confiscation of their property, re-emerged after the 1990 elections. The Bosnian-Muslim *Preporod* (replacing *Gajret* and *Narodna uzdanica)*, the Croat *Napredak,* the Serb *Prosjveta* and the Jewish *La Benevolencia* all came back. In the 1992–5 war they played an important part, both cultural and humanitarian. But looked at from the wider perspective, the re-animation of societies of this kind, with their inevitable monopolization of national cultures and their symbiotic reliance on religious and political organizations, was also retrogressive.

One of the greatest corruptions that the war brought to Bosnia was the collapse of urban society. Bosnian towns were destroyed in many ways: some through tons of shells and explosives (Sarajevo, Mostar, Bihać), others through bloody crime and fear (Foča, Višegrad, Zvornik, Brčko, Bijeljina, Prijedor), still others through a self-destructive renunciation of key elements of their own urban being: the population belonging to other nations or faiths, the cultural and religious buildings of others, and so forth – Banja Luka is an example of such de-urbanization, carried out as a planned policy despite being far from the front line and the war.

There is nevertheless another side to the coin, one that reveals an untapped strength, a knowledge and a creativity that refuse to be crushed, a will to preserve self-respect and authenticity that refused to die even in conditions of the deepest distress, even at the risk of life itself.

This is especially true of cultural life, which does not mean that it is not present in other areas also. All through the war artists, writers, journalists, actors, musicians and scholars lived and worked – in Sarajevo for example – on the very margins of existence, often like pre-historic cave-dwellers, constantly candidates for death and witnesses of the suffering and death of others. In many cases the work they did rose to unimaginable heights. Their achievements were comparable with work being done in the world beyond Sarajevo.

The artists are an outstanding case – painters, graphic artists, designers, sculptors of almost all generations stayed in Bosnia, and only rarely did fate take them away from the country. The amount and quality of what they produced and their experimental approach is an achievement on a world scale. Their work can be recognized as one of the great spiritual and aesthetic achievements of the end of the century.

Theatre had shining moments and so did film, in both the documentary and acting genres. Sarajevo's war photographers achieved fascinating results in both the artistic and documentary senses. Sarajevo's rock-music sub-culture had been the leading one in the former Yugoslavia, but during the war it lost many of its stars who were scattered across the world; nevertheless the ones who were left (temporarily or permanently), as well as those who emerged during the war, continued to demonstrate vitality and originality.

A particular phenomenon is represented by media and publishing: many new media projects, both printed and electronic, appeared during the war, of which an enviable number grew into extremely familiar and influential voices. In this context it is necessary to note those that succeeded completely in nurturing a truly independent, critical-investigative journalism. The production of books was also impressive, especially when we bear in mind not only wartime conditions but the collapse of the market.

Literature, as is well known, is especially subject to various kinds of external pressure, forcing it to fulfil a role which is not naturally its own. Even today some sectors have not fully managed to reaffirm literary freedom. But in large measure, more than might have been expected, they have managed to resume freedom in writing: mostly short forms – poetry, documentary, narrative – without avoiding the subject of what is really happening and at the same time maintaining a high standard. This is especially true of the writers of an older generation, many of whom were exiles in Slovenia or Croatia and in countries all over the world. But it is also true of young, even very young, writers, poets and prose writers unknown before the war, who have produced some of the best works in modern Bosnian literature.

Moreover in the literary field a great reversal has been brought about. Before the war Bosnia was relatively unknown in the world stage. But war and media coverage and the extremity of suffering by the Bosnian people in town and village have (however unfortunately) made the country one of the best-known places in the world. Many leading European and world journalists, historians, writers and others suddenly became interested in Bosnia, resulting in important books and articles in English, French, German and other languages. Texts by Bosnian writers were translated.

Today's cultural and media scene in Bosnia is still creative and dynamic, a witness to the ability of Bosnian society to remain an integral part of the contemporary world of open values. To this extent the Bosnia of today contradicts the primitive ethnocentric model imposed on it by the politicians of the post-Dayton era.

One can hardly expect the healing process to begin and a new civil and cosmopolitan society to develop in Bosnia under the rule of three parallel ethnic parties or movements. The context in which the process might start is one where their total control would be eased, and where a political idea could develop that would outgrow their ethnocentric autism, their regressive and rigid bond with the ethnic-territorial principle, but without ignoring the importance of the national phenomenon. Yearnings for such an idea, as can be seen in the way culture reflects reality, still exist among ordinary people at the level of spontaneous everyday living, despite the trauma of war. How far this will of the people will be able to find political expression does not depend only on developments in Bosnia-Herzegovina.

Culture? Identity? – In place of an Afterword

I

We are constantly faced anew with the problem of selecting from our traditions those which are creative, vital and productive. It is a selection of crucial importance, but it very quickly negates itself the moment we think (which here we so often do) that we can implement it by decree or express it as some single purpose mandated by History and Culture. The process of selection is continuous and invisible, and it takes place as part of cultural and creative life, where inherent and very unexpected virtual criteria are at work. There can be few places where this process emerges as an equation with as many unknowns as in the cultural history of Bosnia, especially its most complicated period, the Ottoman.

In national, political and historical works of the nineteenth and early twentieth century, and in works written between the two world wars that are still current today, the entire Ottoman age was treated only from the standpoint of political history: as an age of foreign military and political occupation, a spiritual and cultural vacuum, a deplorable and historically unproductive *episode*. The pattern and results of cultural processes are completely lost sight of. These are indeed 'brought in' on the wave of great military-political convulsions, but during the course of four centuries they adopt the form of an organic culture-creating process and facts demanding a normal cultural-historical and aesthetic-morphological treatment, unburdened by ideological and civilizational idiosyncrasies. Cultural phenomena cannot be reduced to their political and historical equivalent without running the risk of violating both them and their historical truth. This is especially out of place in the history of cultures like those that developed in the Mediterranean area, which largely resulted from symbiosis and amalgamation, while developing initially through military and political expansion much more often than through some kind of ideal 'natural' course of events. If we do not take these deeper processes into account, our relation to our cultural heritage is reduced to spiritually deadening and ridiculous myths of a 'difficult past', 'centuries of slavery', 'the dark *vilayet*'. This ignores the real cultural movements, transformations and achievements, because such an approach cannot even provide the preconditions for their study, let alone spiritually prepare the ground for active reception of their content. Since this kind of attitude has been dominant for almost a century and a half, it is easy to explain (but no longer today to accept) the fact that whole series of cultural events from that period are still undiscovered. And even when they are discovered, when people do work on them, their work often provokes suspicion rooted in the views we have described.

To those who try to understand the lines that follow and approach them with good will, we must say at the outset that they do not claim to sift the amassed sediment of centuries with painstaking and analytical care for detail. They cannot come up with explicit answers. I do not know anyone who could provide such answers with complete objectivity. These are questions in which past cannot be separated from present concerns, questions relating to a current process in which we are all actively involved. It is impossible to be objective to the point of *sub specie aeternitatis*, where one has a crystal-clear view of everything, dispassionate and coldly logical.

A systematic picture of cultural history in the Turkish period, when it is written, will have to start from the essential spiritual and cultural duality that arose from the co-existence of different cultural, ethnic and religious entities: Muslim-Bosniak, Orthodox-Serb, Catholic-Croat and Sephardic-Jewish.

If we apply the mediaeval distinction between *high* culture and *folk* culture, which is applicable given the mediaeval nature of spiritual and social life in Bosnia right down to the mid nineteenth century, then we can schematically say that the duality lies in this: the sphere of high culture was marked by maximum isolation between the three cultural entities, while the sphere of folk culture was where they blended. Continuing on our path of schematization, we can say that on one hand, in the sphere of high culture, there were three separate cultures, and on the other, in the sphere of folk culture, there was a common fund of cultural models and creative principles. Into this picture of *horizontal* levels we must now introduce *vertical* lines, the organic unity between each of the three high cultures and their share of the folk culture. It is very important not to lose sight of the forms in which the folk culture acted upwards, lending its spirit of *integration* to the spheres of the three separate high cultures.

We must stress that we have introduced the concept of high and folk culture only provisionally, as an aid: the three Bosnian ethno-cultural entities did not all possess them (or at least did not possess high culture) to an equal degree, nor was vertical unity equally developed in all of them. This is historically easy to explain, and is crucial for today's emotional reception of the material. Any future synthesis will have to start by addressing this issue, and until it does so unnecessary misunderstandings will multiply, all equally irrational and limited, whether in their nationalistic or their normative-political variants. If nationalistic, they manifest themselves in ridiculous but malign arguments about whose culture is 'richer' or 'more innate and indigenous', and interpret historical reality and interaction by determinism and some God-given 'potential' or 'unfitness' in this nation or that for this or that kind of self-confirmation or realization. In the second variant, misunderstandings stem from exhaustion brought in by a futile hunt for or invention of a completely symmetrical and strict 'parity', to be asserted at all costs. Both lead directly to falsifications from which our contemporary cultural historiography is not immune. They are the obverse and reverse of the same thing:

spiritual narrowness and provinciality, irrational fear of the *other*, a fear that is contrary to the essence and functions of culture. When we add up everything that we have said about the dynamic component of historical change, we arrive at a complicated spiritual and historical situation, so involved that it is perhaps almost impossible to interpret.

In the period we are considering, the whole cultural and spiritual life of Bosnia-Herzegovina was firmly defined by religion. This is of primary importance for understanding the nature and development of the cultural tradition. As we know, in the theocratic Ottoman state the only possible vehicle for expressing any different ethnic, historical, cultural, political or other interest was the religious community. Hence it is wrong not to accord religion its role in the process of ethnic and national differentiation and identification in Bosnia-Herzegovina, however much the process may be determined by other factors as well.

Religion as the framework of spiritual life had an especially crucial role in the sphere of high culture. Since the Bosnian cultural landscape is threefold (even four-fold) in terms of religion and civilization, and is also scarred by historical antagonism among the three entities, these three cultural spheres clearly had to realize themselves in isolation from one another. Thus it is not only understandable but inevitable that within the small area of Bosnia, quite important creative processes could be taking place at the same time in each other's neighbourhoods, without one entity knowing about the other or having any need to know about it. Here we must try to shed some light on the unequal development of the three *high* cultures.

Islamic high culture in Bosnia naturally came most strongly to expression during the period of Turkish rule, and especially during its first two centuries, when the frontiers of the Empire stretched far to the north of Bosnia and Turkey was legally and economically stable. The mass conversion to Islam (which our historians still find is difficult to come to terms with), oriental urbanization, integration into the oriental economic system, spiritual life and civilization, are all objective and specific historical conditions for the development of culture and art.

This component began to decline visibly in the second two centuries of Turkish rule, after the turning point of the Turkish defeat at Vienna in the late seventeenth century, when the boundaries of the Empire shrank to the Sava and in the western part of the Empire a period of lasting and progressive destabilization began. At this time Bosnia began to go through especially difficult times and crises. Here we can see the connection between a stable system and the development of high culture. This time was also marked by a deep and culturologically very important turning point in Muslim-Bosniak culture (for example, with Alhamijado literature). A feeling began to develop for a creativity different from that of the 'mother' culture. This coincided, in accordance with a strange law of cause and effect, with the intensification of a process by which a specific Bosnian-Muslim ethnos emerged as part of the Turkish-Ottoman commonwealth, through stormy social changes and unrest, through paradoxical and often tragic historical circumstances and events.

In comparison with the Islamic, the spheres of high culture in the Catholic-Croat and especially in the Orthodox-Serb component were much poorer, which is understandable considering their position in the Turkish Islamic state. Despite Islamic tolerance in principle of other monotheistic religions, in practice their members were second-rate citizens. But here, too, it is very important to be aware of great changes in the course of time, depending on many inter-related internal and external factors. Thus, for example, there was a great difference between the position of the Orthodox Church in Bosnia-Herzegovina (and consequently of Orthodox-Serb high culture) in the first centuries, before the abolition of the Peć Patriarchate and the introduction of higher clergy from Greece, and its position in the later period. In the first period, while relations between the Porte and the Patriarchate were harmonious and even very productive, creative processes within the Orthodox-Serb tradition in Bosnia were fruitful too. Frescoes in the Serbian-Byzantine style, created with special intensity during the late sixteenth and seventeenth centuries, are among the peaks of the cultural heritage of Bosnia-Herzegovina in the Ottoman period.

From the eighteenth century onwards the very existential foundations of life began to be eroded. The Turkish offensive in Europe was defeated; church leaders began to increase their ties with the Russian (and Austrian) counter-offensive against Turkey; the Peć Patriarchate was abolished (having been not only the religious but also the political and cultural integrating factor of all Serbs in the Balkans); and higher clergy from Greece were introduced, which not only deprived the Orthodox Serbs of their own authentic representatives but gave them clergy whose activities were strongly anti-national and who introduced much negative tension into relations with the Catholic Croat ethnic and religious communities. For a long time all this destroyed the preconditions for any form of high culture. It might almost be said that from that time on the cultural and creative potential of the Orthodox Serb entity shifted completely into the sphere of folk culture. A strong urban and merchant class, as a social and economic foundation for any form of high culture, did not appear among them until the nineteenth century, when the whole of Bosnia-Herzegovina was in any case entering a completely new cultural age.

The situation of the Catholic Croat entity in Bosnia was similar, but different in some essential elements. Here the Bosnian Franciscan institution of Bosna Srebrena was of primary importance in its continuity and folk character. Through all the four centuries of Turkish rule the Bosnian Catholics had authentic cultural, educational and, of course, religious representatives in the Franciscans. It is important to remember that the Franciscans, although they started by teaching religion, insisted on the kind of education which they themselves had acquired at respectable European schools. Even more important was the fact that their activities did not stop at their primary function, but spread to many other fields and disciplines: history, geography, poetry, the writing of chronicles, and education.

The paradox of the Catholic Croat historical position in Bosnia-Herzegovina had a crucial impact via the profile it gave to the specific mentality and cultural (and not only cultural) activities of the Franciscans, and via the profile it gave to the people themselves. This became especially clear after the European frontiers of the Ottoman

Empire with Venice and Austria were established on the borders of Bosnia-Herzegovina with Dalmatia and northern Croatia, cutting through a natural ethnic-cultural and religious-civilizational continuum. It was approximately at this time that Russia and Austria began to intensify their anti-Turkish policy. Both were seeking to exercise patronage: the one over the Orthodox, the other over the Catholics. They used propaganda and intelligence activities to enlist the population in support of their goals, which were anything but politically altruistic. This made the Turkish authorities even more wary of these ethnic groups, while the lawlessness and rebelliousness that increased after the eighteenth century made relations constantly deteriorate. The Franciscans and their flock, as a social and church structure directly subordinated to Rome (which, from the point of view of a worried Turkish government, was the centre of a dangerous foreign enemy, both political and military), suffered this deterioration especially acutely.

Thanks to the organic unity between the Franciscans and their people, a kind of cultural life continued among the Catholic Croats. It manifested itself most strongly and characteristically in the field of literacy, literature, language and orthography, anticipating ideas which triumphed in Bosnia as a whole in the nineteenth century.

This extremely simplified outline of the Bosnian-Herzegovinian mosaic clearly shows that the three cultural spheres largely developed in isolation from one another, and also makes clear why this is how it had to be. It is intended to show the historical roots of the antagonism that surfaced in various ways and with differing degrees of intensity among the three entities, especially during the long period after the end of the seventeenth century. This is where we can find the roots of Muslim mistrust of Christians, which interpreted rationally and historically was a thoroughly concrete existential fear of foreign European military and political forces that dressed their imperialist strategies in religious motives: 'care' for the faithful and 'the right to practise their religion' for the Orthodox in the Russian variant and for Catholics in the Austrian. Here too lie the roots of reciprocal anti-Turkish and anti-Islamic feelings. Finally, the roots of Orthodox-Catholic rivalry can also be seen here. In the period we are considering, these usually surfaced in the form of completely mundane and banal conflicts about the right to collect taxes. But later, in the nineteenth century, when national bourgeoisies were formed, a dangerous political game began whose countless and intricate strings were pulled from far away in Belgrade and Zagreb, Vienna and Budapest, St Petersburg and Constantinople, and which grew into malignant controversy about the right to Bosnia-Herzegovina, both in Bosnia and outside it. Such controversy always focused on meaningless but dangerous and exclusivist arguments about the priority and primacy of particular national cultures.

It is here, in this context, that I think we must place and solve the question of togetherness and the cultural heritage. The hero of Andrić's story *A Letter from 1920* may have felt (more precisely, *had* to feel) the striking of the clocks in the Christian and Turkish towers in Sarajevo as a metaphor for deadly isolationism, because at that time the isolationism of history was still at work. It had even been increased by the blood-stained acceleration of history from the occupation in 1878 to the first planetary war, which struck in a specially fateful and complicated manner here.

Nothing has changed in the 'reception' of Andrić's story since the time when it was written, long ago in 1938. In the oral culture of Bosnia-Herzegovina it usually continues to be treated as 'that letter in which Andrić said that Bosnia was a land of hatred'. Only the circumstances have changed, widening the circle of its users. Thus we saw the European negotiators (Lord Owen and others), having been given a short course of literary interpretation by the Karadžić-Koljević circle, waving the letter in order to prove that the Bosnian apocalypse was inevitable, indeed almost deserved.

Widely neglected is the simple fact that Andrić's text is a story. It belongs to a separate, autonomous, literary reality with its own rules and relations. The text about hatred in *Letter from 1920* is in a dialogue between two characters. It is spoken by Maks Levenfeld, a Sarajevan Jewish doctor who flees from the hatred of his native land to end up in the Spanish Civil War where as a volunteer doctor he is killed during the bombing of a hospital, which naturally has an enormous red cross on its roof! Given the data in the text, a literary interpretation, to be even basically correct, would have to be something completely different. Incidentally, it may not be very important but it is interesting that this story, set just after World War I, was written (or at least first published) just after World War II, in 1946. Surely this too has a meaning.

There is no doubt that we are still greatly determined today by our narrow interpretation of our cultural tradition and the civilization we belong to: but this is negative only when people do not want to admit it, when it is turned into a taboo. To deny it is useless, untrue, unwise, and above all harmful. But, on the other hand, we are living at a time of truly planetary culture when all the barriers of nation, politics, religion and language have succumbed to the individual reception and organic internalization of cultural values. The only criterion that remains is the universal. To put it figuratively, the symbolic meaning of Andrić's clock towers has changed. They used to guide people through life, now they should act as a fact of culture, a fact of aesthetics and history that by definition *brings together, makes links*. If it is natural, logical and good for us to experience ancient Indian sculpture, Japanese ink drawing, St Basil's in Moscow, Chartres Cathedral, St Naum's at Ohrid, the Holy Cross at Nin, a fresco from Sopoćani and so on through direct aesthetic suggestion and historical evocation, it is not logical and not a sign of personal and cultural maturity if our reception of cultural facts and creative phenomena from our native land is hindered by a feeling, still active though dead, of discomfort and animosity. What I mean is that, given such spiritual discomfort even about the cultural phenomenon that is closest to us, our reception of a Japanese ink drawing cannot be real or complete either. It is here that we must take our test of civilized maturity; and to pass it is more essential in Bosnia than anywhere else.

Let us return to Andrić's picture: it has more to tell us. Materially it is built on the symbol of Sarajevo towers and their clocks 'of various kinds and various sounds', the times of four diverse 'mutually quarrelling calendars' and 'different church languages'. Such images are not only aesthetically suggestive, they are valid and 'true' in terms of civilization and history. But we must ask: how true? Which dimensions of history and culture do they measure, which dimensions do they encompass? Towers, clocks, the measuring of time, calendars, church languages, the urban ambience . . . All these are elements of the high culture, 'snapped', furthermore, at a time still mostly determined by religion.

Andrić's snapshot catches only the upper aspects, it does not include the totality. If we allow ourselves to bring the writer's lens to life it will necessarily, led by a logic of its own, bring us to the bottom of the belfries and clock towers. Where? Into the bustle of life, the noise of centuries of everyday living, the ground floor of history and a different, *folk* culture. This culture lives in the shadow of the towers and their clocks, it cannot avoid being marked by them, each by its own, but these marks are far from able to encompass and imbue it completely. This culture has its own time, origin, laws and functions, elements that sometimes coincide only on the fringes with the world of high culture, and very frequently are quite separate and different. It is essential for our subject to remember that, unlike the three spheres of high culture in their isolation from one another, in folk culture there is a high degree of mutuality among all three entities.

As for our experts in ethnology, folklore, and cultural anthropology, while it would be an exaggeration to say that their subjects are still in swaddling clothes, it is certainly not unjust to say that they have not moved beyond a positivistic stage and are incapable of any kind of synthetic generalization and interpretation. It is really amazing to see how these scholarly disciplines, which are so attractive and highly developed in the world, find no response in Bosnia-Herzegovina. Even a layman can see that the totality of material, social and spiritual folk culture in this region, if studied using the modern methods of these disciplines, would provide an unexpected wealth of many-faceted material for our understanding which would confirm the significant degree of unity among the culture-forming

224 ᴖ Bosnia: A Cultural History

mechanisms and laws that govern this cultural sphere, reflecting the triple cultural and religious schism in a completely different way from the high culture.

The existence of this common substratum throughout the sphere of folk culture is not a mere historical curiosity. Despite the 'high' cultural differences in religion and civilization to which ordinary people have been subjected almost since their arrival in the Balkans, and especially strongly and dramatically in the period we are considering, these people are mostly of common ethnic origin, with a common, very strong, cultural and spiritual mixed Slav-Illyrian heritage. Finally, they are people who speak one language, whose mentality has many common features, and who have for centuries mixed in the closest possible everyday contact, except in a few regions which have been for longer or shorter periods the closed enclaves of a single group.

In the sphere of folk culture Bosnia-Herzegovina's heritage is thus characterized by a high degree of mutuality. The elements by which it is recognized as threefold enter it from above, from the sphere of high culture where they are clearly differentiated in terms of civilization and history. So our heritage is ambivalent and dialectic, as is our nature: we are a 'sum' but we are also a 'product'; we have our different cultural and national traditions but also have the foundation on which they are built and their limited interweaving, and this is a common tradition.

The essence of the Bosnian cultural heritage is the complexity of its civilization, the simultaneity of one shared and three separate traditions. Organically linked as they are (the shared one and the three different ones), not to see, or not to want to see, any one member of this complicated combination means consenting to the impoverishment of one's own being.

II

When we think about the spiritual and historical identity of Bosnia-

Herzegovina only in terms of the national and the political, as has been done for the last hundred and fifty years, the problem seems insoluble. This can be seen quite clearly in the two most notable formulas: that of Kallay and that of ZAVNOBiH. The documents produced by the First Session of the Country-wide Anti-Fascist Council of the National Liberation of Bosnia-Herzegovina, enacted during the night of November 25–6 1943 at Mrkonjić-Grad, said: *'Bosnia-Herzegovina is not Serbian nor Croatian nor Muslim, but Serbian and Croatian and Muslim'*.

Kállay's integral Bosnianism was bound to fail, not because of Bosnianism itself, which is part of a long, active and attractive tradition, but because of the error in the aim itself. He tried to neutralize the existing political models of nations (which were already diversified enough after the Bosnian-Herzegovinian rising and the retreat of Turkey) by introducing one more identical political model: a new nation! The accompanying 'integrally Bosnian' cultural policy was designed to serve the same political goal. Although we recognize its results today, when the political intention has evaporated, as an important part of our scholarly and cultural heritage, this only shows that it was a deliberate cultural policy, while the language of culture corresponds to life and the duration of culture is eternal – both in contrast to politics.

The ZAVNOBiH formula is also based on affirming the integral nature of Bosnia. Unlike Kállay's, it recognizes national identities, but since it too thinks *only in political and national categories*, it does not move beyond its 'not-nor-nor/and-and-and'. That this is not enough to answer the question asked at the beginning of this chapter can best be seen from today's national convulsions, when people are asking the same question in the same way for the who-knows-how-many-th time since the 1870s. What is Bosnia, a mechanical sum of like nations which happen to be here or some kind of integral entity? And if it is an integral entity, how to express it in *national* terms? And this is where the trap lies! This is the necessary and inevitable outcome of any exclusively political, national way of feeling and thinking; within that framework Bosnia is and remains an insoluble enigma and permanent headache.

This is what results from an ideological concept that reduces human individuality and social life to where they *belong* and what they *represent*, when, having used up all the other 'avant-garde' forms, we return to the *national* as our only refuge, and in that *national* category recognize only its *political* content. Is this sometimes retrograde? Is it a return from the individual to the species? Whatever it is, this is the darkness which confronts us. We differ only in whether it fills us with delight or with horror.

The nation is a given concept in modern European history. Whether it will be a productive *advance* of civilization or on the contrary *damnation* seems to depend on the content that is read into it, the kind of value system and hierarchy that it establishes. If the hierarchy is topped by politics, the state and its 'mission' and everything else is derived from these or serves it, damnation cannot be avoided – for the nation itself and for those around it. We do not need a very long memory to see this obvious lesson in our experience of the blood-stained history of twentieth-century Europe, in which we have had an extensive share.

Because of its extraordinary historical structure, Bosnia is a clear, as it were a 'laboratory' example of how an abstract ideological concept and definition of nationhood inevitably gets tangled up in its own web, in a tragicomic clash with history and everyday life. Such a concept has never moved beyond the nineteenth-century urban ideological image of the nation-state. And let us remember, in this framework Bosnia could be 'solved' only as a *national state*, with all the resulting agony: Bosnia as a 'classic Serbian land', Bosnia as a 'classic Croatian land', Bosnia in which 'only the Bosniak Muslims are at home.'

If we feel that Bosnia-Herzegovina today seems to have a kind of identity crisis, in terms of political self-articulation, then is it not historically more accurate to think about the way this crisis has continued throughout modern history, since the first half of the nineteenth century? During this entire period, because of the overriding prevalence of national political processes and exceedingly undemocratic, ideological regimes, Bosnia has never managed politically to articulate and stabilize its historical identity, its multi-cultural and multi-national nature.

If we turn the hierarchical pyramid upside-down, if national identity and feeling are primarily founded, recognized and exhausted in spiritual, historical and cultural content and values (which are all concrete and creative categories and motivations, unlike ideological-political ones, which are abstract and speculative), then the nation can be lived and experienced as a productive fruit of civilization. That this is certainly possible is shown from certain experiences of the modern world, the culturally and economically most productive part of it, which has *really*, and in practice, turned to this model.

By its very nature culture is *open* and *inclusive*, and ideology (every ideology, and especially nationalism) is *closed* and *exclusive*. *National ideology* strives to achieve cleansing; its ideal is the essence of the nation, pure of the admixture of anything *alien*. This means that the alien must be proclaimed as a threat to the purity of the nation, and distaste and hatred must be fostered. The final result is a dried butterfly under a glass case. Self-mummification.

Nation as culture is a dynamic structure, capable of receiving and giving. It does not hold back from what is foreign, but easily makes it its own; it does not fear for its own, but is happy to put it into circulation. This capacity of inclusion, this game of exchange – not cleansing and purity – is a stake in the fullness of identity and communication with others.

If Bosnia is a name for any kind of identity, its content is not the mathematical sum of nations or national cultures, nor is it their drowning in a new (supra) national construction. Its content lies in permanent cultural interaction. The name *Bosnian* is thus not a term for a national order, nor only a regional or territorial one. It is a name for the *process of civilization* we have described, something which through all historical changes and political adversities has lasted for a millennium, to an equal degree practised in everyday life with equal vitality by all. In this process of interaction as a *constant* (its name is Bosnia) national cultures participate as *variables*, retaining their special identities and exposing themselves to continuous culture-creating relations of *receiving* and *giving*. In practice, every national culture in Bosnia is both what it is by name, and something more. National ideology sees this as *impurity*. And since national ideologies by their very nature do not stand still, they will sooner or later and in some way or another begin to act. To cleanse, of course. But from the aspect of culture what we have is an outstanding possibility of connecting the unconnectable, and rich soil for creative articulation of the first order. It is understandable that all travellers of the mind and spirit have emphasized this particular aspect in their experience of Bosnia, just as it is characteristic that the leading writers in our language, Andrić, Dizdar, Selimović, Šop, have found their subject and their nourishment in such a miracle.

How then to think and live in Bosnia today, to approach its spiritual and historical identity with an appropriate language and in an appropriate manner? I do not have a ready answer, nor do I know whether anyone has it. But I know that to do it in the mode of ideology (national or any other), as has been done for the last century and a half, will misfire and be useless. This approach has distanced us even from what it invokes as sacred and in the name of which it unfurls its banners: from the true and full living of national identity. So it may be worthwhile at last to make a systematic attempt at another way – the way of culture. Perhaps this is the only way, the only manner of thinking and living, in which the tension between our *Bosnian* and our *national* components can be resolved.

Glossary

aga	lord or landowner belonging to the lower of the two categories of landowner
alhamáijado (foreign)	term applied to Bosnian literature written in the Arabic script
arzuhal	petition
ayan	elected local official and administrator
ban	Croatian term, used also in mediaeval Bosnia, for ruler (or later regent). Revived in 1939 when Yugoslavia was divided into 'banovinas', each governed by a ban
banovina	territory governed by a ban
bašluk	gravestone
beg	lord or landowner belonging to the higher of the two categories of landowner
beglerbegluk	office of a beglerbeg, the highest rank of pasha, governor of a province (such as Bosnia)
bezistan	cloth market, covered market
Bogoslovija	main seminary of the Serbian Orthodox Church in Belgrade
Bosančica	Bosnian Cyrillic script
čaršija	bazaar, urban quarter of merchants and craftsmen
česma	drinking-fountain
Chetniks	traditional Serbian term for irregular fighters, adopted by forces under Draža Mihailović in World War II and subsequently by Serbian irregulars (e.g. those organized by Vuk Drašković, Vojislav Šešelj and Arkan) fighting in Croatia and Bosnia; also generally applied in Bosnia-Herzegovina after April

	1992 to all Serb forces taking part in the aggression against the country.
čiftluk	private land-holding under the Ottoman Empire
dosluk	friendship
džamija	mosque
eyalet	province of the Ottoman Empire (the largest administrative division)
gazi	hero, war leader
Glagolica, Glagolitic script	original script devised for the Slav languages by St Cyril and St Methodius and used in Croatia and Bosnia for many centuries, though in other Slav lands it was quickly replaced by their later modification known simply as the Cyrillic script
hamam	Turkish baths
han	inn
hajduk	brigand, guerrilla
herceg	duke
janissary	Ottoman soldier, originally recruited as a slave of the Sultan through the 'devširme' or child-tax, but from mid seventeenth century recruited from ordinary Muslims
kapetan	originally military administrator in a frontier zone; in Bosnian history normally administrator of a territorial division with wide-ranging powers, whose office was hereditary
kapetanija	area administered by a kapetan
komšiluk	neighbours, neighbourhood, neighbourliness
krajina	march-land, frontier-zone
mahala	urban quarter
martolos	local Christian (Vlach or Serb) free-booter infantryman
mašet (plural *mašeta*)	mediaeval gravestone, *stećak*
medresa	Muslim theological school
mekteb	Muslim primary school
milet-basha	elders of the people (millets were self-governing religious communities in the Ottoman Em-

	pire that later took on an 'ethnic' connotation)
mimar	master builder
mramorovi	popular local term for stećci (mramor = marble)
mudželit	bookbinder
nišan	gravestone
pasha	general term for territorial governor
pashaluk	territory governed by a pasha
Phanariot	Greeks, called after the Phanar district of Constantinople, some of whom wielded considerable influence under the Ottoman Empire
raya	originally non-Ottoman subject people (Muslim as well as non-Muslim); by the nineteenth century it generally meant non-Muslim subjects only; in modern times often just refers to the 'common people'
sahat-kula	clock-tower
sandžak	largest territorial sub-division of an eyalet, originally a military district
sevdalinka	traditional Bosnian love-song
sljemenjak	stećak with a top in the form of a pitched roof (sljeme = gable)
spahi	Ottoman cavalryman
stećak (plural *stećci*)	Bosnian mediaeval gravestone
šadrvan	fountain, especially in mosque courtyard
šehid	martyr
tarih	occasional verse, inscription, chronicle
tekke	dervish lodge
timar	feudal estate under the Ottoman Empire
turbe	Islamic (domed) mausoleum, often situated near a mosque
uskok	Christian outlaws from Ottoman rule who organized resistance (especially in Dalmatia and along the north Croatian coast), often with Venetian or Austrian backing, as well as operating as normal brigands

Ustasha (plural *Ustashe*)	literally 'insurgent', name taken by an extremist wing of the Croatian Party of Rights which, led by Ante Pavelić, accepted the patronage of fascist Italy in the interwar period; in 1941 the Ustashe were installed in power by the Nazis in the quisling 'Independent State of Croatia', which included the whole of Bosnia-Herzegovina, and in which they pursued genocidal policies against Serb, Jewish, Roma and other minorities
vakuf	religious-charitable foundation, holding property in perpetuity
Velika Škola	first Serbian secondary school, founded 1808, country's pre-eminent educational institution prior to the foundation of the University of Belgrade in 1905
Vlach	descendant of Romanized pre-Slav population of the Balkans
vilayet	province of the Ottoman Empire (replacing the eyalet in 1864)
zadužbina	charitable endowment
zijamet	large feudal estate under the Ottoman Empire

Chronology

10,000 BC
- Palaeolithic rock engraving (Badanj near Stolac)

III Millennium BC
- Neolithic pottery (Obre, Butmir)

II–I Millennia BC
- creation of larger territorial and political Illyrian communities
- iron age culture: pile-dwellings, hill-forts, tumuli graves
- ritual bronze cart from Glasinac
- jewellery (Sanski Most, Jerezine, Ribić)
- Japod reliefs on sarcophagi and urns
- Umbrian-Etruscan inscriptions on earthernware pots (Pod, Bugojno V – IV centuries)
- Celtic invasion IV–III centuries

V–I Centuries BC
- Greek colonization of Adriatic coast and islands
- spread of Hellenism (Herzegovina), centered in Ošanići
- urban architecture, Cyclopean walls, sculpture, pottery, jewellery, carving, Greek writing
- 229–33 BC Roman conquest of Illyricum

I–IV Centuries AD
- spread of classical civilization
- 6–9 AD uprising of Illyrian tribes, *Bellum Batonianum*, establishment of Roman rule
- 14–20 road network built in Illyricum
- urban settlements, military camps, villas, thermae, mines
- architecture and sculpture: Gradac near Posušje, Sipovo, Šovići near Grude, Morgorjelo, Breza, Zenica
- mosaics: Stolac, Ilidža

- development of Illyro-Roman ethnic amalgam

IV–VII Centuries
- 395 division of Roman Empire into West and East
- 476 disintegration of Western Roman Empire
- 480–535 Illyricum under Ostrogoths, then part of Eastern Roman Empire until early 7th century
- late Roman and early Christian era
- mixture of religious cults
- Mithraism – Christianity
- Mithraic sculpture and reliefs (Konjic, Jajce)
- early Christian basilicas and reliefs (Zenica, Dabravina near Breza, Lepenica, Klobuk, Žitomislići, Potoci, Cim, Blagaj on the Sana)

VII–IX Centuries
- arrival of Slavs (614 conquest of Salonika)
- amalgamation of Slavs and palaeo-Balkan (Illyro-Roman) inhabitants
- early forms of territorial tribal organization
- conversion to Christianity
- grave jewellery (Grborezi near Livno, Čipuljić, Višići, Buško Blato)
- traces of contact with Carolingian world – fragments of churches (altar-rails and ciboria from Rapovine, Vrba, Vrutak)

X–XI Centuries
- beginning of feudal statehood in Bosnia, between Hungary and Byzantium, and between Croatian and Serbian sovereignties
- 948 Bosnia mentioned in *De administrando imperio* by Constantine Porphyrogenitus
- poly-alphabetism: Glagolitic and Cyrillic (Humac Tablet 10th–11th century)
- stone carving: relief of Virgin and Child (Vidoštak), altar-rails (Radaslije, Carevac)

XII–XIII Centuries
- political-territorial consolidation and flowering of culture under Ban Kulin (1180–1204)
- political and cultural decline after end of Kulin's reign
- 1189 Kulin's Charter to the people of Dubrovnik
- Miroslav Gospel
- Romanesque carvings: Rogačići, Carevo Polje, Sarajevo, Kreševo, Mujdžići, Zavala

- beginning of stećak art
- 1291 first arrival of Franciscans

XIV–XV Centuries
- political and territorial expansion of Bosnia during reign of Ban Stjepan Kotromanić II (1322–53) and Tvrtko I (Ban 1353–77, King 1377–91)
- building of castles and towns
- development of trade and mining (arrival of miners from Saxony)
- 1340 foundation of Franciscan Bosnian Vicariate
- after reign of Tvrtko I the king loses much of his power; struggle for power among regional lords
- 1432 first fortresses fall into Turkish hands
- religious mosaic: Bosnian Church, Catholicism, Orthodox Church; infiltration of Islam from first half of 15th century
- flourishing of mediaeval culture: golden age of stećak art; art of miniatures and manuscript illumination; architecture of fortifications and castles; art craftsmanship
- 1463 Turkish invasion under Mehmed II. Remnants of Bosnia – banovinas of Jajce and Srebrenica
- 1528 Jajce finally falls to the Turks
- 1592 fall of Bihać – the whole of Bosnia-Herzegovina is part of Ottoman Empire

XVI–XVII Centuries
- Turkish expansion north into Croatia and Hungary
- economic and political stability; urban development
- emergence of multi-civilizational mosaic: Muslim-Oriental, Catholic-Croat, Orthodox-Serb, Jewish-Sephardic
- Oriental-Islamic urbanization and architecture; masterpieces of building (mosques, Islamic schools, gravestones, bridges, inns, baths, caravanserai, clock-towers); calligraphy; literature in Oriental languages; Islamic education
- literary and religious/pastoral influence of Franciscans; painting in western European tradition; relatively stable commercial urban class among Bosnian Catholics
- post-Byzantine frescoes and icons among Orthodox; work of scribes; Goražde printing press 1519–23
- Sephardic Jewish milieu: nurturing of tradition brought from Spain; literacy (Hebrew, Latin); illuminated manuscripts (Haggadah, 13th–14th century)
- flourishing of artistic craft-work

XVIII Century
- decadence of Ottoman Empire
- 1683 Turkish defeat before Vienna, Turks withdraw from lands across the Sava; Bosnia becomes Turkish border region between Ottoman Empire and western Europe
- lawlessness among spahis and janissaries; increasingly bad position of Christian *raya* and poorest Muslims
- end of significant Islamic-Oriental building; decrease of cultural life in all religious/ethnic groups
- 1697 great exodus of Franciscans and Catholics after attack on Sarajevo by Eugene of Savoy; only three Franciscan monasteries left: Kraljeva Sutjeska, Kreševo and Fojnica; decline of Catholic urban commercial class
- 1766 Turkish government abolishes Peć Patriarchiate, after which Greek clergy play increasingly important part in Serbian Orthodox church; people fall into increasing spiritual and cultural stagnation
- manifestation of folk genius: epic poetry and other forms of folk art

XIX Century
- attempts by Porte to stabilize the Empire; 1839 reforms; rebellions against reforms
- moves of Muslim feudal lords for autonomy; 1831 rebellion by Huseinkapetana Gradaščević
- rebellions by Christian *raya*
- 1850–52 bloody pacification of Muslim rebels by Omer-pasha Latas
- 1861–68 Topal Osman-pasha attempts modernization
- reverberations of Yugoslav movements for national and cultural emancipation
- new kind of cultural action – secularization of writing and literature (Ivan Franjo Jukić, Grgo Martić, Vaso Pelagić, Mehmed Šaćir Kurtćehajić)
- beginning of secular painting

1875–8
- rising in Bosnia-Herzegovina

1878–1918
- Austro Hungarian occupation of Bosnia-Herzegovina (1908 – annexation)
- beginning of modern trade and industry
- European way of life begins to become established
- development of media

- interest in cultural history; 1888 National Museum founded in Sarajevo
- mixed styles in architecture: neo-Romanesque, neo-Gothic, neo-Renaissance, 'Moorish style', Vienna secession
- first generation of artists schooled in Europe
- 1881 establishment of regular Catholic church hierarchy, beginning of tension between bishopric and Franciscans

1918-41
- Kingdom of Serbs, Croats and Slovenes founded (from 1929 Kingdom of Yugoslavia)
- stagnation in cultural and all other areas of life
- early writing by Ivo Andrić
- Isak Samokovlija begins to write
- new artists appear: Ismet Mujezinović, Vojo Dimitrijević, Branko Šotra, Danijel Ozmo
- 1939 Cvetković-Maček Agreement: Bosnia-Herzegovina divided between Banovina of Croatia and 'remaining Serbian lands'

1941-5
- Second World War; Bosnia-Herzegovina incorporated into quisling Independent State of Croatia (NDH)

1945-66
- effectively colonial status of Bosnia-Herzegovina in centralist Yugoslav state; unitarist model in culture; Serbianization of language in public life and media
- beginning of serious scholarly and research interest in ancient and mediaeval history and archaeology
- 1961 Ivo Andrić wins Nobel Prize for literature

1966-92
- republican autonomy becomes reality within Federal Yugoslavia; establishment of important cultural, educational and media institutions (Academy of Sciences and Arts, university faculties, Sarajevo TV)
- construction of 3,000 km of asphalted roads
- 1966 novel *Derviš i smrt* by Mešo Selimović; poem cycle *Kameni Spavač* by Mak Dizdar
- 1984 Winter Olympics in Sarajevo
- 1990 first democratic elections, won by national parties: Party of Democratic Action, Serb Democratic Party and Croat Democratic Union

1992–5

- 29 February/1 March 1992 referendum on independence for Bosnia-Herzegovina, almost 64% vote in favour
- March and April 1992 armed forces of Serb Democratic Party and Yugoslav People's Army attack Bosnia-Herzegovina ; 6 April they surround Sarajevo and begin daily shelling and sniper fire on city
- Yugoslav People's Army, later Serb Army, begins to carry out large-scale war crimes especially in eastern Bosnia, Podrinje and the Sana valley
- 1993–4 fighting breaks out between Croat Defence Council (HVO) and Army of Bosnia-Herzegovina (ARB-H)
- 18 March 1994 signing of Washington Agreement, bringing to an end hostilities between HVO and ARB-H: Federation of Bosnia-Herzegovina established
- November 1995 peace negotiations in Dayton (Ohio), ending in Dayton Agreement signed in Paris 14 December

Bibliography

Andrić, Ivo, *The Development of Spiritual Life in Bosnia under the Influence of Turkish Rule*, Durham, North Carolina 1990.

Anđelić, Pavao, *Bobovac i Kraljeva Sutjeska*, Sarajevo 1973.

—— *Srednjovjekovni pečati iz Bosne i Hercegovine*, Sarajevo 1970.

—— *Studije o teritorijalnopolitičkoj organizaciji srednjovjekovne Bosne*, Sarajevo 1982.

Babić, Anto, Desanka Kovačević-Kojić and Sima Ćirković (eds), *Društvo i privreda srednjovjekovne bosanske države*, Sarajevo 1987.

Bakhtin, Mikhail, *Rabelais and his world*, Boston 1968.

Balić, Smail, *Das unbekannte Bosnien*, Cologne 1992.

—— *Kultura Bošnjaka - muslimanska komponenta*, Vienna 1973.

Basler, Đuro, *Arhitektura kasnoantičkog doba u Bosni i Hercegovini*, Sarajevo 1972.

Bašagić, Safvet-beg, *Bošnjaci i Hercegovci u islamskoj kniževnosti*, Sarajevo 1912.

—— *Znameniti Hrvati, Bošnjaci i Hercegovci u Turskoj Carevini*, Zagreb 1931.

Batinić, Mijo Vjenceslav, *Djelovanje franjevaca u Bosni i Hercegovini za prvih šest viekova njihova boravka*, Zagreb 1881.

Benac, Alojz, *Stećci*, Belgrade 1967.

Benac, Alojz, ouro Basler, Borivoj Čović, Esad Pašalić, Nada Miletić and Pavao Anđelić, *Kulturna istorija Bosne i Hercegovine*, Sarajevo 1984.

Benić, Bono, *Ljetopis sutješkog samostana*, Sarajevo 1979.

Bešlagić, Šefik, *Nišani XV i XVI vijeka u Bosni i Hercegovini*, Sarajevo 1978.

—— *Stećci - katološko-topografski pregled*, Sarajevo 1971.

Bogdanović, Marijan, *Ljetopis kreševskog samostana*, Sarajevo 1984.

Bogičević, Vojislav, *Pismenost u Bosni i Hercegovini*, Sarajevo 1975.

Bojanovski, Ivo, *Bosna i Hercegovina u antičko doba*, Sarajevo 1988.

—— *Dolabelin sistem cesta u rimskoj provinciji Dalmaciji*, Sarajevo 1974.

Bordeaux, Albert, *La Bosnie populaire: paysages, moeurs et coutumes, legendes, chants populaires, mines*, Paris 1904.

Božić, Ivan, Sima Ćirković, Milorad Ekmečić and Vladimir Dedijer, *Istorija Jugoslavije*, Belgrade 1972.

Čelić, Džemal and Mehmed Mujezinović, *Stari mostovi u Bosni i Hercegovini*, Sarajevo 1969.

Ćirković, Sima, *Istorija srednjovjekovne bosanske države*, Belgrade 1964.

Collingwood, Robin, *The Idea of History*, Oxford 1946.

Ćorić, Boris, *'Ogled o Ivanu Franji Jukiću'*, in Ivan Franjo Jukić, *Sabrana djela*, vol. 3, Sarajevo 1973.

Ćorović, Vladimir, *Bosna i Hercegovina*, Sarajevo 1925.

Čović, Borivoj, *Od Butmira do Ilira*, Sarajevo 1980.

Deretić, Jovan, *Istorija srpske književnosti*, Belgrade 1983.

Dragojlović, Dragoljub, *Krstjani i jeretička crkva bosanska*, Belgrade 1987.

Džaja, Srećko, *Katolici u Bosni i Hercegovini na prijelazu iz 18. u 19. stoljeće*, Zagreb 1971.

—— *Konfessionalität und Nationalität Bosniens und der Herzegowina*, Munich 1984.

Ekmečić, Milorad, *Ustanak u Bosni 1975-1878*, Sarajevo 1960.

Filipović, Nedim, *Princ Musa i šejh Bedreddin*, Sarajevo 1971.

Gavazzi, Milovan, *Godina dana hrvatskih narodnih običaja*, Zagreb 1939.

Gavran, Ignacije, *Lucerna lucens? (Odnos Vrhbosanskog ordinarijata prema bosanskim franjevcima)*, Visoko 1978.

Georgijević, Krešimir, *Hrvatska književnost od 16. do 18. stoljeća u sjevernoj Hrvatskoj i Bosni*, Zagreb 1969.

Hadžijahić, Muhamed, *Od tradicije do identiteta - geneza nacionalnog pitanja bosanskih Muslimana*, Sarajevo 1974.

Hammer-Purgstall, Joseph von, *Geschichte des Osmanischen Reiches*, vol. 1-4, Budapest 1834-6.

Hangi, Anton, *Die Moslims in Bosnien-Herzegowina. Ihre Lebensweise, Sitten und Gebrauche*, Sarajevo 1907.

Heller, Agnes, *Theorie der Gefühle*, Hamburg 1981.

Hilferding, Aleksandar, *Putovanje po Hercegovini, Bosni i Staroj Srbiji*, Sarajevo 1972.

Huizinga, Johan, *Autumn of the Middle Ages*, Chicago 1996.

Imamović, Enver, *Antički kultni i votivni spomenici na području Bosne i Hercegovine*, Sarajevo 1977.

Imamović, Mustafa, *Pravni položaj i unutrašnji razvitak Bosne i Hercegovine od 1878 do 1914.* Sarajevo 1976.

Islamska kultura, vol. XVII, no. 10, Sarajevo October 1973.

Jelenić, Julijan, *Kultura i bosanski franjevci I-II*, Zagreb 1912, 1915.

Jukić, Ivan Franjo, *Sabrana djela*, Sarajevo 1973.

Kajmaković, Zdravko, *Georgije Mitrofanović*, Sarajevo 1977.

—— *Zidno slikarstvo u Bosni i Hercegovini*, Sarajevo 1971.

Karamatić, Marko, *Franjevci Bosne Srebrene u vrijeme austrougarske uprave*

1878-1914, Sarajevo 1992.

Katoličanstvo u Bosni i Hercegovini, Sarajevo 1993.

Kecmanović, Ilija, *Barišićeva afera*, Sarajevo 1954.

—— *Ivo Franjo Jukic*, Belgrade 1963.

Klaić, Nada, *Povijest Hrvata u razvijenom srednjem vijeku*, Zagreb 1976.

Klaić, Vjekoslav, *Geschichte Bosniens von den altesten Zeiten bis zum Verfalle des Konigreiches*, Leipzig 1885.

—— *Povijest Hrvata*, Zagreb 1974.

Knežević, Anto, *Carsko-turski namjestnici u Bosni-Ercegovini*, Zagreb 1882.

Kovačević-Kojić, Desanka, *Grdska naselja srednjovjekovne bosanske države*, Sarajevo 1978.

Kovačić, Anto, *Bibliografija franjevaca Bosne Srebrene*, Sarajevo 1991.

Kreševljaković, Hamdija, *Esnafi i obrti u Bosni i Hercegovini*, Sarajevo 1961.

—— *Hanovi i karavansaraji u Bosni i Hercegovini*, Sarajevo 1957.

—— *Kapetanije u Bosni i Hercegovini*, Sarajevo 1980.

Kuripešić, Benedikt, *Itinerarium der Botschaftsreise des Josef von Lamberg und Niclas Jurischitz durch Bosnien, Serbien, Bulgarien nach Konstantinopel 1530*, Innsbruck 1910.

Lastrić, Filip, *Pregled starina bosanske provincije*, Sarajevo 1977.

Lašvanin, Nikola, *Ljetopis*, Sarajevo 1981.

Le Goff, Jacques, *Medieval Civilization*, Oxford 1988.

Levy, Moritz, *Die Sephardim in Bosnien. Ein Beitrag zur Geschichte der Juden aus der Balkanhalbinsel*, Klagenfurt 1996.

Lopez, Robert S., *The Birth of Europe*, New York 1966.

Lovrenović, Dubravko, *Utjecaj Ugarske na odnos crkve i države u srednjevjekovnoj Bosni: sedam stoljeća bosanskih franjevaca* (zbornik), Samobor 1994.

Malcolm, Noel, *Bosnia A Short History*, London 1996.

Mandić, Dominik, *Etnička povijest Bosne i Hercegovine*, Rome 1967.

—— *Franjevačka Bosna*, Rome 1968.

Marić, Zdravko, *Depo pronapen u ilirskom gradu Daors*, GZM, new series, vol. XXXIII (1978), Sarajevo 1979.

Martić, Grgo, *Zapamćenja*, Zagreb 1906.

Mazalić, Ooko, *Leksikon umjetnika*, Sarajevo 1967.

Mřnnesland, Svein, *Land ohne Wiederkehr Ex-Jugoslawien: die Wurzeln des Krieges*, Klagenfurt 1997.

Neweklowsky, Gerhard, *Die bosnisch-herzegowinischen Muslime: Geschichte Brauche Alltagskultur*, Klagenfurt 1996.

Nezirović, Muhamed, *Jevrejsko-španjolska književnost*, Sarajevo 1992.

Oaković, Luka, *Političke organizacije bosanskohercegovačkih katolika Hrvata*, Zagreb 1985.

Okuka, Miloš, *Eine Sprache - viele Erben. Sprachpolitik als Nationalisierungselement in Ex-Jugoslawien*, Klagenfurt 1998.

Popović, Miodrag, *Vidovdan i časni krst*, Beograd 1976.

Praistorija jugoslavenskih zemalja I-V, Sarajevo 1987.

Radovi sa simpozijuma Srednjevjekovna Bosna i evropska kultura, Zenica 1973.

Rački, Franjo, *Bogumili i paareni*, Zagreb 1869.

Rizvić, Muhsin, *Književno stvaranje muslimanskih pisaca u Bosni i Hercegovini u doba austrougarske vladavine I-II*, Sarajevo 1973.

Šabanović, Hazim, *Bosanski pašaluk*, Sarajevo 1982.

Šanjek, Franjo, *Bosansko-humski (hercegovački) krstjani i katarsko-dualistički pokret u srednjem vijeku*, Zagreb 1975.

—— *Crkva i kršćanstvo u Hrvata*, Zagreb 1988.

Schmaus, Alois, *Studije o krajinskij epici*, Zagreb 1953.

Šidak, Jaroslav, *Studije o 'Crkvi bosanskoj' i bogumilstvu*, Zagreb 1975.

Spalajkovitsch, M. J., *La Bosnie et l'Herzégovine*, Paris 1899.

Stipčević, Aleksandar, *The Illyrians*, Park Ridge, New Jersey 1977.

Sućeska, Avdo, *Ajani*, Sarajevo 1965.

Südland, L. von, *Južnoslavensko pitanje. Prikaz cjelokupnog pitanja*, Zagreb 1943.

Thaloczy, Lajosz, *Povijest Jajca 1450-1527*, Zagreb 1916.

The Socialist Republic of Bosnia and Herzegovina, Offprint from the Second Edition of *Enciklopedija Jugoslavije*, Zagreb 1983.

Truhelka, Ćiro, *Jajce 1404-1904*, Sarajevo 1904.

—— *Studije o podrijetlu*, Zagreb 1941.

Turčinović, J. (ed.), *Povijesno-teološki simpozij u povodu 500. obljetnice smrti bosanske kraljice Katarine*, Sarajevo 1979.

Vasić, Milan, *Martolosi u jugoslavenskim zemljama pod turskom vladavinom*, Sarajevo 1967.

Vego, Marko, *Postanak srednjovjekovne bosanske države*, Sarajevo 1982.

Vidaković, Krinka, *Kultura španskih Jevreja na jugoslavenskom tlu*, Sarajevo 1986.

Vodnik, Branko, *Povijest hrvatske književnosti*, Zagreb 1913.

Wenzel, Marian, 'Bosnian History and Austro-Hungarian Policy: Some Medieval Belts, the Bogomil Romance and the King Tvrtko Graves', in *Bosanski stil na stećcima i metalu – Bosnian Style on Tombstones and Metal*, Sarajevo 1999.

—— *Ukrasni motivi na stećcima - Ornamental Motifs on Tombstones from Medieval Bosnia and Surrounding Regions*, Sarajevo 1965.

Zbornik radova o Matiji Divkoviću, Sarajevo 1982.

Zirdum, Andrija, *Filip Lastrić Očevac*, Zagreb 1982.

Index